Effective
Accounting
Reports

EFFECTIVE ACCOUNTING REPORTS

Bruce Joplin

and

James W. Pattillo

PRENTICE-HALL, INC.
Englewood Cliffs, N.J.

PRENTICE-HALL INTERNATIONAL, INC., *London*
PRENTICE-HALL OF AUSTRALIA, PTY. LTD., *Sydney*
PRENTICE-HALL OF CANADA, LTD., *Toronto*
PRENTICE-HALL OF INDIA PRIVATE LTD., *New Delhi*
PRENTICE-HALL OF JAPAN, INC., *Tokyo*

LIBRARY OF CONGRESS
CATALOG CARD NUMBER: 79–77902

PRINTED IN THE UNITED STATES OF AMERICA
13-240721-3 B & P

About the Authors

Bruce Joplin is a member of the Management Consulting staff of Peat, Marwick, Mitchell & Co. in Los Angeles. Formerly, he was Controller of a diversified West Coast Company. In addition, he has served as Deputy Controller of the City of Los Angeles and on the staff of the Auditor General of California. Mr. Joplin is a CPA, holds a BA from Golden Gate College in San Francisco and an MBA from California State College at Sacramento. He is a frequent contributor to professional accounting magazines and was awarded a certificate for outstanding contribution to accounting literature by the National Association of Accountants.

James W. Pattillo is Professor of Accounting at Louisiana State University. Previously, he taught accounting at the University of Southern California in Los Angeles. He has worked with the staffs of Ernst & Ernst, CPAs, and Tilley & Roth, CPAs, both in Los Angeles. He currently has his own CPA practice in Baton Rouge, and is also associated with Tilley & Roth. He has served as consultant for the Los Angeles staff of the U.S. General Accounting Office. Dr. Pattillo received his PhD degree from Louisiana State University, his MBA from Texas Technological College, and his BS in Commerce from St. Edward's University. He has written numerous articles for accounting periodicals.

What This Book Will Do for You

This book was written for the practicing accountant who wants to prepare better—more readable and more effective—reports. The modern accountant's reports go directly to action-oriented managers from the foreman to the president. These reports are the basis for both day-to-day operating decisions and major company policy. Reports prepared by today's accountant must be both informative and comprehensive. The progress of his company and his own personal success depend on it.

Accounting reports convey information to busy, hurried people who cannot and will not take the time to analyze page after page of undistinguishable numerical tabulations. The accountant must know how to select the report content, format and media which will make information meaningful to the reader. Good reports grasp the reader's consciousness. They communicate, they convince, they motivate. *Effective Accounting Reports* is designed to aid the accountant in producing such reports.

Anyone connected with the handling of financial data will benefit from this book. Treasurers and Controllers will find their repertoire of reporting techniques broadened. The straightforward presentation will appeal to busy financial executives. Line accountants in industry and government will be able to achieve versatility in report preparation and presentation. Remember, your report is often the only portion of your work which is seen by your superiors. Junior accountants will find that the how-to-do-it approach of the book bridges the gap from school to the work situation.

Systems analysts, consultants and public accountants will find *Effective Accounting Reports* a reference source which can be used beneficially on most assignments. The book should be part of the traveling library of anyone involved in the design of information systems.

Effective Accounting Reports covers the entire gamut of report presentation. It is unique in its emphasis on the use of computers in preparing reports. Computer reports which can be submitted directly to operating management without the necessity for retyping are described and illustrated. Attention is directed to reporting aids of the future such as computer connected microfilm and visual display systems. The growth of computers being what it is, no practicing accountant should fail to read the chapters on automatic data processing.

One of the most important parts of the book tells how to design a reporting system for your company. An outline of the steps in building an effective series of reports is given. The material is not theoretical. Examples are presented to illustrate each point as the reader is taken through the pyramid system of reports.

One chapter is devoted to illustrating the various types of reports commonly in use today. A position statement which reflects price-level adjustments is shown. Income statements in single and multiple steps are illustrated. Reports for decision making in the areas of capital investment, production, distribution, and personnel are presented. Reports from various departments such as sales, credit and purchasing are included.

Oral presentations? Yes! The proper use of visual aids in assisting such presentation is developed step-by-step. Charts and graphs to aid the reader or viewer in quickly grasping the essence of information are thoroughly reviewed and demonstrated. Many actual, work-a-day examples taken from established reporting systems are included in the book.

This book shows how the eye appeal or readability of accounting reports can be improved without undue cost or delay. The concept of exception reporting is analyzed in detail, setting forth its advantages and disadvantages. The very necessary function of control and distribution of reports is discussed and a report control, inventory, and evaluation program set forth.

Effective Accounting Reports brings together in one handy reference the various reporting methods and techniques used by accountants today. Emphasis is placed upon the preparation of reports through the use of computers and other modern techniques. The accountant who masters the material in this book will be qualified to fulfill his role as the interpreter and reporter of all quantitative information necessary to the proper operation of his organization.

Contents

Effective Accounting Reports

1

Effective Reporting Techniques

The choice of the form and the techniques of presenting information to management is a major determinant of whether the report will be understood and used. The forms of presentation include written, oral, and visual. The written form includes tabulations of numbers, charts and graphs, narrative, and a combination of these. Oral forms include chart-room discussions, personal contacts, and audio-inquiry devices. Visual forms include personal inspection and visual display devices.

These forms of presentation are covered in this and other chapters throughout this book. The emphasis in this chapter, however, is upon the techniques which may be used in connection with all these forms to make the report presentation more effective. To have value, the report must be used. The information must be seen or heard, and be understood by the receiver before it can be used. Certain techniques, correctly used, can increase understanding.

TECHNIQUES FOR EFFECTIVE REPORTS—
CONSIDER PERSONALITIES FIRST

The report recipient is a part of the communication system at work, having individual goals and helping to achieve company goals. He is a block in the pyramid of authority and responsibility relationships.

In this chapter we view the recipient as a personality. We attempt to bring out considerations which we may turn into techniques for more effective reporting.

1

Who Is Going to Read the Report?

This is a critical point in report preparation. The report must be written and presented so that the reader is able to understand the contents and take action based upon the report. It must be prepared for him and be neither above nor below his understanding, for maximum effectiveness. The more the report writer knows about the reader, the better. His prior knowledge, position in the company, his authority and responsibilities, his personal characteristics and preferences, his temperament and biases should all be considered. Receivers vary in their desire for detail and in the presentation methods preferred. Some want great detail so as to draw their own conclusions; others want the writer's conclusions and recommendations supported by a minimum of information. Some want figures, tables, charts, graphs; others prefer narrative or oral presentations. Some want all the evidence and no recommendations; others want only recommendations.

Considering the personality of the report recipient is a key technique for effective reporting. Find out what kind of report gets the desired reaction from the reader, and use it.

Who Is Going to Receive and Act on the Report?

Reading, receiving and acting on the report are different actions, and may be performed by different people. The initial recipient may read the report, but pass it on to his subordinate for action. The subordinate, of course, must also read the report, so it must be written for him, too.

The report writer may know the report will go to the subordinate, but wish to direct the report to the supervisor. This is either because the ultimate responsibility lies there, or in order to appeal to the authority of the supervisor in getting action out of the subordinate.

Why Does the Reader Want the Report? How Will He Use It?

It may be that the reader wants the report in order to serve as the basis for a certain decision; he may want it for the purpose of controlling future events; he may wish to review the performance of his subordinates. All are legitimate bases for receiving a specific report. But the personality of the reader may be such that he relies on his intuition first and uses the reports as justification or rationalization for his decisions. The report preparer must know the receiver and his personality, and the uses to which he *actually* puts the information contained in the report.

What Does the Reader Expect to Get from the Report?

Does he expect the solution to his problems? Clarification of problem areas? Alternative approaches to a solution? Facts surrounding the cause? Facts pertinent to the solution? Background information only?

The requirements of the reader must be known before effective reports may be prepared. Frequently, if asked, the manager cannot give an accurate statement of the information he needs to do his job. Here the accountant must understand the situation and be imaginative and creative in his suggestions. A principal technique for effective reporting, therefore, is first to consider the personalities involved in the reporting situation.

TECHNIQUES FOR EFFECTIVE REPORTS— CONSIDER CONTENT NEXT

Chapter 3, "Designing and Building an Effective Reporting System," covers many ideas, most of which when cast into a do-it-this-way mold, become techniques for better reports to management. The report content is the next major consideration.

Emphasize the Principal Items

Management's time is limited, and reports must compete for their share along with many other things that demand attention. The principal items in the report should be given first, and emphasized by various mechanical aids illustrated later in this chapter. Principal items may be summarized in the first pages. A transmittal letter accompanying the report may state the problem and the material covered in the report.

Pinpoint Responsibilities for Results

All costs and revenues should be the responsibility of some individual somewhere in the responsibility pyramid. For effective reporting these people should be identified by name and job title, and included in the report itself. This pinpoints responsibility for corrective action or reward. It shows the manager who within his sphere of responsibility is or is not performing as planned.

Putting names of the responsible individuals in the report is most easily done in narrative reports. These could be incorporated within the narrative itself, or set off to the right or left margin in a separate column. If the latter is done, the person's telephone extension could also be included for the reader's convenience if he wished additional information.

If tabular reports are prepared, the names could be put in the accompanying comments. If no comments are prepared, the names could be put in the heading and within the body of the report. In Figure 3-7, Operating Summary for Vendco Service, Inc., the title could include the name of the Northeast Area Manager, and the body of the report could include the names of his subordinates in charge of each of the three regions for which he is ultimately responsible. The point is, responsibility should be pinpointed and names given; this focuses attention where it should be, on the individual, and not on the figures themselves or an impersonal segment of the firm.

Compare Actual with Planned Performance

Pinpointing responsibility does little good if there are no standards against which to measure actual performance. The accountant must present information which illustrates these differences. The standards may be composed of forecasts, plans, or budgets. Or they may be actual figures of the past—either last month, or the same month or period last year. As pointed out earlier, these comparisons of actual with actual should be on a normalized basis; that is, the past figures should be restated on the basis of today's conditions. Effective reports use the technique of including meaningful comparisons in the main report.

Show the Effects of Operations upon Position

Whether the report covers a division or a foreman's responsibility center, the current operations have had an effect upon the previous status of that center. Not only should the change be shown, but the responsible manager should also be told his current position. There will then be two related measures for his comparison: actual operations against planned, and previous against current status.

Carefully Plan Information Classification and Arrangement

Careful placement of the information, and the titles used, is as much an effective reporting technique as the data itself. All accountants know items are easily "buried"; conversely, items may be easily emphasized. It is up to the accountant to classify the data and arrange it in the order most useful for the intended purpose of the report. Psychology plays a large part in determining the arrangement. Reports that highlight and emphasize the exceptions will probably receive more attention and induce quicker action than ones showing columns of figures in routine fashion.

Feature Controllability of Elements

Following the responsibility reporting concept, the technique of featuring controllable elements is very important. Showing uncontrollable costs on a report may be interesting information to the receiver, but if they are uncontrollable by him, they are irrelevant and useless. Only controllable events should be reported to him.

Match the Level Reported To with the Appropriate Detail

In addition to reporting only controllable costs and revenues to specific responsibility levels, the detail included should be commensurate with that level. The lower the management level, the greater detail that is needed to plan and control operations, because the span of responsibility is small. Going up the reporting levels, the span grows broader, and less detail about lower-level operations is needed. This technique requires close attention to the purpose of the report, the reader's preferences, and the uses to which he puts the report information.

Make Reports Timely, Prompt, and Regular

This technique is largely psychological; the reader comes to look forward to receiving regular reports (if they have proved useful), and to receiving information contained in special reports when they are requested. Some executives use the regular receipt of reports at a definite hour or day to regulate their own operations and plans. From this viewpoint, reports should be prompt. They also must be timely. In order to issue reports promptly, the right information must be readily available. All that should be needed is its assembly into the proper form, and even here some preplanning and standardization can cut down the receive-request, fill-request lag time. Effective reporting heavily relies on this technique of availability of information when and where needed.

Sacrifice Details, But Not Accuracy

No matter how detailed a report is, or how broad its coverage, it should be numerically accurate. The reporting process may be speeded up by using flash reports, in which only preliminary or even estimated data is included. This is acceptable to get some results faster, but they should still be arithmetically accurate. If they are otherwise, it causes the reader to lose faith in the whole content of the report.

TECHNIQUES FOR EFFECTIVE REPORTS— MECHANICS OF PRESENTATION

As the need to exercise operational control increases, the need for effective tools to help do this job also increases. The creative accounting report that stresses action is such a tool. Action reports motivate management to take the desired action, be it corrective or planning action. These reports should stress the figures significant for the user's purpose. It is hard to say what is significant here, because each situation is different. But volume, rate, dollar, trend, and percentages are possibilities; performance indicators, indexes, statistics, analyses will be pertinent in specific circumstances.

Techniques That Command Reader's Attention

The "how" of presenting reports is a most critical area. Whether the report lives in the manager's mind or dies in his files is based to a large extent upon the eye appeal of the report package. A constant stream of information competes for the manager's attention. The reading of reports or other communications that look difficult to digest or time-consuming is likely to be put off as long as possible. Unless it is useful or indispensable, this may be forever. If the report deserves the manager's attention, producing an attractive report deserves the accountant's attention.

Clearly Identify the Report. We have noted that a descriptive and interesting title is preferable. But avoid making it too long or complex, which may cause uncertainty about what is really in the report. It may be worth the cost to invest in a typewriter with quarter inch characters, and use it to prominently display report titles and other material. (This type shows up well in view-graph transparencies, too, for aiding oral presentations.)

Leave Plenty of White Space. Too much detail in one place is both confusing and un-appealing. It may be a sign of too much information. It is a sign of too much information on one page, at least. The information should be reduced to more significant figures or presented in several pages or reports instead of one. Charts and graphs especially should have plenty of white space; too much detail on a single graph is forbidding and many readers are lost in trying to figure it out. Ease of visual interpretation is fostered by presenting only one or two ideas on each graph. White space has eye appeal; use this technique to good advantage.

Produce Neat Reports. Eye appeal is also gained by neatness; attention is distracted by things that make the report unneat. Dirty typewriter keys (where "o's" and other loop letters are blackened in), inferior reproduction methods that leave ink spots or smudges, erasures and over-strikes, a poor typing job generally, all these contribute to the man-ager's unwillingness to read the report. Computer prepared reports are especially suscep-tible to sloppy production. Overused ribbons and light or smudged carbon copies are prime offenders. The report that is to command careful reading, first commands careful preparation.

Be Consistent in Writing Style and Exhibits. Writing style is covered in Chapter 2, and the subject of exhibits is treated in considerable detail in Chapter #6. The technique to point out here is that the report should be consistent in writing style and exhibits. Report techniques become habitual, which is both good and bad. Changes are usually desirable when conditions change, but consistency is desirable otherwise, generally. If a certain format has proven successful, it should be changed when it can be improved, but not before. Even then, erratic changes are undesirable; the changes should be introduced gradually. You should be consistent in presenting similar tabular reports for the different managerial levels.

Details in the reports should be given attention for consistent treatment. Likewise, within each sheet the same information should be given for each category. For example, if there are several divisions being detailed in a specific report, the same information should be given for each one—sales, costs, profits, or whatever is the subject of the report. Also, each month's actual performance report should be matched line-for-line with the forecast or budget of the future months, and with the actual for those months when they occur, for the year-to-date, and for the total year. Reports prepared this way require a minimum of reader reorientation, and quicker interpretation is made possible. Speed and accuracy in preparing the report is likewise facilitated.

Be Consistent in Pagination and Indexing. A method of numbering the report pages should be devised—whatever best fits the company and its managers' preferences. There are at least two obvious possibilities:

- Numerical sequence—straight numbering of pages. These should be keyed to a table of contents.
- Number the major reports—give a number in numerical sequence to the major reports, and letters to the supporting schedules. The income statement (num-ber 4 for example), would have supporting schedules for cost of sales (4A), direct operating expenses (4B), etc. A table of contents is again desirable. If

this system is retained month after month, this technique becomes a time saver in preparing and reading the report.

Indexing should follow the standardized pagination plan. By indexing reports is usually meant listing them on the first page as a form of table of contents. This index should have a full page (or more) to itself, comprising the introduction to a group of reports that are basically tabular. A table of contents page would usually be prepared for a narrative report.

Be Consistent in Punctuation and Mechanics. Tabular reports appear almost exclusively without punctuation. Narrative reports and the narrative comments in tabular reports should show consistent and correct grammatical use of the various punctuation marks. Carelessness in punctuation, mechanics, and spelling is seldom excused, especially by the boss, even though he may be interested chiefly in the content of the report. Most college-size dictionaries have an appendix covering the elements of punctuation and their correct usage. Your office should not be without this writing aid. Some secretary's handbooks have similar sections, but are a second choice to a good dictionary for the office.

Be Consistent in Using Covers, Binding, Tabs, and Paper. Although this technique is fairly obvious, frequently it is overlooked. The report covers, binding, tabs and dividers, and report paper should be standardized as much as possible. Again, this facilitates the recognition and use of the report.

Report covers should be heavy enough to withstand the expected use, and attractive. Using colored covers is a personal preference; psychologists tell us that blue is the most eye-pleasing color, so readers are more initially receptive to reports with blue covers than others. In any event, a certain (preferably soft pastel) color should be chosen and consistently used. The covers should be slightly larger than the paper so as to allow a small outside margin. A cover that lies flat is preferable to one that does not, and care should be taken to see that none of the information is hidden under the binding. There should be a uniform cover for all accounting reports to management; frequently, companies standardize binders for all reports issued within the company.

The binding is also a matter of preference and cost. A staple in the upper left-hand corner is the simplest, and may suffice for short informal reports. Acco, Prestong, and other two-hole left-margin fasteners are available and widely used. Probably the most attractive and relatively inexpensive binding for reports of five or more pages is the multiple-punch plastic backbone binder sold under a number of brand names. Again, this should be standardized.

Using tabs and dividers facilitates reference and reading. This technique saves reader look-up time and invites ready reference to specific report sections. Tabs and dividers may be used with a table of contents or may take its place. In the latter situation, the divider usually would have printed on it the contents of that section. Preferably the contents would appear at the beginning of the report and on each of the section dividers.

The paper used in reports should be standardized as well. For non-computer operations, usually two sizes will cover all situations: 8½" x 11" and 11" x 16". The latter would be used for a wide spread of data, and folded once to conform to the basic 8½" x 11" sheet size. This system eliminates having to turn the report from a vertical to a horizontal position in order to read the page.

Computer operations pose a bigger paper problem. The standard sheet size is 11″ x 14″. This may be folded to the regular 8½″ x 11″ page size and bound on the left margin along with the narrative comments. But frequently no narrative comments accompany the report, and being oversized, the reports are not bound. They are transmitted loose, and are less effective. Reproduction machines are available to reduce standard computer printouts to 8½″ x 11″, but the cost of this would probably be prohibitive for most firms. Report covers should be used if at all possible, as well as good paper and good carbons.

Make Every Report Self-Explanatory. The manager should not have to search the report for additional information he needs, nor have to ask the accountant for another report. The accountant should find out what the manager's information requirements are, and fill these with understandable and complete reports.

Techniques That Increase Eye Appeal

There are several techniques that may be employed to increase eye appeal. These techniques emphasize the numbers, the narrative, the readability, and the understandability by various means. Comments on and illustrations of these follow.

Emphasize the Figures. This may be done by using color, boxes or gutters, lines and spaces, and half-tone overlays.

Color may be used effectively to highlight current figures or variances. This is often hard to do unless the accountant has access to special printing equipment. Less expensive devices are available, however, such as simply using a different color (for example, blue) ribbon on the typewriter, or by using different colored Ditto masters if this brand of machine is available.

Color also may be used to identify reports of a certain division or department. Differently colored paper may be specified for separate departments, making the combined report easily identifiable. Or, a color scheme can be used on tabs and dividers; this helps the reader to find a particular segment of the report immediately.

If reproduction equipment is used which cannot print colors, using the box or box-and-gutter technique is a good substitute. These two techniques focus the reader's attention on an easily digested or important segment of the report. At the same time they emphasize related data so that relationships may be quickly appreciated.

The *box-and-gutter* technique is illustrated in Figure 1-1a. The material is separated into six boxes, each of which is divided from the others by a "gutter." Total revenue from sales and operations is shown in the upper center box. Cost of sales, operating costs and gross margin is in the lower center box. The left side columns show data for this month; the right side columns show year-to-date information. Each box is related to the others in both importance of the information and in its layout. But each may be viewed separately if desired. Too many boxes would probably be confusing; a maximum of eight for an 8½″ x 11″ sheet, or 16 boxes for an 11″ x 16″ sheet, is recommended. On Figure 1-1a, six boxes are shown, which presents an eye-appealing arrangement. An alternative would be to segregate the budget variances into separate boxes as well, but this seems unnecessary.

The *box around significant items* is also easy to use to guide the reader's attention. This is illustrated in Figure 1-1b. The amount columns for the month and year-to-date are enclosed in boxes to relate them to the account titles, to each other, and to make them stand out from the other columnar data which was deemed (in this case) to be less important. The boxes may be drawn in by hand before reproduction, or if a single report is to be issued, afterward.

The box-and-gutter technique is also illustrated on Figure 1-3. On this position statement, the significant sections are assets, liabilities, and equity. Here the separation is not so much to divide the information into digestible portions as to relate the traditional sections of this statement to one another: the assets on the left, and on the right the liabilities and owner equity.

Half-tone overlays may also be used to emphasize significant items. This technique is illustrated in Figure 1-2. There the amount columns, this month and year-to-date, are set out. Half-tone overlays are made by Para-tone, Inc., and other companies, and consist of pressure-sensitive, thin film sheets of various screen patterns. They come in a matte or gloss finish, and in a number of colors and special symbols. Office supply and architect supply stores normally carry a variety on hand, or can order specially from available catalogues. The overlay is merely cut to the desired size and pasted over the figures or other items to be emphasized. If desired, the overlay may be written, typed, or drawn upon. A light (10% to 20%), fine (60 to 85 line) dot screen is recommended so as not to obscure the figures that you desire to emphasize. Graduated dot screens, line screens, or special pattern screens are especially helpful in making charts and graphs.

Lines and spaces may be used when presenting figures to emphasize items and enhance readability. Using plenty of white space improves the appearance of the report; using lines to divide the information improves the comprehension. This technique is illustrated in Figure 1-6. The three most significant items are shown separately: sales, cost of sales, and gross profit. The detail of cost of sales is in a section by itself. This technique eliminates the need for additional lines and double underlining of totals. For certain types of reports this works well. The information must be separable and significant in itself, and not include too many items in each section.

Guidelines may also be used to good advantage. Although it is recommended that the reports not contain more information than can be easily comprehended, occasionally it is necessary to have listings of items. The eye does not follow very easily single-spaced columnar data, so it should be broken by eye guidelines at no more than every sixth item. The fourth or fifth is even more preferable. This technique is illustrated in Figure 1-1a also, where guidelines exist in each of the upper and lower boxes across the page. The standard computer stock paper is preprinted with guidelines or alternating white and shaded areas. Whether lined or shaded, the area enclosed is usually only two or three lines wide, which makes the data even easier to read. The guideline should be a fine line, lighter than that used as data boundaries in the boxes or box-and-gutter. The reader thereby distinguishes it as a guideline and not as a total line.

Emphasize Titles and Particulars. These may be emphasized by various techniques. These include lead-off captions, indentation, enumeration, print types, and preprinted headings.

Personal preference governs in the use of *lead-off captions*. Some say that lead-off cap-

DEEP SOUTH DEVELOPMENT COMPANY

OPERATING STATEMENT

MONTH ENDING JULY 31, 1969

CORPORATE

( ) Indicates Under Budget
Figures in thousands

ACCOUNT	AMOUNT THIS MONTH (000)	PERCENT OF INCOME	BUDGET VARIANCE (000)	AMOUNT YEAR TO DATE (000)	PERCENT OF INCOME	BUDGET VARIANCE (000)
Gross sales						
Subdivision real estate	$ 652	50	$21	$ 3,805	49	$84
Investment properties	190	15	-0-	1,152	15	(5)
Joint ventures	54	4	2	324	4	2
Operating revenue						
Rental property	127	10	-0-	748	10	4
Oil, gas and mineral	82	6	(3)	490	6	5
Joint venture	164	12	5	986	13	8
Other	44	3	(1)	255	3	(6)
Less sales deductions	(4)	-0-	-0-	(25)	-0-	-0-
TOTAL REVENUE	$1,309	100	$24	$7,735	100	$92
Cost of sales						
Subdivision real estate closed	$322	24	$(4)	$1,633	21	$ 8
Investment properties	50	4	1	300	4	(2)
Joint ventures	38	3	(1)	235	3	(4)
Operating Expense						
Rental property	87	7	2	625	8	6
Oil, gas and mineral	58	4	3	350	5	5
Joint ventures	89	7	(2)	546	7	(7)
Other	114	9	1	685	9	(3)
GROSS MARGIN	$551	42	$24	$3,361	43	$89

(continued below)

Figure 1-1a.

10

CORPORATE OPERATING STATEMENT

(Continued)

Page 2 of 2

BUDGET VARIANCE (000)	PERCENT OF INCOME	AMOUNT THIS MONTH (000)	ACCOUNT	AMOUNT YEAR TO DATE (000)	PERCENT OF INCOME	BUDGET VARIANCE (000)
			General and administrative overhead			
$ 3	8	$108	Division	$ 548	7	$10
3	7	158	Corporate	1,052	6	(4)
(7)	13	102	Other	128	9	(3)
$(1)	28	$368	TOTAL OVERHEAD	$1,728	22	$ 3
$25	14	$183	NET PROFIT – Deep South Development Company (Parent)	$1,633	21	$86
			PROFITS FROM SUBSIDIARIES			
$-0-		$ 5	Better Made Construction Company	$ 25		$-0-
–		9	Diversified Property Rentals	30		5
-0-		1	Sherwood Forest Land Corporation	4		-0-
-0-		(4)	Unified Water Company	(20)		-0-
$26	15	$194	COMBINED PROFIT BEFORE INCOME TAXES	$1,672	21	$91
		89	Estimated income taxes	648		
		$105	COMBINED NET PROFIT	$1,024	21	

Figure 1-1b.

11

DEEP SOUTH DEVELOPMENT COMPANY

OPERATING STATEMENT   ( ) Indicates Under Budget

MONTH ENDING JULY 31, 1969

CORPORATE ADMINISTRATION

BUDGET VARIANCE	PERCENT OF TOTAL OVERHEAD	AMOUNT THIS MONTH	ACCOUNT	AMOUNT YEAR TO DATE	PERCENT OF TOTAL OVERHEAD	BUDGET VARIANCE
$(3,500)	66	$ 105,000	Salary, wages and commissions	$ 650,000	62	$(25,000)
1,500	9	13,500	Rentals and utilities	85,000	8	(2,000)
			Supplies, maintenance and repairs	62,000	6	(1,000)
0	2	3,000	Depreciation and amortization	22,000	2	0
4,700	22	35,000	Interest, insurance and taxes	225,000	21	22,000
500	1	1,700	Miscellaneous	8,500	1	2,000
$ 3,200		$ 158,200	TOTAL ADMINISTRATIVE OVERHEAD	$1,052,500		$(4,000)

Figure 1-2.

12

DEEP SOUTH DEVELOPMENT COMPANY

POSITION STATEMENT

MONTH ENDING JULY 31, 1969

ASSETS

	July 31, 1969	July 31, 1968
CASH	$ 1,009,432	$ 703,717
MARKETABLE SECURITIES	462,310	508,910
RECEIVABLES:		
Installment notes	4,623,115	4,737,745
Other receivables	628,073	810,458
	5,251,188	5,548,203
REAL ESTATE HELD FOR DEVELOPMENT AND SALE:		
Land	16,960,105	16,735,732
Buildings	2,645,100	2,645,100
	19,605,205	19,380,832
REAL ESTATE HELD FOR INVESTMENT:		
Land	7,756,711	5,556,714
Buildings	965,106	1,710,100
Leaseholds	1,856,100	856,100
	10,577,917	8,122,914
JOINT VENTURE REAL ESTATE:		
Land	1,020,110	920,110
Buildings	150,620	150,620
Leaseholds	102,969	102,969
	1,273,699	1,173,699
EQUIPMENT, net of depreciation	1,677,329	2,033,914
OTHER INVESTMENTS	3,861,306	3,451,283
PREPAID EXPENSES AND OTHER ASSETS	808,180	1,250,047
TOTAL ASSETS	$42,849,237	$42,173,519

LIABILITIES

	July 31, 1969	July 31, 1968
ACCOUNTS PAYABLE	$ 2,220,120	$ 1,820,167
ACCRUED EXPENSES	577,682	1,042,657
NOTES AND CONTRACTS PAYABLE		
To banks	16,582,391	17,862,561
To others	1,961,385	6,621,632
	18,543,776	24,484,193
ACCOUNTS WITH AFFILIATES		
Notes payable to Sherwood Forest Land Corporation	1,000,000	1,350,000
Other affiliates	10,067	24,278
Current federal taxes payable to Sherwood Forest Land Corp.	52,678	174,473
Deferred federal taxes payable to Sherwood Forest Land Corp.	1,502,385	1,232,086
	2,565,130	2,780,837
TOTAL LIABILITIES	$23,906,708	$30,127,854

EQUITY

	July 31, 1969	July 31, 1968
CAPITAL STOCK AND SURPLUS		
Capital stock	$ 2,000,000	$ 2,000,000
Capital surplus	2,732,119	2,732,119
Retained earnings	14,210,410	7,313,546
TOTAL EQUITY	$18,942,529	$12,045,665
TOTAL	$42,849,237	$42,173,519

Figure 1-3.

13

tions should be descriptive, even if this makes them somewhat long; others say they should be used sparingly, or not at all. For example, in Figure 1-1a, the lead-off captions of Gross Sales, Operating Revenue, Cost of Sales, and Operating Expense conceivably could be eliminated altogether. However, the report seems more readable with them included; certainly the uninitiated would find them helpful. Lead-off captions are used to explain or classify the details in the report. Whether this caption clarifies or clutters depends upon the individual case. Where the caption may be eliminated without significant loss of understandability to the reader, it may be eliminated. Then the details should be reworded to include the information formerly contained in the caption. For example, in Figure 1-1b the caption "General and Administrative Overhead" could be eliminated and the section revised:

> Division Overhead
> Corporate Overhead
> Other Overhead
>
> Total General and Administrative Overhead

Figure 1-2 also shows no lead-off caption, and includes a reworded total line.

Another technique that increases eye appeal is the use of *reverse indentation*. The main items are listed on the margin and less important items and details are indented in step fashion. Practice varies as to placing totals: they may either be indented further or placed at the margin. Figures 1-1a and 1-1b show this reverse indentation: captions, details and total. Figures 1-2 through 1-5 also show the totals indented, since the authors consider this to be more eye-appealing. Placing the total on the margin causes the section to be somewhat unsymmetrical, and sometimes it competes for attention with the lead-off caption for the following section. By indenting to the left, that is, using reverse indentation, it can be seen that the amounts at similar indentations add down. Indenting to the right obscures this relationship.

The reader might contrast the reverse indentation technique used in Figures 1-1 through 1-5 with Figure 1-6 which uses "regular" indentation for the items. Regular in this case refers to the normal procedure for narrative writing, indenting the first word of the paragraph several spaces, that is, indenting to the right. You will agree, we think, that this report is not so eye-pleasing as those preceding it. Further, it is hard to know just which item is important. Reverse indentation makes the important items and relationships stand out.

Lists of items in narrative are almost lost if they are placed within the line separated only by commas. Both eye appeal and emphasis are gained by listing the items in a column, either indented or on the margin. For example, the manufacturing variances for the period and the explanations are:

Variance	Cause	Amount
• Material price	favorable purchase of material X	$10,000 fav.
• Material usage	excessive waste	4,000 unfav.
• Labor rate	10% wage settlement boost	8,000 unfav.

- Labor efficiency   shutdown from strike   12,000 unfav.
- Overhead-fixed   idle capacity from
                   strike   8,000 unfav.
- Overhead-variable   savings in cost of
                   services   4,000 fav.

Instead of placing a bullet or asterisk before these items, they may be numbered one through six. Frequently, an out-of-the-ordinary treatment (such as arrows, stars, periods) can be more eye-catching.

Using *different print types,* or strategically using upper and lower case letters is another effective emphasis technique. The variety helps the reader to distinguish differences and perceive the relative importance of the item without knowing its technical content. One of the things helping to differentiate and emphasize is the use of upper and lower case type. Also, different type faces are relatively easy to acquire now without resorting to a complete printing shop. Specifically, by using the IBM Selectric Typewriter with the interchangeable typing elements, or a VariTyper which has a greater variety of type faces available, differentiation is possible.

Figures 1-1 and 1-2 show the use of both upper and lower case in captions and details, and all uppercase letters for totals and column headings. In the former, only the first letter of the first word is capitalized. This is easier to type than having all first letters capitalized, and easier to read, too.

Using first-letter capitalization on all words in the detail is shown on Figure 1-4. Upper case is used on all captions and totals. This form seems less desirable than that used in the previous paragraph, which we recommend. Capitalized captions are shown also in Figure 1-3.

Only capitalized letters are used on Figures 1-5 and 1-6. Where the information shown is relatively sparce and spread out, using all capital letters looks all right. However, as noted above, we recommend capitalizing only the first letter of the first word in the detail items.

Computer printed reports are a problem. Since type faces are all capitalized, differentiation can be effected only by other means. Indentation to the left (reverse indentation), spacing, white space, and the other hand-drawn devices mentioned above are possibilities. In any event, emphasis of certain items must be gained by using the most practical and effective means.

Preprinted heading forms are both a time-saver and an eye-catcher. When the format of the report is set and prospects are that it will remain so for some time, serious thought should be given to this technique. Although preprinted forms (headings, column titles, eye guidelines and column dividers) are more expensive than stock paper, the appearance and readability is enhanced, and is normally worth the added cost. The headings may be color coded for emphasis or segmentation, such as for the various management levels, and easily tied in to each other by standardizing the form to be used for each report.

Emphasize Readability of Figures and Titles. Various techniques are available to emphasize readability. These include having columns add down, rounding off figures, eliminating dollar signs, putting particulars in the middle, and logical placement.

Having the columns add down increases readability and comprehension. You should

DEEP SOUTH DEVELOPMENT COMPANY

CASH FLOW PROJECTION

MONTH ENDING JULY 31, 1969

CORPORATE

( ) Indicates Under Budget
Figures in thousands

	ACTUAL YEAR TO DATE	ANNUALIZED FISCAL VARIANCE	ANNUALIZED FISCAL PROJECTION	ANNUALIZED FISCAL BUDGET
NET CASH FLOW FROM OPERATIONS:				
Texas District	121.5-	14.0-	385.9-	371.9-
Central and Gulf Coast District	326.9-	20.6	53.9-	74.6-
Northern Coast District	293.2-	50.0-	194.3-	144.3-
Southern Coast District	298.4	120.4	823.0	702.7
Oil, Gas and Mineral	54.2	6.9	313.5	306.6
Unified Water Company	48.2-	.8	149.2-	150.0-
TOTAL OPERATING DIVISION CASH FLOW	337.2-	84.6	353.1	268.5
LESS:				
HOME OFFICE REQUIREMENTS:				
Mortgage Principal Payments	6.5	---	---	58.0
Repayments--Project Line-of-Credit	900.0	62.0	4,259.7	4,197.7
Interest	640.0	40.0	1,115.0	1,075.0
Administrative Overhead	100.1	9.9-	760.1	770.0
TOTAL HOME OFFICE REQUIREMENTS	1,646.6	92.1	6,134.8	6,090.7
NET CASH FLOW	1,983.8-	7.6-	5,781.8-	5,822.2-
BANK BORROWINGS REQUIRED	1,790.0	---	5,570.0	5,070.0
TOTAL CASH AVAILABLE	193.8-	---	---	752.2-

Figure 1-4.

DEEP SOUTH DEVELOPMENT COMPANY

PROPERTY STATUS REPORT

JULY 31, 1969

PROPERTY NAME	CODE	ESTIMATED FAIR MARKET VALUE	BOOK VALUE	LESS TOTAL BORROWINGS	EQUITY INVESTMENT	NET INCOME % OF EQUITY YEAR-TO-DATE	INDEX
TOWN & COUNTRY APTS.	13-60	708 999	750 000	Bank 600 000	108 999	10%	1.10
TOWN & COUNTRY SHOPPING CENTER	13-71	42 768	573 000		42 768	(2)	1.15
TOWN & COUNTRY CAFETERIA	13-72	60 433	379 950		60 433	5	.65
MILKY WAY GOLF COURSE	13-73	491 075	531 000	Note 5 000	486 075	(6)	1.50
NEW ORLEANS LEASEHOLD	13-85	2 431	145 000		2 431	(25)	1.00
TOTAL		1 305 706	3 378 950	605 000	700 706		

Figure 1-5.

never expect the reader to be able to add across more than two or three items, and if one column is a subtraction item, the chore is even more difficult. Where several items are added together, they should be listed so that they add down all in one group. From this total should come the subtraction item noted by the word "less" or by the figure being in parentheses.

If the sum of several items is subtracted from another total, the items to be added to get the total minus figure should be set off to the left of the main column, drawing only the sum to be subtracted into the main column. If guidelines are not used, a single line should separate the details from the total figure. Preferably the total figure should be double underlined. This technique is demonstrated in Figures 1-2, 1-3, and 1-5. The lines within the boxes in Figure 1-1 take the place of addition lines and double underlining, as do the divisions in Figure 1-6. Figure 1-4 is reproduced without addition lines or double underlining; you can see that this procedure is clearly less desirable than the other presentations.

Computer printouts are no exception. They can be made to look better by using addition underlining and totals double underlining. The dash may be used for the addition line, and while not a solid line, is more desirable than no line. The equal sign is used to double underline; again the lines are not solid, but are preferable to nothing. An alternative that is sometimes used is to place a single asterisk to the right of intermediate totals and a double asterisk by final totals. Although this does distinguish these figures somewhat, they are still not as prominently displayed as by using the line. Asterisks are also used to denote unfavorable variances; your practice should be consistent and eye-catching.

Rounding figures to significant levels is a readability-must item. The extent of the rounding depends upon many factors: the personality and preferences of the reader, the level of management reported to, the information contained in the report, and the finality of the figures. This is demonstrated most consistently in Chapter 3, "Designing and Building an Effective Reporting System." There the pyramid structure of the reporting system is illustrated by a set of coordinated reports through seven responsibility levels. The figures in these reports are rounded to progressively higher amounts as the reporting level increases.

Rounding to significant levels is also demonstrated here in several ways. Figure 1-1 is stated in thousands of dollars; the "000" has been eliminated because the zeroes do no more than clutter up the statement. Because the corporate administration is responsible for its own overhead expenditures, the schedule of administrative overhead is slightly more detailed than in Figure 1-1, being rounded in Figure 1-2 to the nearest $100. No rounding has been done in Figure 1-3; you can see that at first glance the appearance is somewhat cluttered by the detailed figures.

A different type of rounding was used in Figure 1-4. Here the figures are stated in terms of thousands, but rounded to the nearest $100. The reporter must be cautious with this technique, however, for it may be difficult for the reader to understand that to the left of the decimal place represents thousands and to the right represents hundreds. This type of rounding is especially good for projections.

The accountant *must* round off figures to levels significant to the manager being reported to. Do not clutter up the mind of the manager with useless and needless cents,

DEEP SOUTH DEVELOPMENT COMPANY

TEJON RANCH - SUBDIVISION PROJECT

PROJECTED PROFITABILITY

MONTH ENDING JULY 31, 1969   ( ) Indicates Under Budget

ACCOUNT	LATEST FILING INCOME AND EXPENSE PROJECTED-TO-DATE		CURRENT WORK IN-PROCESS		PROJECT BUDGET VARIANCE	PROJECT TOTAL PROJECTED	PROJECT TOTAL BUDGET
	UNITS	AMOUNT	UNITS	AMOUNT			
SUBDIVISION SALES	10	468 800	10		(50 000)	5 138 000	5 188 000
COST OF SALES							
LAND COSTS	10	60 000	10	60 000		600 000	600 000
SUB-CONTRACTING COSTS	10	345 000	10	22 000	(9 200)	3 520 800	3 530 000
MATERIAL COSTS		28 100		4 000	(5 500)	214 500	220 000
LABOR COSTS		8 500		800	(4 300)	115 700	120 000
OTHER DIRECT CHARGES		8 000				80 000	80 000
TOTAL COST OF SALES		449 600		86 800	(19 000)	4 531 000	4 550 000
TOTAL GROSS PROFIT		19 200			(31 000)	607 000	638 000

TOTAL SALES	%
ACTUAL: 1,253 000 to date	24%
PROJECTED: 5 138 000 for project	100%

TOTAL COST	% of SALES
ACTUAL: 1 615 400 to date	129%
PROJECTED: 4 531 000 for project	88%

% OF ROI
2%
13%

Figure 1-6.

dollars, hundreds, and even thousands. The time and effort it takes for the accountant to do the rounding is no excuse for neglecting it. The accounting department exists to serve management; preparing effective reports (rounded figures!) is simply one way to serve.

Rounding to significant levels follows two simple rules:

- If the number being eliminated is four or below, round down to the lower zero; if it is five through nine, round up to the higher zero. Ignore all digits to the right. For example:

  3,4̲46 is rounded to 3,400 (ignore the 6).
  7,7̲62 is rounded to 7,800 (ignore the 2).

- In rounding figures added to each other vertically or horizontally, round the most significant figures (that is, the most important) first, next round the intermediate totals, making them agree with the most significant ones, then round the details to the intermediate totals. This process will not always result in following the first rule precisely, but it will minimize the overall distortion.

Eliminating dollar signs and thousands' commas also helps to increase eye appeal and emphasize readability. Accountants traditionally have put dollar signs on the main statements—the balance sheet and income statement. They need go no further, and there is serious question whether they are needed on these either. Unless there are unit figures or percentages (and these may be clearly marked as such) there is usually no need to put dollar signs on the reports. Again, they merely clutter the statement and add nothing to the understanding of the figures. Spaces left where the thousands' and millions' commas go also enhance readability.

In Figure 1-1, the thousands' comma was eliminated in the rounding; the millions' comma is retained. The dollar sign also is retained on the first figure of the series and the total of that series. In Figure 1-3, because there are so many series to be added, the dollar sign was placed only on the first and last items in each of the three sections. Dollar signs have been eliminated from Figures 1-4, 1-5, and 1-6, with no loss of understanding and with an increase in readability. On Figures 1-5 and 1-6, the thousands' and millions' commas have been eliminated. This latter technique depends upon the reader's preference; many prefer the comma to a blank space. If no commas are used, there must be a larger-than-usual space between the columns so as to differentiate sufficiently the columnar data and so that there will not be too much data on the page itself.

Rounding percentages to significant levels also increases readability. Where the figures used as the basis for percentages are projections, or are themselves of questionable accuracy, there is no need to carry percentages out to several decimal places. And frequently more detail simply is not needed. In either case, percentages carried to several decimal places are not needed and may even be misleading. Normally one decimal place is sufficient, and usually percentages with no decimal points are preferable. Figures 1-1 through 1-6 are all presented in this latter fashion. The illustrative pyramid reports in Chapter 3, "Designing and Building an Effective Reporting System," are presented to one decimal place. The latter procedure is preferable when the rounding of the dollar amounts is not extensive and the figures themselves are relatively small in some cases and less than 1% of the total.

Particulars should be put in the middle if at all possible. This helps the reader's eyes easily to follow the figures across the page on both sides of the particulars. This is demonstrated especially in Figures 1-1 and 1-2. In addition, this format helps to separate the numbers into their two distinctive groups. Figures 1-3 and 1-5 do not lend themselves to this format. However, Figures 1-4 and 1-6 could have easily been recast with the particulars in the middle for increased readability.

Emphasize Understanding by These Techniques. Several techniques are available which are easy to use and quite essential for increased comprehension of the information presented. These techniques revolve around various presentations of differences.

Using comparison bases without further interpretation in themselves enhances understandability. This is demonstrated in the illustrations in Chapter 3. There the reports give this month and year-to-date figures for the current year forecast, the current year actual, and previous year actual. For each of these a further comparison base is provided by giving both the sales and contribution margin figures, and these are provided for the various areas of responsibility encompassed by the report.

Comparison bases exist, therefore, between:
- the same item
  —at different points in time
  —over different periods of time
- two related items as contrasted to each other
  —at different points in time
  —over different periods of time.

Presenting *absolute difference amounts* is one way to interpret further the comparison bases. Instead of relying upon the comparison bases themselves to tell the story to the reader, the accountant may make the subtraction and present the dollar difference between them. This may be titled "difference" or "variance." If the variance is given, depending upon the reader's desire, the least significant of the comparison bases may be eliminated. This is illustrated in Figures 1-1 and 1-2. The actual this month and year-to-date figures are given, as is the amount by which these varied from the budget. The budget figures themselves are not shown. Figure 1-4 presents the two comparison bases and the dollar difference. Thus, the "fiscal variance" is the absolute difference amount between the annualized fiscal projection and fiscal budget. Also, the actual year-to-date column provides a comparison base between it and the other annualized figures.

Figure 1-6 also presents absolute difference amounts in the "project budget variance" column. This is the difference between the project total projected and budget columns.

In making the comparison and stating the difference, you should correctly label that difference. Several alternatives are available:
- over or (under)
- increase or (decrease)
- favorable or (unfavorable)
- better or (worse)
- over or (under) budget

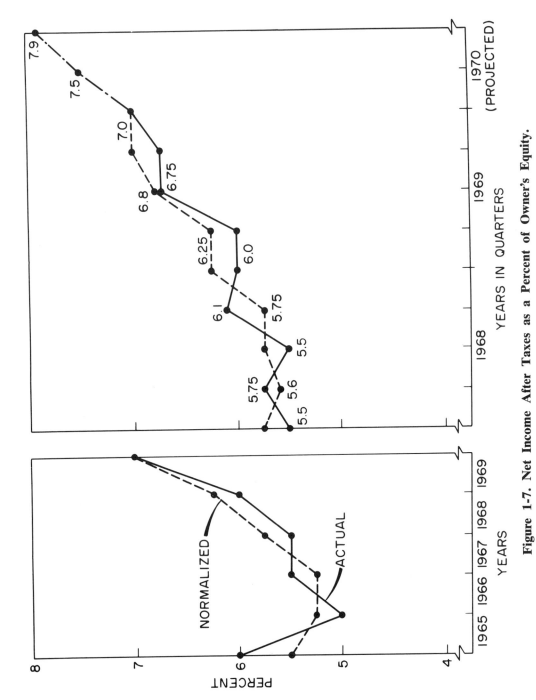

Figure 1-7. Net Income After Taxes as a Percent of Owner's Equity.

Adapted from Robert L. Seaman, "Elements of Effective Reporting," *Reporting Financial Data to Management,* American Management Association Management Report No. 83, 1965, p. 40.

To generalize, the more specific the column heading, the more understandable it will be. "Over or (under)" leaves the reader unsure of the figure being used as a base against which the comparison is made, even though only two columns are given for comparison. This is clearly the least desirable alternative. "Increase or (decrease)" is little better; the reader must himself decipher whether the difference is good or bad. An increase in some items is good; an increase in others is undesirable. To have both these interpretations in close proximity is very confusing and is to be avoided. "Favorable or (unfavorable)" and "better or (worse)" are more specific and tell the reader whether the difference was desirable or undesirable rather than merely pointing the direction of the change. "Over or (under) budget" and variations on this in each particular case is the best for it gives the comparison base and tells whether the actual was under or over budget, which the manager readily recognizes as good or bad. This, too, may be refined to a more readily understandable "favorable or (unfavorable) variance from budget."

Percentage comparisons are one more aid to emphasize comprehension. The percentage comparisons in the reports illustrated in Chapter 3 are relatively simple calculations of the details to the total on a vertical basis. Likewise, Figure 1-1 gives the breakdown of total revenue (being 100%) and the expenses as a percent of total sales. Where separate schedules of details are given, such as in Figure 1-2, the details are given as a percent of the total item in the schedule, administrative overhead in this case. Figure 1-6 gives some percentage comparisons outside the regular presentation in order to highlight these relationships.

Balance sheets commonly show the individual items stated as a percent of total assets. Where figures differ significantly from one period to another, a comparison of percentages is for some purposes more meaningful and effective than comparing dollar amounts. In this case, a difference between percentages may be stated. Statement percentages may be compared with other periods for the same firm, with other firms, or with an industry average.

Trend analyses are an important technique for emphasizing understanding. When comparisons of yearly data are made, the data should be made comparable by converting prior data to fit current circumstances. This is very difficult because of the many variables involved. Where adjustments must be made, or when comparing budgets and forecasted data on an annual basis, it may be necessary to annualize and normalize the data. *Annualizing* means to make the time periods comparable by considering holidays, differences in length of quarters or years (e.g., 52–53 week fiscal year). *Normalizing* the data means conforming certain historical information to the present or expected future conditions. This involves recognizing and effecting changes in accounting policies, product lines, volume, production methods, and other factors influencing the data. This is the only valid comparison between historical data of different periods. Figure 1-7 demonstrates a graphic trend analysis for accounted-for and normalized data comparisons of past years based upon current conditions (1969).

The supplemental analytical report is another technique used to obtain greater understanding. These reports are usually prepared by special request and may cover almost any financial and/or operating statistic. Such things that may be analyzed in greater detail include the following:

- sales: sales returns and allowances, customers
- earnings: per share, as a percentage of sales, as a percentage of stockholder equity
- cash flow
- income before taxes: as a percentage of sales, as a percentage of assets
- payroll paid: regular, bonus on profit share plan
- interest and debt service
- square feet of facilities in use: square feet idle
- cost of facilities: invested, depreciated
- accounts receivable: bad debt allowance
- working capital: current assets, current liabilities
- long-term debt: current portion
- shareholder equity: book value in dollars per share
- number of employees

Visual interpretation by the accountant for the manager is probably the technique that emphasizes understandability most. Several are illustrated in Chapter 5, "Using Visual Aids in Reporting," so they will only be listed here; others will be discussed briefly.

Flow charts have boxes and arrows to show the positions and flow of documents, responsibility, objects, or any other thing. They are often useful in clarifying and illustrating matters discussed in accounting reports. Since these are easily found and explained in great detail in systems and computer books, they will not be illustrated here.

The layout chart is a form of flow chart. It places machinery and other facilities on an area drawn to scale. It is used in reports covering various procedures or layouts. Before-and-after charts facilitate comparison of proposed and present layouts.

Charts and graphs are discussed extensively in Chapter 6.

Tabular presentation is the form most familiar to accountants. Unfortunately, unless carefully constructed, the tabular presentation is the least comprehensible. If tabular data must be presented, the techniques described in this chapter should be utilized.

Ratios can frequently improve comprehension of the report data. Ratios express relationships in meaningful terms. Percentages are a form of ratio: a true ratio is stated as "x to y," or "x : y," or "x/y." Thus, the current ratio is "current assets : current liabilities"; attaching figures we may get as an answer the ratio of 2:1, or 0.5:1—the base should always be expressed as 1. Stated as a percentage, the current ratio would be 200%, or 50%; but many "ratios" should be expressed as such, and not as a percentage.

Many ratios can be successfully applied in analyzing financial statements and operating reports. Outside-the-firm comparison figures are frequently helpful in evaluating your own firm's effectiveness. Dun and Bradstreet, Inc. annually publishes a booklet of comparative ratios for the past year. Fourteen important ratios are presented for 12 retail lines, 24 wholesale lines, and 36 manufacturing lines. The ratios are as follows:

- current assets to current debt (times)
- net profits on net sales (percent)
- net profits on tangible net worth (percent)
- net profits on net working capital (percent)
- net sales to tangible net worth (times)

- net sales to net working capital (times)
- collection period (days)
- net sales to inventory (times)
- fixed assets to tangible net worth (percent)
- current debt to tangible net worth (percent)
- total debt to tangible net worth (percent)
- inventory to net working capital (percent)
- current debt to inventory (percent)
- funded debt to net working capital (percent)

For each of the lines of business the number of reporting companies is given. For each ratio, there are three figures stated: upper quartile, median, and lower quartile. Also given is a table of median ratios for the prior four years for 70 lines of business activity, and an explanation of the computation and meaning of the ratios. These ratios have been published annually since 1931 as a yardstick for financial analysis by management, accountants, credit men, and financial analysts. In addition to this publication there are other similar publications by Robert Morris Associates and several of the nation's largest banks.

Other ratios may be calculated and included in reports to operating management. The accountant should be imaginative in relating meaningful operating statistics to derive ratios. For example, the following, and variations on them, may be helpful:

- efficiency ratio of standard to actual (material units or price, production machine or labor hours or cost, variable overhead)
- activity ratio of standard (or allowed) hours in production to normal (or budgeted) hours

Ratios may be prepared by cost or responsibility center. Frequently the efficiency ratios assist in judging the effectiveness of those in charge of the responsibility center. They should not be overlooked as an effective technique in management reporting.

2

Effective Narrative Reporting

A report—whether oral, tabular, or narrative—is a tool. It should be conceived, planned, prepared and delivered with the understanding that maximum effectiveness to the reader is its primary objective. All reports, and particularly those predominately narrative, should be shaped to the needs and purposes of the readers for whom they are intended.

Accountants Must Sharpen Narrative Reporting Skills

Because of the increased demand from management, labor, government, creditors and the general public for accounting reports of all kinds, accountants have found themselves in a dilemma. They are trained in the use and reporting of figures, but often lack the skills to put those figures into words that clearly tell the whole story and yet are brief.

Narrative reports are largely based on numbers. But being based on numbers does not mean that the accountant must merely rehash the tabular report. More is needed. Management really wants objective information of past happenings and future projections so that they can translate this into action wherever needed in the company. The normal presentation of financial results is not the whole story. Accountants should gather and integrate into their report information relating to the activities of competitors, of the present economic conditions (in their industry and in general), and of any other data that is appropriate.

Thinking and writing are very different from calculating and listing. Skill is needed in the latter, but creativity is essential to the former operations. The accountant must be able to do all these, and be better than the average person. For not only is his job at stake, but also the integrity and usefulness of the accounting profession.

27

Thinking and writing are hard jobs, but essential. The writing must be such as can be read and interpreted accurately and quickly; the report must be exact, clear, and concise. The information must be presented tactfully but firmly, and in a flexible but objective style.

Narrative reports must tie in to oral presentations. The accountant has to be objective in his reporting of internal and external data. The information should be unbiased, yet forceful enough that the manager takes the desired action. Accountants' reports contain facts describing past operations and projecting future operations; accountants, in their position as providers of this information, have become a part of the top management team. As a part of this team, accountants are becoming more involved in presenting their reports orally to others. This aspect of reporting is discussed in more detail later in this book; suffice it to say here that the narrative and tabular reports must tie in closely with the oral presentation. Likewise, the narrative must tie in closely with the exhibits and visual aids presented both in the written and the oral reports.

PLANNING THE REPORT

Planning is the necessary first step to any effective action. Preparing reports is no exception. A finished report must represent careful investigation of the problem area and alternative solutions or data to be presented, as well as sound thinking, logical organization and effective presentation. With a well-conceived plan, time and energies will be best spent, and the prospects will be improved for preparing the report that will make the desired impression.

Preparing any accounting report requires understanding its objectives and gathering and organizing the material according to a plan. For narrative reports, outlining is an essential part of the plan. The better the outline, the easier the report is to prepare.

Planning the report itself is a process of determining the steps leading toward the objective. By planning the report the accountant is able to determine the nature and amount of work required to gather the information to be presented. The plan will be affected in part by the nature of the report to be prepared and the time and resource limitations under which the accountant must work.

Planning Requires Hard and Careful Thinking

Report preparation should not be routine, for all reports are different. However, there are certain steps in the planning process that are common to all reports. These steps must be followed systematically and thoroughly; they include:

- studying the request or charge to produce the report in order to determine its uses and purposes
- listing the internal and external information needed to fulfill the purpose of the report
- determining what information is available and what must be generated or otherwise obtained

- outlining the steps to take and the methods to use in getting the information
- outlining the format of the narrative and tabular exhibits and determining the precise information to be included in each part
- estimating the time and cost necessary to prepare the report as planned, and making the necessary revisions if either is over the set limitations.

The report must fit into a carefully planned company reporting structure. Otherwise the time required to produce the information probably will be excessive and the cost exorbitant. The details of building a reporting structure are discussed in the following chapter.

Periodic reports are planned largely around past activities and to a growing extent around projections of future activities. Special inquiry reports are planned around special investigations on a particular topic. Both of these report types, and all reports in general, require meticulous thinking and careful planning about the technical contents and their effective presentation.

Planning the Time for Complete Preparation

Probably one of the most important phases of planning is to "nail down" the time requirements for the reports. Many considerations enter here. All reports require time for the following:

- data accumulation
- decisions about the form to use and techniques to incorporate
- reproduction of the finished copy
- distribution of finished copies to the proper people.

These considerations will all bear differently upon whether the report is issued:

- for control, planning, or informational purposes
- in written (narrative, tabular, or both), or oral form
- for top executives, middle management, or supervisory levels
- periodically, irregularly, or to meet a special request.

Certainly it is an oversimplification to say that time must be provided for complete report preparation. Yet this requirement for complete reports must be weighed against the timeliness factor. For most reports, the later they are after the event they are meant to clarify, the less useful they are. Therefore, accountants must make every effort to speed up the process of issuing the report. This may involve keeping the records more current so less catch-up time is needed when the reports are required; using standardized forms for periodic reports; using faster reproduction methods; or issuing "flash reports" from incomplete data. Sufficient planning must be done in order to be able to issue the reports when needed.

Planning the Narrative Portion—Building Good Outlines

To save time (and money) many accountants dictate their reports. But this requires skill developed through practice, based upon a detailed plan. This plan usually is in the form of an outline. In building the outline, you must keep foremost in mind: (1) the reader's requirements and viewpoint, (2) the orderly presentation of the information, and (3) the necessity of maintaining reader interest.

There are several basic elements in outlining, an understanding of which is essential to building a good outline. The first element is to *accurately define the problem*. From this you may organize your discussion in the most logical sequence. This sequence may be chronologically, by place, by quantities, or qualitatively. The objective in outlining is to subdivide the topic into relatively equal and comparable parts. The subdivisions should be made on the basis of the common characteristics of the data. This *division by relationships* is the second basic element of outlining. The last element is the caption used; should it be a *topic or talking caption*? The topic caption is a short one- or two-word construction which only serves to identify the topic or area of discussion. The talking caption identifies the subject matter also, but in addition indicates what is said about the subject. Talking captions briefly summarize the material covered. For example:

FINANCIAL   FINANCIAL OPERATIONS MIXED

    Profits   Profits below budget although sales are up
    Working capital   Working capital position strong
    Rate of return   Rate of return below budget
    Finance   New financing needed for expansion
    Stock market prices   Stock prices advance beyond DJI average

MARKETING   MARKETINGS OPERATIONS IMPROVE

    New orders   New orders up 6%
    Product line   Product line changes

The talking caption—the right-hand column above—takes more time and talent to construct, but definitely improves reports, especially narrative reports to management. Whichever form is adopted, you should maintain parallelism in the construction. All captions in the first degree of division should be parallel—all sentences or all noun phrases or all clauses. The captions in the second and third degree of division need not be of the same construction as the first degree, but they, too, should be consistent within their level of division in the outline. Keep the captions talking; keep them descriptive of the material they cover; keep them parallel in construction—by these means you will keep your reader interested. These subheadings, taken as a whole, tell the story concisely and prepare the reader to receive the details that follow.

Developing a good outline requires a thorough comprehension of the entire project. Before constructing the final outline, all the preliminary work should be finished—research, calculations, statement of objective, solution to the problem or recommendations formulated. The controlling ideas should be clarified and categorized in this preliminary phase. These ideas form the main headings and the body of the report; facts supporting these central ideas form the meat on the skeleton outline. A personal but objective style of effective writing fills the body with life and vigor.

Plan the Title and Lead Paragraphs

For narrative reports especially, but also applicable to any written comments in any report, the accountant must decide upon the title and lead paragraphs. These are an important part of the planning phase. They indicate the value of the report, so this helps the preparer focus upon what the report is to do for the recipient. Further, the lead paragraphs tell the story of the material they contain; this technique forces the preparer to examine the adequacy of the data to tell that story.

All reports should have a title. Whether the report is on a single page or comprises a book-length presentation, all reports should have a descriptive title and show the company name. It may seem needless to repeat the company name on each internal report. In a sense, it is. Yet this is a good way to build company pride and loyalty. The title is the most important display element in the report. The title must make the reader want to read the report; it must show the recipient why he should read the report; and it must implicitly or directly reveal the benefit to be derived from reading the report. The title should not necessarily be short; its meaning is the important thing.

Plan the Feature Material

Recommendations, items of special interest, and other material to be emphasized should be written down while it is still fresh, and arranged in the order of importance. These, along with the lead paragraphs, will direct the accountant toward what additional material is required to support the featured material. It forces a review of the purpose of the report and how adequately the assembled material meets that purpose.

Plan the Order and Emphasis of the Parts

Once the feature material has been decided upon, the supporting data should be assembled and arranged in the order of importance. The length of each section should be determined, and the emphasis appropriately placed according to the report purpose. Emphasis may be gained by placement, visual aids, and a number of other techniques that will be demonstrated later in this chapter.

Planning the Illustrations and Exhibits

Whether the report is to be written or orally presented, the exhibits it contains carry a large burden for ease of comprehension and understanding. They should be carefully planned in order to attain maximum effectiveness—at what point in the presentation they should be introduced, the things to illustrate and highlight.

These exhibits should supplement and complement the narrative, and not just repeat in a different way what was already said. The construction of visual aids and their relation to oral and written reports is covered in other sections of this text, so will not be elaborated upon here.

PREPARING THE REPORT

After the proper planning has been done, and that is a major and critical operation in itself, the actual report preparation may begin. This has two main phases: writing the draft of the narrative to be presented either in written or oral form, and devising the exhibits to accompany the narrative.

Accountants have traditionally tended to present more exhibits than narrative. Unfortunately, this emphasis seems to be misplaced.

Having planned which material to include, the accountant probably will have developed in his mind several possible outlines of his report content. These should be written down, revised, thought over, and revised again. Eventually one will satisfy the report requirements. With this settled, the rough draft writing begins.

Frequently, accountants' reports are built around the exhibits and illustrations. If these were not prepared in the course of formulating an outline, they should be done immediately after. Not only are they a guide to the narrative, but once they are prepared the process of writing will not have to be interrupted to arrange data, determine relationships, make calculations, or prepare graphics.

Good writing requires hard work, and is achieved by rapid writing, based on the presentation of ideas, tabular or graphic materials, followed by carefully revising and checking the details, style and mechanics.

The first objective is to record the main framework of ideas. This is done most effectively by overlooking inexact expression or the lack of finality in organization. Substance and vigor comes first, polish and emphasis follows. Few people are able to write the finished product the first time; most people follow the write-edit-rewrite routine as the most desirable course. As the writing continues, jot down any pertinent thoughts; later they may be effectively integrated into the report.

Three R's: Review, Revise, Rewrite

After quickly writing the first draft, careful review, revision and rewriting of each section is necessary for a well-written final report. Follow a plan again for this phase, just as was done for the rough draft. Separate readings are desirable for specific purposes:

- sound structure and organization
- clear expression and meanings
- accurate facts
- pleasing style and appropriate format
- overall readability and excellence after revision.

Other details concerning the mechanics of report preparation are found later in this chapter. Once the draft has gone through at least one revision and rewriting, it should be ready for reproduction in final report form.

DEVELOPING A PERSONAL BUT OBJECTIVE STYLE
OF EFFECTIVE WRITING

Style means two things. *Literary style* encompasses the author's writing characteristics; these result from the sentence structure, length, and arrangement, and from the choice of words. The *mechanics of style* is established by a particular use of capital letters, symbols, abbreviations, punctuation, spelling, numbers, and italics. Both these types of style are important for the report writer. They are important because they largely determine the interest of the reader, how easily he reads and understands it, the impression he gets of the accountant who prepared the report, and the action he takes based on the information in the report. Keep in mind that these elements of style are largely controllable by the report writer.

Practical Rules of Mechanics

Rules for mechanics of style are mostly common sense statements directed toward consistency and understandability. Variations in style will slow the reader by requiring him to adjust his "intake" of information. Several rules may be stated:

- Use elements of mechanics in such a way that they will be easily understood, especially numbers, symbols, and abbreviations. Use them logically. For example, the "%" symbol may be used in tabular as well as written material more effectively (and logically) than "percent" or "per centum." And "$6.25 million" in the narrative is preferable to "six and one-fourth million dollars." Further, unless you are indicating accuracy to the cent, $34,320 is preferable to $34,320.00 in the narrative comments.
- Use the mechanics common to a particular field when reporting to people in that field, since it will be the style most readily recognized by them. For example, the abbreviations peculiar to engineers should be used in reports directed to engineering personnel. Reporting to a first-line supervisor should take into consideration his job and the technical jargon and style mechanics surrounding that job.
- Follow consistently throughout the report the style mechanics adopted. For example, unless warranted by being obviously separated and unrelated, do not use 0.762 in one place, .762 in another, and .76200 in another; be consistent (the first form is most logical and understandable, and is preferable).

Specific elements of style will not be commented upon further. Many English books, writer's guides, secretary's handbooks exist that give rules and illustrations. Every accountant's desk should have a good dictionary, such as the latest edition of Merriam Company's *Webster's New Collegiate Dictionary;* this and other good dictionaries have a section on style mechanics. The dictionary named also has a section on preparing copy for printing; the standard proofreader's marks should be adopted by your department so that reviewing report drafts will be facilitated. One other reference may be mentioned:

the U.S. Government Printing Office (GPO) Style Manual (abridged 1967 revised edition) is very complete and inexpensive. These references should be consulted for the correct use of the elements of style mechanics: capitalization, spelling and compounding, punctuation, abbreviations, numerals, italics, symbols, tables, footnotes, and indexes.

Use Objectivity in Writing

Good narrative writing requires that the material be objectively presented. Statements that tell facts and analyze situations are preferable to a persuasive style. Unless the reporting situation clearly demands it, the report should be free from the biases and subjective opinions of the writer. Objective writing avoids emotional words.

The assumptions underlying the report and the opinions that are stated should be identified as such. Statements of opinion made by accountants might be accepted as fact were it not for this requirement. The reader has a right to know that the statement is fact or opinion. Recommendations are often called for in report situations. The reader should understand the basis for the recommendation; the basis usually is developed in the body of the report, and if it is not the basis should be specifically stated.

Expression of Thoughts Through Writing

You must remember that reporting is a form of communication. The facts and their interpretation are put into words, numbers and symbols so that the reader may act upon this information. In preparing reports, the accountant draws upon several learned and intuitive skills. These are knowledge, reasoning, judgment, creativeness, and persuasion. The better he uses these skills, the more effective will be his report to management. Expressing thoughts, facts, and interpretations through writing is an art that is difficult to master. But it can be mastered through hard work and study, unending patience, and diligent practice.

A Simple Procedure to Aid Clear Statement

The most effective device for obtaining clear statement is to carefully construct the paragraph for easy reading and complete comprehension. First, the writer must pick *key words* which are the most relevant in explaining the concept or item, and build each phrase around these key words. Next, form these phrases into sentences, all of which contribute to and are built around the central thought. This central thought is the paragraph; this should convey the message to the reader. The ideas set into words and paragraphs must be in a logical and obvious sequence; the words used must relate to each other to provide clear statements of the ideas.

Carefully design the sentences and paragraphs so that the appropriate words will be in that sequence which will express to the reader the same facts and the understanding the writer has of these facts. The sentence should be complete, concise, correct, clear and convincing: these are the five "C's" that should govern all accountants' writing.

TECHNIQUES FOR PUTTING READABILITY INTO THE NARRATIVE

Probably the key to readability—and understandability—of accountants' reports is the effective use of the techniques described below.[1]

1. Use Common Language and Definitions Extensively

An obvious but often overlooked technique is to write the way you talk. By this is meant not to use accounting terms but rather to use a conversational tone and common language.

Accountants frequently fall into the trap of using their own jargon—their technical language—in their reports. This is simply confusing, and certainly not amusing, to the reader. Common language should be used as much as possible; that language by which people communicate in everyday life. Certainly the use of slang is not advocated; understandable construction and words we do recommend. Percentages, ratios, graphs, and charts fit within the scope of understandable language. Saying we sold four items this year for every three sold last year is more readily comprehensible than merely stating dollar figures.

Definitions are helpful when technical terms are necessary. They are easy to write and should not be avoided; in fact, a section early in the report stating definitions is frequently desirable. Definitions have three parts:

- the *term* being defined . . . . "revenue"
- the *family* to which the term belongs . . . . asset inflow
- the *differentiation* that makes the term different from all
    others in the family . . . . from sales of products

(Thus, revenue *is* an asset inflow into the firm from the sale of its products and services. This differentiates it from other inflows: interest, dividends, borrowings, disposals of capital assets.)

Sun Oil Company annually publishes a pamphlet entitled "Understanding Sun's Accounting Terms." This explains the terms used in the company's financial statements issued to stockholders. Each definition is cross-referenced to the financial statements. This very commendable effort helps the report readers to understand more fully the financial statements presented to them. This booklet is partially reproduced in Figure 2-1, with the permission of Sun Oil Company.

2. Write Clearly, Concisely, and Correctly

Several items are included here which, when taken as a whole, make the narrative more clear, concise and correct. You should closely examine your narrative to see that the words and sentences are in the best possible form.

---

[1] Many of the items presented here were adopted from Laura Grace Hunter, *The Language of Audit Reports,* U.S. General Accounting Office, published by the U.S. Government Printing Office, Washington, D.C., 1957. This excellent booklet is on sale by the Superintendent of Documents, GPO, for 35 cents; every report writer's library should contain a carefully studied and frequently referred-to copy.

Consolidated Statement of Income and Stockholders' Equity

Sun Oil Company SUNOCO and Subsidiaries

For the Years Ended December 31

	1967	1966
① REVENUES		
Sales and Other Operating Income	$1,151,698,000	$1,047,278,000
Other Income	21,552,000	24,063,000
	1,173,250,000	1,071,341,000
② COSTS AND EXPENSES		
Costs and Operating Expenses	709,728,000	652,260,000
Selling, General and Administrative Expenses	142,210,000	122,999,000
Taxes, including Income Taxes	102,768,000	93,431,000
Intangible Development Costs	29,814,000	34,565,000
Depreciation, Cost Depletion and Retirements	69,686,000	59,877,000
Interest and Debt Expense	10,386,000	7,554,000
Minority Interest	82,000	81,000
	1,064,674,000	970,767,000
③ NET INCOME		
④ EARNINGS EMPLOYED IN THE		
BUSINESS AT JANUARY 1		
⑤ DIVIDENDS PAID		
Cash		
Common Stock		
1967-5%-1,222,126 shares		
1966-6%-1,383,029 shares		
EARNINGS EMPLOYED IN THE		
BUSINESS AT DECEMBER 31		
⑥ COMMON STOCK, NO PAR VALUE		
Authorized, 1967–35,000,000 shares		
Authorized, 1966–25,000,000 shares		
Issued, 1967 –25,664,741 shares	905	
Issued, 1966 –24,433,620 shares		
Less Treasury Stock, at cost–1967–546,593 shares	1,047	
–1966–636,344 shares	21	
⑦ STOCKHOLDERS' EQUITY AT DECEMBER 31	$1,026	

Consolidated Statement of Financial Position

Sun Oil Company SUNOCO and Subsidiaries

At December 31

	1967	1966
ⓐ CURRENT ASSETS		
Cash	$ 51,246,000	$ 51,099,000
Short Term Investments, at cost	54,195,000	34,792,000

ASSETS

LIABILITIES AND STOCKHOLDERS' E...

ⓒ CURRENT LIABILITIES		
Accounts Payable and Accrued Liabilities		
...e Taxes		
...ies		
...Future Oil Produc...		

Indicates pag...

April, 1968

THE CONSOLIDATED STATEMENT OF INCOME

The **Consolidated Statement of Income** is a financial summary of the operations of the Company for a specified period of time, such as three, six, nine or twelve months. "Consolidated" means that the statement includes the operations of all subsidiary companies in which Sun owns more than 50 per cent of the voting stock. The full operations of several affiliated companies in which Sun does not have a controlling interest are not included. However, included in "Other Income" is Sun's equity or share in the undistributed net earnings of the affiliated companies in which it owns a proprietary interest.

① REVENUES **Revenues** are the funds received by the Company during the period, excluding gasoline taxes and other taxes collected on behalf of Federal and state governments.

Sales and Other Operating Income, which is the major part of Sun's revenue, includes all of the money taken in by the Company from the sale of crude oil, natural gas and refined products, including chemicals; tires, batteries and other accessories sold through service stations; and all other products sold by the Company and subsidiaries in the normal course of business. It also includes the money received for services rendered, such as payments for tankers chartered to other companies and for shipping other companies' oil through Sun's pipelines.

Other Income is income which is not generated directly by Company operations. It includes income from the sale of used, worn out or obsolete equipment or facilities such as a tanker, truck, piece of land or other property which the Company no longer needs. Other Income also includes interest on Government and other securities and investments and the equity or share in undistributed earnings of the several affiliated companies in which a proprietary half interest is held.

UNDERSTANDING SUN'S ACCOUNTING TERMS

Many shareholders of corporations do not fully understand financial terms used in annual reports, according to a survey conducted by Opinion Research Corporation of Princeton, N.J.

ORC explains the situation this way: Traditionally, U.S. companies have leaned over backwards to report their activities fully and accurately. In doing this, the tendency has been to use technical terms which have precise meanings for financial analysts and others in the field of finance. The trouble is that these terms often are so technical that they have little meaning for shareholders.

It is the purpose of this booklet to help Sun shareholders and others better understand the terms used in the **Consolidated Statements of Income and Financial Position** which are reproduced on pages 4 and 5.

Figure 2-1.

a. Arrange words in their best order—watch modifying words and phrases.

b. Make it sound logical—make the subject do the action.

c. Say what you mean—be accurate in word choice and arrangement.

d. Be as specific as possible—economize on words, but repeat if necessary for clarity; excess words merely clutter the message.

e. Stop when you are through—no need to repeat unless clarity is jeopardized.

f. Don't lose the subject—put the doer and its action close together.

g. Avoid using the same word in two senses in a sentence—the reader must stop to figure out your meaning.

h. Place transitional words within the sentence—the beginning and end of the sentence should be reserved for emphatic words.

i. Use the positive statement—negative statements detract and confuse.

j. Avoid splitting phrases—put transitionals and other phrases between whole phrases.

k. Put the message at the end of the sentence—a strong sentence needs a strong ending; the position of greatest emphasis is the end of the sentence.

3. Keep the Sentences Short

Most accountants tend to write sentences that are too long. Even for technical material, sentences should not average more than 17 words. It is not uncommon to have longer sentences; but there should be short ones too. A 30-word sentence should be looked upon with suspicion, for most likely it can be broken up into more bite-sized pieces. If your sentences are too long, here are some techniques to shorten them.

a. Add some periods at appropriate breathing spots—usually that is where one idea ends and another begins. One idea to a sentence, please.

b. Put qualifying ideas in separate sentences—to include qualifying clauses and phrases in the central sentence merely confuses the reader. Watch *except for, although, while,* and *since,* especially.

c. Express the idea in fewer words—frequently a whole phrase or clause can be replaced with a single word. Prepositional phrases are the worst offenders; avoid the "*in connection with*" construction especially.

d. Use paragraphs to break the pace and separate groups of ideas—make the idea groups relatively narrow in scope and make these separate paragraphs.

e. Use enumerations or lists rather than straight narrative—this helps imprint your message in the reader's mind.

f. Use figures only—avoid both spelling out numbers and then repeating them in parentheses; only in legal documents is this duplication desirable.

4. Use Summary and Transition Statements to Advantage

Statements or paragraphs which summarize the previous material and which lead into the material to follow are very helpful to the reader. This technique shows him quickly where he's been and where he's going; it may go at the end of the old section or the beginning of the new one.

Personal preference and clarity govern the frequency. Major sections of the report should be so divided. Minor sections and subsections may or may not use this device, depending upon how big the break in train of thought between subsections. Summary statements should not duplicate what was said; they should abstract the major ideas and succinctly state them. Headings themselves serve as transitional devices, but the report should read smoothly even without using headings.

5. Use Parallel Construction When Appropriate

When two or more words or ideas in a sentence are parallel in meaning, they should be placed in parallel form. This form of construction is implemented by the following techniques:

a. Make the verbs into "*-ing*" form—"he will be responsible for collecting, depositing, and reporting cash receipts."

b. Repeat the word if this is necessary for clarity—if the form is not parallel then it is better to substitute a synonym.

c. When contrasting two or more things, keep the sentence unchanged in order to emphasize the contrast.

d. Two or more parallel thoughts in a single sentence should be parallel in word order.

e. When two verbs are used, use the same voice for both—preferably use the active voice rather than the passive voice.

f. When using the either-or construction, the phrases they govern must be parallel—the same rule applies to neither-nor constructions.

g. When listing a series of items in a sentence, make each item logically relate to the common introduction—*of, to, the* are frequently repeated for each item.

h. All items listed in tabular form should be parallel in construction—each should be in item form or in complete sentence form.

6. Eliminate Floundering Sentences

A sentence that starts off with a positive statement is more readable than one that begins with a qualifying word or phrase. Using *although, while, since* and other qualifiers puts the reader on notice that the more important idea comes later. Separate these qualifications into separate sentences if possible. Here are some *do's* regarding floundering sentences:

a. An introductory phrase must modify the subject of the sentence—if it does not the sentence should be rearranged. Especially be cautious of implied subjects.

b. Make introductions have their own subject and verb—then the reference is unmistakable.

c. Make a sentence start off with its subject rather than a prepositional phrase—especially watch out for *in addition to* and *based on* as the first words in the sentence.

7. Use Action Verbs Where Possible

This involves three phases of word use: (1) present vs. past tense, (2) passive vs. active voice, and (3) noun vs. verb form.

(1) Present vs. Past Tense. The verb tense in report writing is like that in any other writing. You should describe things as they happened, as they are happening, or as they will happen; this helps the reader understand your story. Using entirely the past tense, or the present tense, is illogical and confusing. Anything done or happening before the report's preparation is stated in past tense. Anything you call attention to in the report is stated in present or future tense. When speaking of the report itself, take the viewpoint of the section you are in relative to the other sections: you *call* his attention to a graph in this section; you remind him that a preceding section *explained* certain information; you refer him to a later section that *will show* other details.

(2) Passive vs. Active Voice. Even though we do not talk in the passive voice, we tend to write that way. Instead of "I made the report" we tend to write "The report *was prepared by* me." Not only is the word order illogical, but also the emphasis is shifted from the end of the sentence to the beginning. Passive voice results in dull writing and should be avoided at all costs.

(3) Noun vs. Verb Form. Verbs make the sentence move, have vigor and vitality. Give them the chance to do their work; use the verb form rather than the noun form of the word. Long abstract nouns that are made out of verbs make your writing heavy and hard to read. If you do use the noun form by making it the subject of the sentence, you will usually be left searching for another verb to use. More often you must resort to some dull substitute such as *achieved, effected, occurred,* or *accomplished*. The abstract noun form normally ends in either *-ation, -ment, -tion, -ance,* or *-ence*. By avoiding the "the . . . -ation of" construction and by using the *ing* form, the sentence is more concise, clear, and correct. For example, "by *the* alloc*ation of* the plant costs . . ." is improved by saying "by allocat*ing* the plant costs. . . ."

8. Break the "It" Habit

One of the main contributors to foggy writing is the incorrect or inaccurate pronoun reference. The worst offenders are *it, that, this, those, theirs,* and *these*. Watch the antecedents to which these (that is, these pronouns!) refer. Ask yourself if the reference is logical and clear to the reader. Also be sure the antecedent and the pronoun reference agree in number—both should be singular or both plural.

9. Use Uniform but Interesting Headings

Headings are guide posts, direction signs to degrees of importance. Headings of the same degree of importance must assume the same physical position throughout the narrative of the report. This is illustrated in Figure 2-2. First degree headings are chapter titles and part designations. Second degree headings include text covering several broadly related paragraphs. Third degree headings introduce one or possibly two or three paragraphs of closely related material. Fourth degree headings are included in the text of the paragraph itself, and the material to which it relates normally does not extend to another paragraph. More than one of these fourth degree headings may appear in the same paragraph. Figure 2-2 also shows the normal letter and number designations attached to the

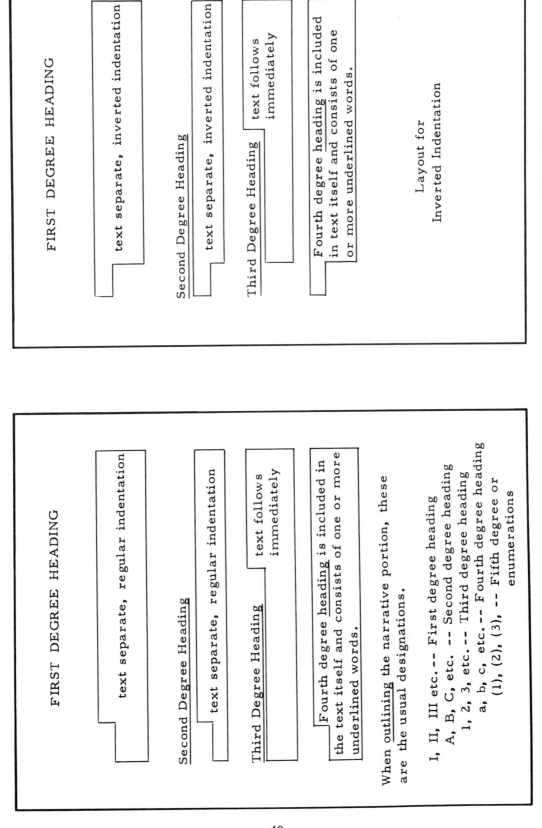

FIRST DEGREE HEADING

    text separate, inverted indentation

Second Degree Heading

    text separate, inverted indentation

Third Degree Heading   text follows immediately

Fourth degree heading is included in text itself and consists of one or more underlined words.

Layout for
Inverted Indentation

Figure 2-3.

FIRST DEGREE HEADING

    text separate, regular indentation

Second Degree Heading

    text separate, regular indentation

Third Degree Heading   text follows immediately

Fourth degree heading is included in the text itself and consists of one or more underlined words.

When outlining the narrative portion, these are the usual designations.

I, II, III etc.-- First degree heading
A, B, C, etc. -- Second degree heading
1, 2, 3, etc.-- Third degree heading
a, b, c, etc.-- Fourth degree heading
(1), (2), (3), -- Fifth degree or enumerations

Figure 2-2.

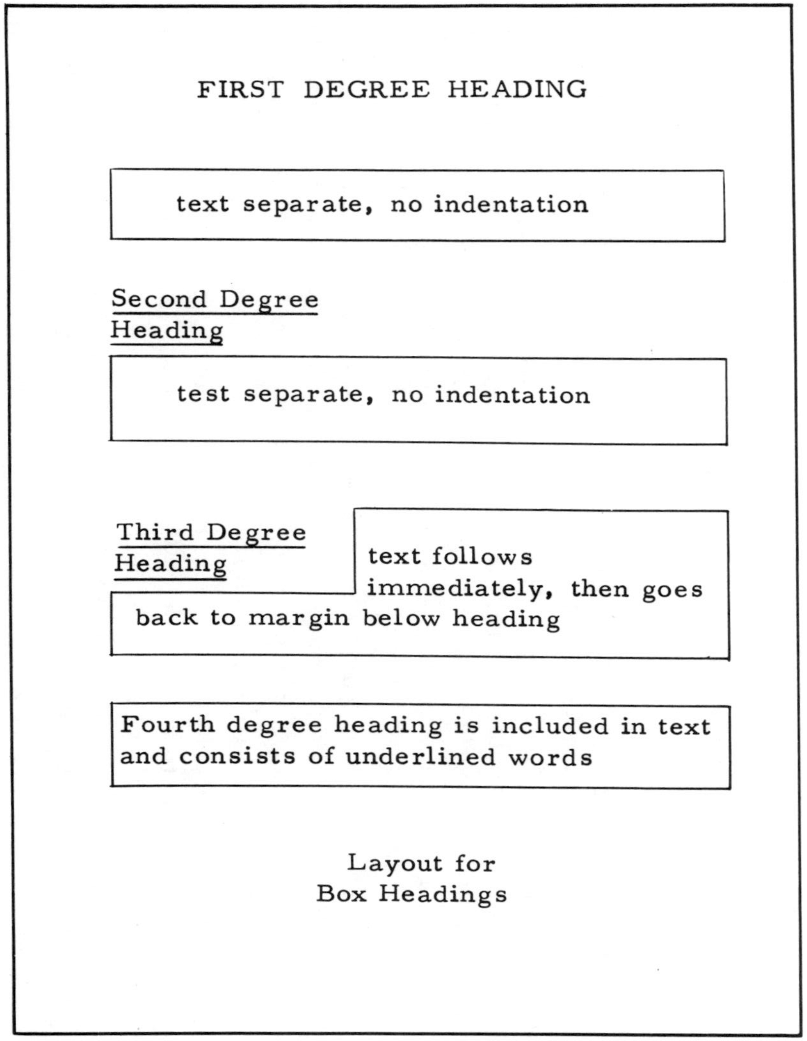

FIRST DEGREE HEADING

text separate, may indent if
desired

Second
Degree
Heading

text follows, may indent if
desired

Third
Degree
Heading

text follows, may indent
if desired,
heading not underlined

Fourth degree heading is
included in text, underlined

Layout for
Hanging Headings

Figure 2-5.

FIRST DEGREE HEADING

text separate, no indentation

Second Degree
Heading

test separate, no indentation

Third Degree
Heading

text follows
immediately, then goes
back to margin below heading

Fourth degree heading is included in text
and consists of underlined words

Layout for
Box Headings

Figure 2-4.

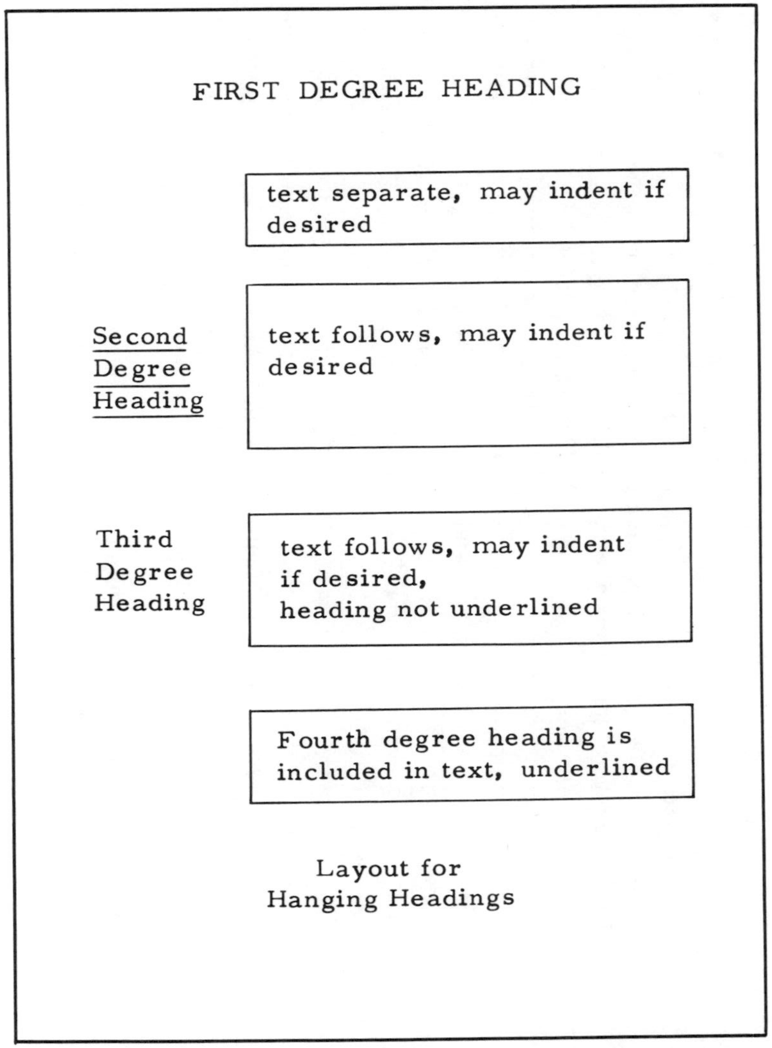

41

various degrees of headings. These letters and numbers are not carried over to the finished report, however, but exist merely to structure similar degrees of importance.

There are several interesting alternatives for positioning the headings and text. Figure 2-2 shows the *"regular" indentation* style. That is, the text is below the first and second degree headings, indented three, five, or seven spaces, depending upon preferences. The third degree heading itself is similarly indented, with the text immediately following.

Figure 2-3 shows the headings and text position using *inverted indentation*. This is a more eye-catching layout than the regular indentation. But those styles shown in Figures 2-4 and 2-5 are even more appealing and readable. These are self-explanatory and will not be discussed further.

There are many existing schemes for headings which you will find in various reports and communications books. Actually, any combination of position and type (upper and lower case, underlined or not underlined) which shows the relative importance of the captions is acceptable. One governing rule is that no caption have a higher ranking type or position than any of the captions at a higher level. Position itself is subordinate to type, but combined the relative importance of the caption is designated. Again, consistency in use is the password to more comprehensible reports.

In your headings, you should be creative and use more than one- or two-word descriptions. As illustrated above, make the captions "talk" by describing the content nature of the section; these are especially effective. Such headings of the same degree must be parallel in grammatical construction. For headings of the same degree within the same section of the report, use all nouns, all phrases, all clauses, or all complete thoughts. Keep the structure parallel; do not mix the structure elements.

ALL-PURPOSE STANDARDIZED FORMAT FOR NONFORMALIZED REPORTS

This all-purpose format is generally adaptable to most accountants' narrative reports. It contains seven elements designed to indicate an effective arrangement of the material.

1. Binder or Cover Page. This binder should be the most important display element in the report. It should make the reader want to read the report and indicate directly or indirectly what benefit he is to receive by reading it. The binder or cover page should be standardized, and show the title, a routing list, preparer's name and department, and the release date.

2. One-Page Transmittal Letter. This transmittal letter should state (a) the nature of the report, (b) the purpose of the report, (c) how the report may be used or benefit the reader, (d) any important items in the report that need highlighting, and (e) a closing courtesy paragraph, if appropriate.

3. Table of Contents. This serves the purpose of the reader's locating specific material without having to thumb through the whole report. The main sections of the table of contents may be divided within the body of the report by using divider tabs or different colored paper. Reports over five pages long should have a table of contents—even for this length the table is helpful.

4. Summary of Recommendations or Findings. This section summarizes the recommendations detailed later in the report, or gives the solution to the problem posed in the report, if appropriate. The object is to give the reader what he is most interested in as quickly as possible.

5. Body Supporting the Recommendations or Detailing the Investigation. This section, organized according to the table of contents, contains a description of the procedures followed and the work done in support of the conclusions and recommendations made.

6. Supporting Exhibits and Illustrations. These may either be placed near the related narrative or grouped together at the end of the section to which they are relevant. The type of report and personal preferences govern. The exhibits should be titled and explained in a caption so the picture is complete. Do not make the reader search through the narrative to find the reference. Number and title the exhibits consistently, and refer to them properly in the narrative.

7. Summary, Conclusions and/or Recommendations. These elements should be concisely stated. The summary need not repeat arguments or narrative; it should abstract the main ideas. The conclusions and/or recommendations should be enumerated for easier reading and differentiation. Be sure that the purpose of the report, as stated in the transmittal, has been met as specifically detailed in this section.

LONG FORMALIZED REPORTS

Occasionally it is necessary to prepare a longer, more formal report. This document records the steps of the investigation in the order that they were taken. The pattern these reports follow is typically similar to that presented by Paul Douglas.[2] This pattern consists of 12 parts. Depending upon the purpose of the report and the formality required, all or only a portion of these parts may be incorporated.

1. *Cover* that is attractive, strong enough to stand heavy use, and clear in its statement of the subject of the report.
2. *Title page:*
    a) Subject of the report.
    b) Author's name and title, his division and company affiliation.
    c) Person, group, and firm for whom the report was prepared.
3. *Syllabus:*
    a) Summary highlights.
    b) Concise statement of findings.
    c) Summary of conclusions.
    d) Summary of recommendations.
4. *Negotiating documents:*
    a) Letter of authorization.
    b) Letter of acceptance, acknowledging the authorization and summarizing the problem to be investigated.

---

2 Paul Douglas, *Communication Through Reports* (Englewood Cliffs, N.J.: Prentice-Hall, Inc., 1957), pp. 288–289.

   c) Letter of submittal of the finished report to a superior committee.
   d) Letter of transmittal of the finished report to the authorizing party, summarizing the report's significance and uses.
   e) Letter of approval by authorizing party acknowledging receipt.
5. *Table of contents:* key word or sentence descriptions of the sequence of major topics referenced to pages on which discussion of the topic begins.
6. *Table of illustrations:* list of tables, charts, figures, illustrations, and legal cases referenced to the pages on which they appear.
7. *Report narrative:* the story of the problem, procedures, and work performed.
   a) Statement of the problem and scope of the investigation.
   b) History of the problem; its background, why the study was undertaken, and the probable significance of the results of the study.
   c) Definition of special terms used in the report.
   d) Method and procedure used in the study.
   e) Materials and apparatus required in the study.
   f) Discussion of data gathered in the investigation.
8. *Synthesis and critique:*
   a) Findings produced in the study.
   b) Conclusions, a discussion and evaluation of the importance of the findings.
   c) Recommendations on a solution to the problem, based on the findings and conclusions.
   d) Summary critique of the whole study.
9. *Footnote references:* gathered into one section unless they are already listed at the bottom of the referenced page.
10. *Exhibits:* a consolidated reference section that has not already been included within the text.
11. *Bibliography:* references considered important for the reader, and a record of materials used in developing the report.
12. *Index*

ILLUSTRATION OF A NARRATIVE REPORT

The following report, originally appearing in *The Arthur Andersen Chronicle,*[3] demonstrates a monthly management report that is largely narrative. This report is broad in scope, yet brief and informative. It divides the typical business into its functional divisions, and also gives information on business conditions and competition trends. Names and telephone numbers are available to obtain more detailed information from each division.

This report is typical of what could be prepared for any type of business and for any level of management. The format would change, but the underlying principles of the

---

[3] Albert J. Bows, "Broadening the Approach to Management Reporting," *The Arthur Andersen Chronicle,* Vol. 22 (April 1962), pp. 7–25. Reprinted with permission.

information to be included would be similar. This Monthly Management Report for the XYZ Safety Razor Company is presented in Figure 2-6.

THE ARTHUR ANDERSEN CHRONICLE

XYZ SAFETY RAZOR COMPANY
Monthly Management Report
July, 1961
HIGHLIGHTS

XYZ OPERATIONS   **Page**

New orders fall off 14% in Southwest sales region.   2

Profits of $8,000,000 are below budget, but 3% ahead of 1960.   3

Second quarter earnings per share of 42 cents are 3 cents greater than 1960.   4

Liquid position remains strong with a 2.4 ratio of current assets to current liabilities.   4

Safety razor sales are 6% below budget.   5

Product line changed to meet consumer preferences.   5

Inventories at 17% above budget are heavy at all manufacturing plants — accumulations too much?   6

Anticipate significant increase ($3.50 per ton) in steel prices.   6

New research on steel alloys to start in August.   7

Labor turnover problem improved at California plant.   7

RAZOR INDUSTRY

Number one competitor undertakes extensive market research program.   7

Manufacturers of electric shavers accelerate advertising programs.   7

U. S. ECONOMY

An increase in consumer spending forecasted for third quarter.   9

DECISIONS NEEDED

Decisions needed on product line changes, inventory levels, and financing Ontario plant.   10

Figure 2-6.

THE ARTHUR ANDERSEN CHRONICLE

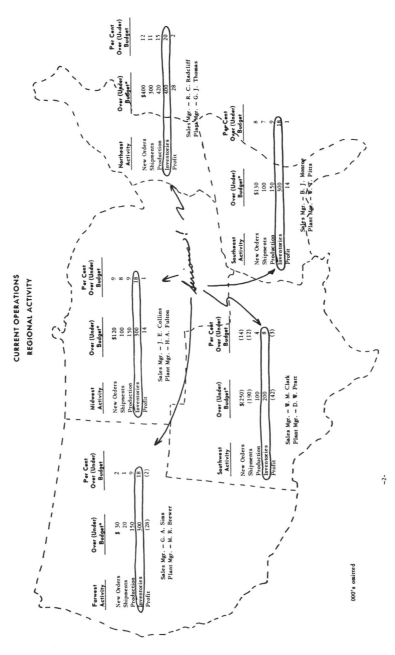

Figure 2-6 (Continued).

THE ARTHUR ANDERSEN CHRONICLE

FINANCIAL

Questions
Call   Dial

PROFITS

Profits for July are $14,000 below budget. While total sales are up, profits are slightly below budget because of lost business in the Southwest and accelerated advertising expenditures. T. L. Brown, Controller, reports that advertising expenditures are $71,000 above budget. Our year to date gross profit remains 5% favorable because of the acceptance of the profitable deluxe blade.

Brown 324

000's Omitted

Operating Results July, 1961	Amount		Budget Comparison Favorable (Unfavorable)			
			July		Year To Date	
	July	Year To Date	Amount	%	Amount	%
Net sales	$7,283	$51,000	$ 330	5	$ 2,300	5
Cost of sales	4,569	32,000	(190)	(4)	(1,400)	(5)
Gross profit	$2,714	$19,000	$ 140	5	$ 900	5
Operating expenses—						
Selling	$ 714	$ 5,000	$ (66)	(10)	$ (550)	(12)
Advertising	500	3,000	(71)	(14)	(325)	(12)
Administrative	350	3,000	(17)	(5)	(125)	(4)
	$1,564	$11,000	$ (154)	(10)	$(1,000)	(10)
Operating profit	$1,150	$ 8,000	$ (14)	(1)	$ (100)	(1)

Product line profits for safety razors are below budget. The Southwest and Farwest Divisions are below budget. Increased sales did not overcome higher advertising expenditures in the Farwest.

Brown 324

July Profit Budget Comparison Favorable (Unfavorable)	Deluxe Blades		Standard Blades		Economy Blades		Safety Razors		Total	
	Amount	%	Amount	%	Amount	%	Amount	%	Amount	%
Northeast	$17	6	$(2)	(1)	$17	3	$ (4)	(1)	$ 28	2
Southeast	(1)	1	3	1	7	1	5	1	14	1
Southwest	(15)	(5)	(9)	(2)	(7)	(1)	(11)	(3)	(42)	(3)
Midwest	10	4	12	2	1	—	(9)	(2)	14	1
Farwest	3	2	3	1	(11)	(2)	(23)	(5)	(28)	(2)
Total	$14	3	$ 7	1	$ 7	1	$(42)	(4)	$(14)	1

Figure 2-6 (Continued).

THE ARTHUR ANDERSEN CHRONICLE

FINANCIAL (CONTINUED)

	Questions	
	Call	Dial

WORKING CAPITAL

Liquid position remains **strong** with working capital **$800,000** over budget. **Current liabilities** are **up** significantly to finance **higher inventories**. Our **inventory position** is **17%** higher than **planned** and should be watched closely for the next few months to **avoid** an **excessive build-up**.

Brown   324

Working Capital Status	000's Omitted		Per Cent Over (Under) Budget
	Amount	Over (Under) Budget	
Current Assets—			
Cash	$ 6,500	$ (300)	(4.4%)
Receivables	9,500	600	6.7
Inventories	10,200	1,500	17.2
	$26,200	$1,800	7.4
Current Liabilities	11,000	1,000	10.0
Net Working Capital	$15,200	800	5.6

RATE OF RETURN

With **profits** running **below budget**, the **rate of return** is slightly **lower** than **planned**.

	1960	Budgeted 1961	Anticipated 1961
Rate of Return on Invested Capital	6.68%	6.95%	6.82%

FINANCE

B. M. Blair, Treasurer, reported that the **study** on methods to **finance** the **proposed plant** in Ontario, Canada has been completed. The study recommends the **issuance** of **$3 million** of 5-1/2% subordinated notes, due 1982 and **$2 million** of 5-3/4% **capital debentures**, due 1982.

Blair   323

The Company **paid** its usual quarterly **dividend** of **25 cents** for the quarter ended June 30. The dividend was paid on **July 15** on stock of record June 25. Second quarter **per-share earnings** were **42 cents**, up 3 cents over **last year**.

Blair   323

Figure 2-6 (Continued).

THE ARTHUR ANDERSEN CHRONICLE

FINANCIAL (CONTINUED)

		Questions
	Call	Dial

STOCK MARKET PRICES

The price of **ABC Razor stock increased 9%** over the previous month, while **our stock increased 8%** for the same period. ABC's new issue, accompanied by a meeting with financial analysts probably helped them. Blair 323

	Per Cent Over (Under) Last Month	Price Index		
		July	Year Ago	5 Years Ago
Dow Jones (Industrials)	+1%	133	126	101
XYZ Razor Company	+8%	137	132	106
ABC Razor Company	+9%	125	118	102

MARKETING

NEW ORDERS

New Orders in July were **up 6%.** All sales regions showed gains **except the Southwest.** The Southwest region is **down because we lost our best salesman** in the Fort Worth-Dallas district. W. M. Clark, regional sales manager for the Southwest, expects the new salesman to **recover** the lost **business** within two months. Jones 320

Sales for all items in the razor blade line are up. Safety razor sales are slightly off. Jones 320

July, 1961		
	000's Omitted Over (Under) Budget	Per Cent Over (Under) Budget
Deluxe Blades	$200	8
Standard Blades	100	5
Economy Blades	86	6
Safety Razors	(56)	(6)

PRODUCT LINE

The Product Evaluation Committee reports that the **5-BLADE** package of **STANDARD** blades is being **eliminated** from the product line. Consumers have **shifted** almost completely to the **10-BLADE** and **25-BLADE** packages. Jones 320

According to the Market Research Department, field tests indicate that **consumers have a strong preference** for the **50-BLADE** packages of **ECONOMY BLADES.** Plans have been made to introduce this package in **September** of this year. Baker 329

Figure 2-6 (Continued).

THE ARTHUR ANDERSEN CHRONICLE

MARKETING (CONTINUED)

	Questions	
	Call	Dial

ADVERTISING

Within our own organization, some question has been raised as to the merits of associating our products with **sporting events** through the **advertising program.** The main argument is that we are directing our **advertising efforts** primarily at the **male audience** when in reality we are selling to a **mixed market.** Our marketing consultants conducted a survey of consumers in several large cities to resolve this question. The results of this survey indicated that while **wives** usually do the **purchasing of razor blades**, they usually **cater** to their **husbands' preference.**   Davis   322

G. P. Davis, Director of Advertising, reports that the **advertising program** has been **accelerated** to **offset** the advertising programs of **electric shaver manufacturers** and ABC Razor Company. This **extra expenditure** was **approved** and explains why we are over the budget.   Davis   322

MANUFACTURING

PRODUCTION

All **manufacturing** facilities have been producing at **near capacity** for the months of June and July. S. E. Dawson, Director of Manufacturing, reports that both finished goods and raw materials **inventories** are being **accumulated** in anticipation of a **price increase** for domestic **steel** during the fourth quarter of 1961. However, the **inventory** is **heavy** and a **cut-off** on this **should be established.**   Dawson   325

RAW MATERIALS

L. N. Kemp, Purchasing Agent, **predicts an increase** in the **price** of **steel** for the **fourth quarter** in **1961.** Steel consumers, in **anticipation** of a **steel strike** during the **first half** of **1962,** will begin building inventories during the last quarter of 1961 thus causing prices to rise.   Kemp   331

PLANT AND EQUIPMENT

For the first time since modernizing the equipment at the **California plant,** anticipated **operating capacity was reached** this month. M. R. Brewer, plant manager, explained that the **delay** in reaching normal operating capacity was **caused** by the **excessive labor turnover rate** realized during the first half of 1961.   Smith   326

Figure 2-6 (Continued).

THE ARTHUR ANDERSEN CHRONICLE

RESEARCH AND DEVELOPMENT

	Questions	
	Call	Dial

CURRENT PROJECTS

C. K. Emerson, Director of the Research and Development Division reports that all current projects will be completed by mid-August.

FUTURE PROJECTS

At the conclusion of current projects, all research personnel will work on projects to evaluate the possibility of using different steel alloys to produce blades comparable in quality, but lower in price to our present line. If their research is successful, we may offset the adverse effects of rising steel prices.   Emerson 327

INDUSTRIAL RELATIONS

LABOR RELATIONS

J. P. Scott, Personnel Manager at the California plant, reports that the problem of turnover rates at the California plant has been improved. We were losing many skilled workers to the aircraft industry in this area, but apparently the instability of the aircraft business has lessened the tendency for workers to seek aircraft employment.   Thompson 328

COMPETITION AND INDUSTRY TRENDS

MARKET CONDITIONS

Our advertising agency reports that the wet shave market continues to appear strong even though manufacturers of electric shavers have stepped up their advertising programs, especially through television media.   Davis 322

COMPETITION

Our chief competitor in the wet shave market, ABC has recently commissioned the K–T MARKET RESEARCH AGENCY to conduct field studies to establish characteristics of their razor blades which "in the consumer's opinion" are superior to ours. E. L. Kelly of our market research department estimates that this study is costing them approximately $250,000 and will probably be the basis for an extensive advertising program.   Davis 322

Figure 2-6 (Continued).

The Arthur Andersen Chronicle

COMPETITION AND INDUSTRY TRENDS (CONTINUED)

	Questions	
	Call	**Dial**

LABOR RELATIONS

In a recent speech, George Meany, President of the A.F.L.–C.I.O., was intimate and definitive regarding the unions' plans to seek higher wage rates during the next round of contract negotiations. J. B. Thompson of the industrial relations department reports that our competitors will be weaker at the bargaining table than our firm, because they have raised prices since the last union contract and we have not.   Thompson   328

EXPANSION DEVELOPMENTS

G. H. Edwards of our Atlanta plant reports that the M.N.O. RAZOR COMPANY has started a program to modernize its manufacturing facilities in Tennessee. They appear to be moving towards a semi-automated system similar to ours. They enjoyed a labor cost advantage in Tennessee in the past, but with the construction of synthetic textile plants in the immediate proximity, this advantage has been rapidly disappearing.   Smith   326

NEW PRODUCTS

C. D. Jones, general sales manager, reports that a razor blade, lower in price than our ECONOMY line and interchangeable between our line of safety razors and others, has recently been introduced by M.N.O. This addition to their product line has not been accompanied by an extensive advertising program.   Jones   320

FINANCIAL TRANSACTIONS

An offering of 100,000 shares ($1,217,000) of ABC Razor Company common stock was oversubscribed after reaching the public market at $13.50 a share. Our underwriters, Davenport & Stewart, reported that Mellon, Tucker & Fritz managed the underwriting group.   Blair   323

IMPORTANT TRENDS IN BUSINESS CONDITIONS

INDUSTRIAL PRODUCTION

The Federal Reserve Board's industrial production index hit a new peak in July -- 2% above June and 10% above the recession low of February, 1961. The previous high was in January, 1960.   Fowler   332

PLANT AND EQUIPMENT OUTLAYS

A key factor in determining the rate of economic recovery in the months ahead will be the volume of spending for fixed investment. Planned outlays at the annual rate of $34.6 billion for the third quarter mark the beginning of the upturn in spending.   Fowler   332

Figure 2-6 (Continued).

THE ARTHUR ANDERSEN CHRONICLE

IMPORTANT TRENDS IN BUSINESS CONDITIONS (CONTINUED)

	Questions	
	Call	Dial

RETAIL TRADE

Retail sales, after rising in May and June, declined from a seasonally adjusted level of $18.3 billion in June to $18.1 billion in July.

Forecasts indicate an increase in retail sales for August and September.   Fowler 332

INCOME

Personal income rose in July for the fifth consecutive month, advancing $4.5 billion from the June seasonally adjusted annual rate of $417 billion. The July national income was at a seasonally adjusted annual rate $18.7 billion above the February low.   Fowler 332

PERSONAL CONSUMPTION EXPENDITURES

Consumer spending on nondurable goods increased for the first quarter in 1961 and preliminary estimates show an increase for the second quarter 1961. An increase in spending is forecasted for the third quarter.   Fowler 332

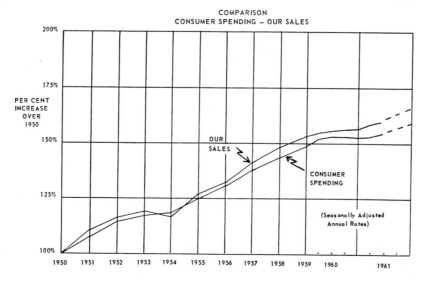

Figure 2-6 (Continued).

THE ARTHUR ANDERSEN CHRONICLE

ACTION REQUIRED

	Questions	
	Call	Dial

PRODUCT LINE

Since the sale of safety razors has been below budget all year, the **Product Evaluation Committee** has prepared a list of **recommendations** for **upgrading** the **safety razor line.**   Jones   320

INVENTORIES

S. E. Dawson, Director of Manufacturing, and L. N. Kemp, Purchasing Agent, have prepared a special report **recommending** the **levels** of **raw materials** and **finished goods inventories** to carry until a **new union contract** in the steel industry is negotiated next year.   Kemp   331

Dawson 325

EXPANSION

Recommendations on **financing** the **proposed plant** in **Ontario,** Canada, have been made. Our **plans** should be **firm** by the **first** of **September** if the **securities** are to be **issued** during the **first quarter of 1962.**   Blair   323

- -

RELEASE DATE   August 15, 1961

DISTRIBUTION

1. All members of Executive Committee

2. All Vice Presidents

3. Controller

Figure 2-6 (Continued).

3

Designing and Building an Effective Reporting System

The basic requirements of a good management reporting system can be described by the following "secrets." We call them

THE BASIC

- S—Define *strategic* factors
- E—Include *external* and internal information
- C—Use *comparisons* extensively
- R—Show *relevant* data only
- E—Cover the *entire* range of operations
- T—Be *timely* in reporting
- S—Set *standards* wisely

OF EFFECTIVE

- R—Recognize and report by *responsibilities*
- E—Focus upon *exceptions* existing
- P—Follow a *pyramid* report structure
- O—Include *operating* statistics
- R—*Review* reporting needs of management
- T—Reveal significant *trends* and relationships
- S—Promote *simplicity* and clarity in reports

These elements of report content and techniques are further investigated in the sections that follow.

Establish Profit Responsibility

One of the first requirements for effective management reporting is to establish responsibility for cost incurrence and for profit generation. This in turn requires that the organization structure be studied to determine who makes the decisions, when, where, and based on what information. The answers to these questions ultimately determine which reports will be prepared for each level of decision maker. Further, they determine that the reports are responsive, timely, understandable, relevant, and motivating.

The profit responsibility may be, and usually is, tied to the organization structure. The structure may be functional, or firms could also be divided by product divisions, having the sales, production, engineering and finance functions separately operating in each division, or similarly by geographical region.

Organization structures are vertical as well. This is the line of authority and responsibility which is established in the organization. Staff groups may be organized also, at various levels, where a need exists for technical and expert advice.

Effective management reporting is built on closely defined authority and responsibility relationships. These relationships must be determined so that the reporting system will provide pertinent information to the person having a certain area of responsibility.

Profit responsibility can be easily tied into the regular reporting system. Establishing cost centers as the basic profit responsibility centers is a first step. Minimizing costs at these points (thus contributing to increased profit) becomes the objective, given certain standards as to quantity and quality of inputs. Responsibility accounting and reporting is not a cost accounting system but may be closely tied to it as well as to general accounting. Standards, budgets, forecasts, and exception reporting are also vital refinements.

Classifying costs as controllable and noncontrollable is a key characteristic of responsibility accounting and reporting. Cost items must be associated with the person responsible for them; all costs are ultimately and in some fashion controllable by someone. Responsibility accounting reports to the person only those costs for which he is responsible and over which he has some control. Profit responsibility planning and control reports are illustrated in a later section.

Establish Report Content

The second basic requirement for effective management reporting is to establish the report content. This content will depend upon the needs of its user. The following principles should be considered.

Report Purpose. As noted above, the reports prepared should be directed toward their use in planning or control, or to convey information. Planning and control are the most numerous. Information reports (for the sake of merely giving information) should be minimal. The report with a purpose is one that motivates action of some kind; these are the most important. This means the accountant must determine precisely the purpose of the report and the use to which it will be put.

Information Adequacy. The accountant must next determine that the information in the report is adequate for these uses and this purpose. The report should be complete, but not too detailed for his particular level of operations. Lower levels of management should be given detailed information. More summarization is called for as we move to higher levels of management. At the higher management levels the scope of the information should be limited to that which highlights problem areas and pinpoints responsibility for their correction.

Included in the reporting system should be a provision for a superior to receive information on the performance of his immediate subordinates who, in turn, receive reports on the performance of their subordinates, and so on down the chain of command. This aspect of responsibility accounting, the "pyramid" structure, will be investigated in a later section.

Information Relevancy. Adequacy and relevancy go hand in hand. Only those facts necessary for the decision at hand should be included, and they should be clearly and concisely stated. The facts presented should be those the reader considers relevant—if you do not know the information he considers relevant, ask him.

Information Arrangement. A fairly obvious requirement (but one so often overlooked) is that the information be presented and arranged in a manner that permits its optimum use. Reports in tabular form are probably least useful, yet most often presented. Financial and other management reports should be recast into graphs, charts, and other easily grasped visual aids to understanding. Trends, comparisons, ratios and other relationships and significant data should be prominently displayed. Deviations and responsibilities should be pinpointed so corrections can be made or rewards given.

Establish Reader Preference as to Form

The form the report ultimately takes and the arrangement of information within the report should be determined to a large extent by the preferences of the person receiving it. It would be useless to present a report in tabular form to a manager if he disliked this form. Graphic or narrative reports should be devised to communicate the same information in a different form.

Standardization of report forms for specific functions and purposes is desirable. This cuts down cost of preparation and increases the usefulness, generally. But it has the disadvantages of becoming habitual; conditions may change, requiring different reports, but the old form is clung to because it is "tried and true." Nevertheless, there should be a constant review of the information system and the report structure, with periodic revisions when necessary.

Establish Timing of the Reports

A late report is virtually useless. Information of past operations and results of decisions may be useful if it is not too old; current information is desirable; projections of future data are the most relevant for planning and control decisions.

The proper timing of reports to the various levels of management is vital to an effective management reporting system. The lowest level manager should be given his report first, and be given time to analyze it before his superior calls him in. Therefore, a short lag time is appropriate before the report's submission to managers up the line. In effect, the top man is the last to know, but this disadvantage is outweighed by the increase in morale and effectiveness of each level of managers.

The lag time between the event, the report and the corrective action determines the effectiveness of the control maintained. The reliability and relevancy of the information determines the effectiveness of the planning accomplished.

Related to timing is the matter of frequency. Reports that are too infrequent lose validity and relevancy. But reports presented too frequently may be too costly for the benefit derived, or may not give a representative picture. A delicate balance is required in the frequency of report to provide immediate control over certain activities and to provide periodic control over more general operations, all while preserving the timeliness of the report. Factors affecting this balance are the promptness required by management, making the report cover a period long enough to be representative, and the availability of data. The benefit of usefulness must be carefully weighed against the cost of timeliness.

The timing of specific regular reports must be established for first-line supervisors, operating managers, officers, board of directors, and staff personnel. All have different requirements that must be met. First-line supervisors need certain daily reports. Other reports may be prepared monthly, quarterly, or yearly depending upon their purposes and the level of management to which they are directed.

PRINCIPLES OF RESPONSIBILITY REPORTING

Drawing on the foregoing discussion of the basic requirements for effective management reporting, and adding a few additional concepts, we may derive several principles of responsibility reporting.

Establish Responsibility and Authority Relationships

It was stated earlier that in establishing profit responsibility, we must determine the existing authority and responsibility relationships. These will generally follow the outline of the organization chart. But this formal structure does not show the whole picture. Informal relationships exist as well. These should also be determined. Both formal and informal authority-responsibility relationships, therefore, should be established within the reporting system.

Fix Responsibility for Profit Control with Specific Individuals

Clearly assigning responsibility is essential to an effective management information system. Responsibility accounting builds upon this principle. The system gathers data on revenues, costs, and profits, then organizes the data into information tailored to the authority-responsibility structure of the firm.

Responsibility reporting relates to controlling costs at the level at which they are approved and incurred, and to maximizing revenues at the points at which they are generated, and tieing the authority, responsibility and accountability for these to specific persons at these levels or points. The revenues and/or costs must be attributable to the particular person's efforts and be under his control.

Establishing responsibility for costs is not always as easy as it sounds. The organization chart does not always provide the answer, either because it is faulty or because informal relationships exist, as noted before. Responsibility may be according to function or job that can be done anywhere in the firm. It may be according to a product line, or a department. Service efforts are the most troublesome since the benefits are the most widespread across the firm.

When organizational responsibilities for costs are finally determined, then two kinds of cost information are provided for each element of cost within the responsibility area. These are planned costs and actual costs. The comparison of these fits into another principle, the discussion of which follows in a separate section.

Establishing responsibility for revenues and profits covers a smaller number of people usually, but is no less important than controlling costs. Only the top management has the direct responsibility for profits. Middle managers (or perhaps vice-presidents) in charge of sales, and their subordinates, have the direct responsibility for generating revenues. They also have costs which they must control.

The process of establishing responsibility here is very similar. First, clearly assign responsibility for results to the person having the authority to exercise control. Second, establish goals and standards representing satisfactory performance. Third, collect and report actual revenues and profits, compared to the prior plan, to the person responsible.

Such a profit responsibility plan is presented in the illustration—Figure 3-1. This plan shows: (1) the responsibility of the president for net income. (2) The manufacturing vice-president responsible for the total costs of manufacturing, including a direct responsibility for noncontrollable manufacturing costs. (3) The manufacturing department heads directly responsible for controllable costs and indirectly responsible for noncontrollable but identifiable costs, for product costing purposes. (4) Direct service department costs chargeable to the respective department heads, and the noncontrollable costs as the responsibility of the service vice-president. (5) Division sales directors responsible for direct costs incurred in their area, as well as for revenue generation, and the sales vice-president responsible for noncontrollable costs identified with the sales areas and function.

The sales forecast is the key to this profit plan. Other sales levels could be projected under different volume assumptions and the planned costs established for those volumes.

Establish Responsibility Centers Separate from Cost Centers

It was mentioned earlier in this chapter that cost centers are a starting point for responsibility assignment. This is true, to an extent. A cost center is assigned, in traditional cost accounting, costs which benefited that center. Assigning costs by origin, however, is more relevant to responsibility accounting. Where costs originate is important for control purposes because a certain person is given the authority for approving and incurring the expenditure. The lowest level administrative units at which costs may originate are, therefore, responsibility centers. These should be the focal point for control and reporting purposes. A cost center would have both controllable and noncontrollable allocated costs assigned to it through the benefit criterion. Responsibility centers would have only controllable costs assigned, according to the origin-authority criterion.

Measure Performance of Individual Against Original Plan

Comparing actual against planned revenue and cost performance provides the manager responsible for a particular center with an excellent means of planning and controlling his operations. Continuous control is facilitated; further planning is made easier. Deviations from standard may be analyzed and corrective action taken.

Actual performance may be superimposed upon the profit responsibility plan shown in Figure 3-1. Then it becomes a "Profit Responsibility Report." For example, the planned and actual performance for the North sales division may be shown as:

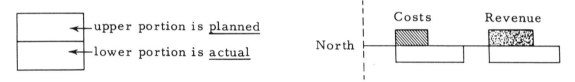

Actual costs exceeded planned costs; this is an unfavorable variance. Actual revenues exceeded planned revenues; this is a favorable variance.

As an alternative, the variances themselves could be shown on a profit responsibility control report, as presented in Figure 3-2. In this case only the deviations are shown. The size and shade of the box indicates the favorable or unfavorable amount of the deviation. This report would be presented to the upper levels of management. The department head would get more frequent reports covering specific controllable costs within his department and the amount of variance from the planned costs. This report would show weekly or monthly and year-to-date totals, and may be in tabular form or in a form similar in concept to the profit responsibility plan and control reports presented in Figures 3-1 and 3-2.

The participation of various managers in setting planned revenues and costs and other standards of performance is closely related to responsibility accounting. Responsibility consists of two aspects: the obligation to attain planned results, and the reporting back to higher authority of the results achieved. Accountability is that part of responsibility which identifies the obligation to report actual performance to higher authority. This brings us to the next principle of responsibility reporting.

Establish Reports for Action Points

This involves, principally, establishing a pyramid structure of reports. This structure permits the various managerial levels to be linked in a chain of reciprocal information.

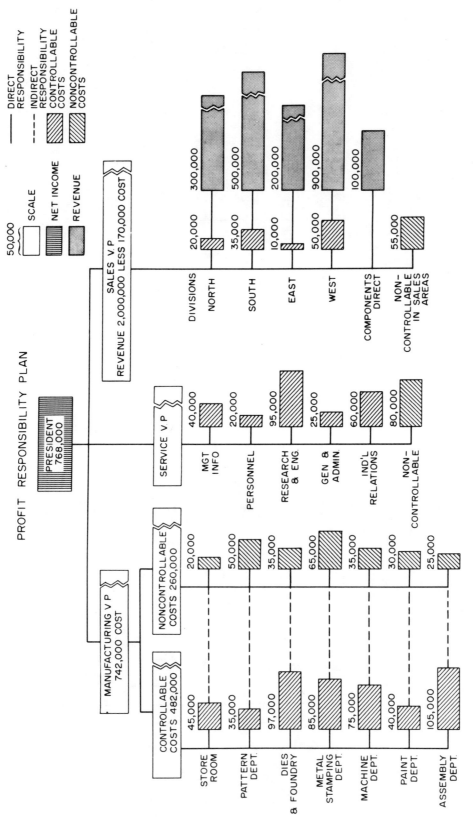

Figure 3-1.

Adapted from Frank Wallace, "Creating Cost Consciousness," *Manufacturers' News*, July 1948, p. 5.

61

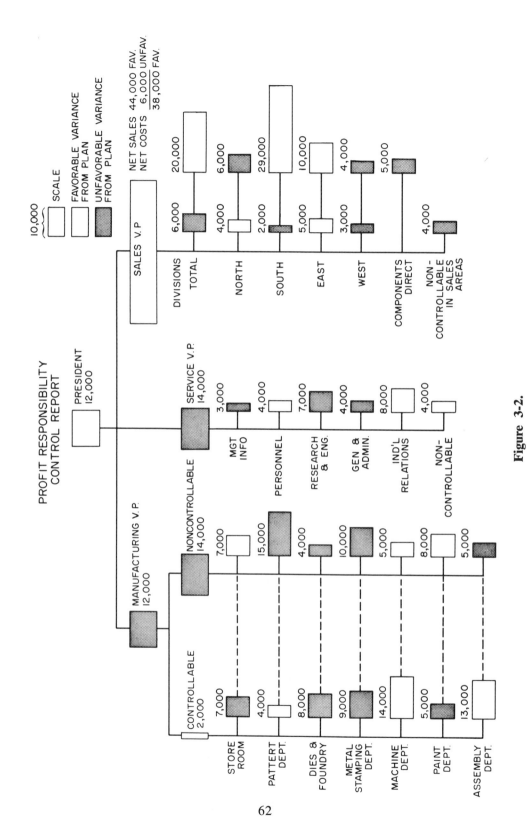

PROFIT RESPONSIBILITY
CONTROL REPORT

SCALE

FAVORABLE VARIANCE
FROM PLAN

UNFAVORABLE VARIANCE
FROM PLAN

10,000

PRESIDENT
12,000

SALES V.P

NET SALES 44,000 FAV.
NET COSTS 6,000 UNFAV.
          38,000 FAV.

DIVISIONS

TOTAL   6,000   20,000
NORTH   4,000   6,000
SOUTH   2,000   29,000
EAST   5,000   10,000
WEST   3,000   4,000
COMPONENTS   5,000
DIRECT
NON-   4,000
CONTROLLABLE
IN SALES
AREAS

SERVICE V.P.
14,000

NONCONTROLLABLE
14,000

MGT INFO   3,000
PERSONNEL   4,000
RESEARCH   7,000
& ENG.
GEN &   4,000
ADMIN.
IND'L   8,000
RELATIONS
NON-   4,000
CONTROLLABLE

MANUFACTURING V.P.
12,000

CONTROLLABLE
2,000

STORE ROOM   7,000   7,000
PATTERT DEPT. 4,000   15,000
DIES &   8,000   4,000
FOUNDRY
METAL   9,000   10,000
STAMPING
DEPT.
MACHINE   14,000   5,000
DEPT.
PAINT DEPT.   5,000   8,000
ASSEMBLY   13,000   5,000
DEPT.

Figure 3-2.

Adapted from Frank Wallace, "Creating Cost Consciousness," *Manufacturers' News*, July 1948, p. 5.

62

Each manager is concerned with two areas of responsibility—his own to his superiors, and that of his immediate subordinates to him.

In this system relevant, controllable cost and revenue information is presented at each operating level in the detail necessary for that station's requirements, decisions, and action. Action points are responsibility centers; these should be the focus of the accountant's reporting attention.

Responsibility Reporting in Action. The organization chart is the key to effective reporting. Figure 3-3 presents an organization chart for the imaginary Vendco Service, Inc.

This chart shows the company directed by a president and three vice-presidents in charge of the industries, institutions, and serv-o-mat divisions. The figures in parentheses are internal code numbers signifying functions and organizational levels. Below the vice-presidents there are managers in charge of the various areas, regions, subregions, and local districts. These are levels 5, 4, 3, and 2, respectively. The detailed organization chart is shown only for the industry division; other divisions would be similar in structure, however. The dark vertical line signifies the direct chain of command existing within the industry division for certain lower levels of the organization structure. Details of the structure for the other divisions have been omitted in the interest of brevity.

The seven levels of responsibility have been numbered. This emphasizes the parallel and pyramidal relationship of these responsibility levels and the reports directed at each of these levels. The numbering also provides a ready reference point for discussion on the reports which follow.

"Lower" Management Reports. The first level of responsibility is that of the individual salesmen in the field. These men must prepare daily and other periodic reports of sales and costs and report this to the manager of the local district (level 2). The individual salesmen's reports are not shown here since they involve only a bookkeeping function. These individual reports are accumulated periodically and summarized at level 2. All the details of sales, other operating income, cost of sales, payroll and other costs are shown from the combined salesmen's reports. This report does show several items of depreciation and amortization and shop expense which have been charged to salesmen. But it does not show any expenses incurred at the next higher level (level 3) for the benefit of the local districts. For all practical purposes, therefore, the "contribution margin" figure (the last shown) is within the control of the manager of the local district.

Within Figure 3-4 certain level 2 figures have been indicated A–D, and others E–H. These signify revenue and contribution margin, respectively, for this month and year-to-date for actual and forecasted amounts. These amounts are similarly keyed on the level 3 operating summary, Figure 3-5a.

The previous year's actual amounts are not included on the level 2 operating statement presented, although they could have been. Also, the dollar difference between the actual and forecasted figures could be presented in a separate column. Or, instead of presenting actual, forecasted, and the difference, we could present just the actual and the favorable or unfavorable deviation from forecast. Management must decide what information would be most useful to them, and in what form. The management in this case has decided that total forecasted figures are preferable to differences, and that, at the upper levels, the previous year's figures also should be shown.

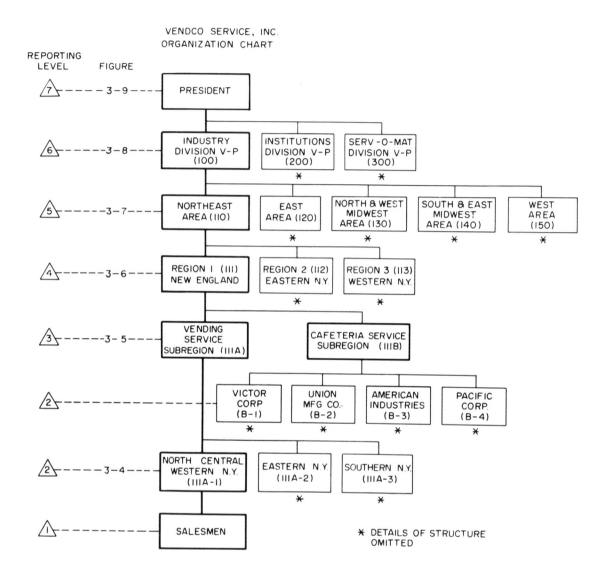

VENDCO SERVICE, INC.
ORGANIZATION CHART

Figure 3-3.

VENDO SERVICE, INC,
OPERATING SUMMARY
NORTH - CENTRAL - WESTERN NEW YORK--111A-1--INDUSTRY DIVISION

LEVEL 2 REPORT
DATE 4/30/69

ACCOUNT	APRIL ACTUAL	APRIL FORECAST	YEAR-TO-DATE ACTUAL	YEAR-TO-DATE FORECAST
SALES				
1.00 CIGARETTES AND CIGARS	6 210	6 300	41 160	43 320
2.00 FOOD THROUGH VENDING MACHINES	510	680	2 550	4 660
3.00 HOT BEVERAGES	65 500	67 370	496 040	463 160
4.00 COLD BEVERAGES	1 800	3 400	13 780	23 330
5.00 CANDY, GUM, NUTS	4 300	6 300	42 890	43 320
6.00 MILK, JUICES, ICE CREAM	10 790	11 920	78 590	81 970
7.00 PASTRIES	670	970	7 870	6 670
10.00 SERV-O-MAT SALES	-0-	-0-	-0-	-0-
TOTAL SALES	89 780 (A) 100.0 0/0	96 930 (B) 100.0 0/0	682 860 (C) 100.0 0/0	666 410 (D) 100.0 0/0
OTHER OPERATING REVENUE				
102.00 VENDING COMMISSIONS RECEIVABLE	230 .3	190 .2	1 830 .3	1 330 .2
103.00 PROMOTION ALLOWANCES	150 .2	120 .1	460 .1	850 .1
105.00 CASH DISCOUNTS	340 .4	390 .4	2 690 .4	2 670 .4
199.99 OTHER OPERATING INCOME	590 .6	970 1.0	5 670 .8	6 670 1.0
TOTAL OPERATING INCOME	1 310 1.5	1 690 1.7	10 797 1.6	11 580 1.7
TOTAL INCOME	91 090 101.5	98 610 101.7	693 660 101.6	677 990 101.7
COST OF SALES				
201.00 CIGARETTES AND CIGARS	4 900 78.9	4 850 77.0	32 160 78.1	33 350 77.0
201.01 CIGARETTE TAX	650 10.4	-0-	650 1.6	-0-
202.00 FOOD THROUGH VENDING MACHINES	320 61.7	440 65.0	1 440 56.6	3 030 65.0
203.00 HOT BEVERAGES	20 140 30.7	19 540 29.0	158 660 32.0	134 320 29.0
204.00 COLD BEVERAGES	450 24.9	820 24.0	3 390 24.6	5 600 24.0
205.00 CANDY, GUM, NUTS	2 190 51.0	3 280 52.0	21 890 51.0	22 520 52.0
206.00 MILK, JUICES, ICE CREAM	6 020 55.8	6 200 52.0	42 140 53.6	42 620 52.0
207.00 PASTRIES	450 68.1	680 70.0	5 440 69.1	4 670 70.0
251.00 LOSSES, MATCHES, SALES TAX *	170 .2	100 .1	1 210 .2	680 .1
TOTAL COST OF SALES	35 291 39.3	35 900 37.0	266 970 39.1	246 800 37.0
GROSS PROFIT	55 790 62.1 0/0	62 710 64.7 0/0	426 690 62.5 0/0	431 200 64.7 0/0
301.00 PAYROLL COSTS *	13 990 15.6	13 070 13.5	99 990 14.6	101 520 15.2
310 OTHER EXPENSES *	30 420 33.9	29 440 30.4	213 950 31.3	211 860 31.8
TOTAL OPERATING EXPENSES	44 410 49.5	42 510 43.9	313 940 46.0	313 390 47.8
CONTRIBUTION MARGIN	11 390 (E) 12.7 0/0	20 210 (F) 20.8 0/0	112 750 (G) 16.5 0/0	117 820 (H) 17.7 0/0

ALL FIGURES ROUNDED TO NEAREST 10 DOLLARS
* DETAIL OMITTED FOR ILLUSTRATION PURPOSES

Figure 3-4.

"Middle" Management Reports. Figure 3-5a shows the operating summary for level 3, the subregion vending machine operations. The totals line lettered I is carried forward to Figure 3-6, reporting level 4. Likewise, the totals line lettered J on Figure 3-5 is carried to Figure 3-6. Figure 3-6 then summarizes the responsibility of the manager of region I, New England. His operating summary presents the activities of his subordinates, the managers of the vending service subregion and the cafeteria service subregion, as well as the additional costs for which he is responsible. These costs are incurred for the benefit of the two subregions, but are not allocated to them because the subregion managers do not have control over them. The manager of the region does, and it therefore shows on his operating summary.

The grand totals, indicated as line K in Figure 3-6, are carried to the level 5 operating summary, Figure 3-7. This is the operating statement for the northeast area and shows, in addition to the amounts mentioned, total revenue and contribution margin of the other two New York responsibilities, regions 2 and 3. Also, the report shows the unallocated costs incurred at this level 5, but uncontrollable at the lower levels. The totals line, indicated as L, is carried to the level 6 statement.

"Top" Management Reports. Figure 3-8 presents the accountability for the operations under the authority of the industrial division vice-president, which is level 6 in the managerial hierarchy. This operating summary shows revenue and contribution margin totals for five areas below him, as well as a separate but affiliated support group. Also given is the controllable expense incurred by this manager for the benefit of his responsibility areas. The grand totals, indicated as line M, are carried to the final report to the president, Figure 3-9.

The operating summary in Figure 3-9 is given to the president, level 7, and highest in this managerial hierarchy. (Other reports would be devised for the board of directors, mostly in graphic form.) The three main subdivisions are clearly shown, as well as an amount forecasted to be derived from acquisitions during the year. National overhead is also given, being the responsibility of the president.

It can be seen from these illustrations that responsibility accounting emphasizes the information useful to operating management and de-emphasizes the nonessential items (for decision purposes) that are found in so many operating statements today.

An overall picture of a responsibility reporting system for manufacturing costs is presented in Figure 3-10.[1] This shows four levels of responsibility for incurring manufacturing costs. Each report indicates in its top portion the controllable expenses incurred at that level and the variation from budget. In its bottom part, each report shows the standard for productive labor and the variance from standard, for this month and year-to-date. The accountability to the next highest managerial level is presented by the arrows showing the upward flow of specific information.

From the reported results, as illustrated in both these examples, each person is able to determine how successfully he has controlled the activities he is responsible for, and his superiors are able to use this same responsibility reporting to judge how effectively each person is carrying out his delegated responsibilities.

---

[1] This is adapted with permission from charts 3 and 12 in John A. Higgins' "Responsibility Accounting," *The Arthur Andersen Chronicle,* Vol. 12, No. 2 (April 1952).

VENDO SERVICE, INC,
OPERATING SUMMARY
VENDING SERVICE SUBREGION--111A--INDUSTRY DIVISION

LEVEL 3 REPORT
DATE 4/30/69

		Current Year - Forecast Sales	Current Year - Forecast Cont. Margin	Current Year - Forecast 0/0	Current Year - Actual Sales	Current Year - Actual Cont. Margin	Current Year - Actual 0/0	Previous Year - Actual Sales	Previous Year - Actual Cont. Margin	Previous Year - Actual 0/0
111A-1	NORTH-CENTRAL-WESTERN NEW YORK									
	MONTH	96 930 (B)	(F) 20 210	20.8	89 780 (A)	(E) 11 390	12.7	86 330	17 210	19.9
	YEAR-TO-DATE	666 410 (D)	(H) 117 820	17.7	682 860 (C)	(G) 112 750	16.5	598 410	108 980	18.2
111A-2	EASTERN NEW YORK									
	MONTH	85 390	10 410	12.2	79 910	4 240	5.3	71 820	5 620	7.8
	YEAR-TO-DATE	600 550	61 500	10.2	570 720	55 910	9.8	409 550	33 710	8.2
111A-3	SOUTHERN NEW YORK									
	MONTH	91 300	7 360	8.1	101 130	11 740	11.6	82 710	8 620	10.4
	YEAR-TO-DATE	668 050	62 680	9.4	712 410	92 570	13.0	615 830	57 920	9.4
	(I) TOTAL VENDING SERVICE									
	MONTH	273 620	37 980	13.9	270 810	27 360	10.1	240 860	31 440	13.1
	YEAR-TO-DATE	1 935 010	241 990	12.5	1 965 990	261 220	13.3	1 623 780	200 610	12.4

Figure 3-5a.

VENDO SERVICE, INC, LEVEL 3 REPORT
OPERATING SUMMARY DATE 4/30/69
CAFETERIA SERVICE SUBREGION--111B--INDUSTRY DIVISION

		Current Year - Forecast Sales	Cont. Margin	0/0	Current Year - Actual Sales	Cont. Margin	0/0	Previous Year - Actual Sales	Cont. Margin	0/0
111B-1	VICTOR CORPORATION									
	MONTH	1 400	1 160-	83.0	1 570	840-	53.6	1 390	1 080-	77.3
	YEAR-TO-DATE	9 500	7 810-	82.2	11 320	5 890-	52.1	9 370	7 060-	75.3
111B-2	UNICN MANUFACTURING CO.									
	MONTH	10 770	1 080	10.0	9 550	950	10.0	10 770	1 080	10.0
	YEAR-TO-DATE	81 840	8 180	10.0	75 110	7 510	10.0	81 820	7 540	9.2
111B-3	AMERICAN INDUSTRIES									
	MONTH	33 000	2 780	8.4	32 190	2 410	7.5	33 480	3 150	9.4
	YEAR-TO-DATE	246 000	20 350	8.3	256 780	18 840	7.3	246 620	17 610	7.1
111B-4	PACIFIC CORPORATION									
	MONTH	11 000	2 750	25.0	13 010	2 050-	15.8	11 200	3 190	28.5
	YEAR-TO-DATE	73 700	18 123	24.6	92 870	23 790	25.6	72 990	22 310	30.6
111B-5	NEW BUSINESS									
	MONTH	6 740	540	8.0	-0-			-0-		
	YEAR-TO-DATE	33 040	2 640	8.0	-0-			-0-		
	(J) TOTAL CAFETERIA SERVICE									
	MONTH	62 910	5 990	9.5	56 310	470	.8	56 840	6 340	11.2
	YEAR-TO-DATE	444 080	41 490	9.3	436 080	44 250	10.1	410 790	40 400	9.8

Figure 3-5b.

VENDO SERVICE, INC,
OPERATING SUMMARY
REGION 1- NEW ENGLAND--111--INDUSTRY DIVISION

LEVEL 4 REPORT
DATE 4/30/69

	CURRENT YEAR - FORECAST			CURRENT YEAR - ACTUAL			PREVIOUS YEAR - ACTUAL		
	SALES	CONT. MARGIN	O/O	SALES	CONT. MARGIN	O/O	SALES	CONT. MARGIN	O/O
111-A ① TOTAL VENDING SERVICE - SUBREGION A									
MONTH	273 620	37 970	13.9	270 810	27 360	10.1	240 850	31 440	13.1
YEAR-TO-DATE	1 935 010	241 990	12.5	1 965 990	261 220	13.3	1 623 780	200 610	12.4
111-B ① TOTAL CAFETERIA SERVICE - SUBREGION B									
MONTH	62 910	5 990	9.5	56 310	470	.8	56 840	6 340	11.2
YEAR-TO-DATE	444 080	41 490	9.3	436 080	44 250	10.1	410 790	40 400	9.8
TOTAL OPERATIONS									
MONTH	336 530	43 960	13.1	327 120	27 840	8.5	297 690	37 780	12.7
YEAR-TO-DATE	2 379 090	283 480	11.9	2 402 080	305 470	12.7	2 034 570	241 010	11.8
REGIONAL OVERHEAD									
MONTH		7 070-	2.1		5 950-	1.8		-0-	
YEAR-TO-DATE		54 380-	2.3		39 560-	1.6		-0-	
Ⓚ GRAND TOTAL REGION 1									
MONTH	336 530	36 890	11.0	327 120	21 890	6.7	297 700	37 780	12.7
YEAR-TO-DATE	2 379 090	229 100	9.6	2 402 080	265 910	11.1	2 034 570	241 010	11.8

Figure 3-6.

VENDO SERVICE, INC,
OPERATING SUMMARY
NORTHEAST AREA--110--INDUSTRY DIVISION

LEVEL 5 REPORT
DATE 4/30/69

		CURRENT YEAR - FORECAST			CURRENT YEAR - ACTUAL			PREVIOUS YEAR - ACTUAL		
		SALES	CONT. MARGIN	O/O	SALES	CONT. MARGIN	O/O	SALES	CONT. MARGIN	O/O
111	(K) REGION 1 - NEW ENGLAND									
	MONTH	336 500	36 900	11.0	327 100	21 900	6.7	297 700	37 800	12.7
	YEAR-TO-DATE	2 379 100	229 100	9.6	2 402 100	265 900	11.1	2 034 600	241 000	11.6
112	REGION 2 - EASTERN NEW YORK									
	MONTH	472 500	23 200	4.9	457 600	9 600	2.1	416 200	1 900	.5
	YEAR-TO-DATE	3 621 200	186 200	5.1	3 376 700	86 800	2.6	3 124 400	82 000	2.6
113	REGION 3 - WESTERN NEW YORK									
	MONTH	539 200	34 600	6.4	543 300	42 400	7.8	506 400	52 200	10.3
	YEAR-TO-DATE	3 882 600	285 500	7.4	4 233 600	373 200	8.8	3 452 100	352 400	10.2
	TOTAL OPERATIONS									
	MONTH	1 348 300	94 600	7.0	1 328 000	73 800	5.6	1 220 300	91 800	7.5
	YEAR-TO-DATE	9 882 900	700 700	7.1	10 012 400	725 900	7.3	8 611 000	675 400	7.8
	AREA OVERHEAD									
	MONTH		4 000-	.3		4 500-	.3		17 100-	1.4
	YEAR-TO-DATE		30 200-	.3		33 700-	.3		99 500-	1.2
	(L) GRAND TOTAL AREA 110									
	MONTH	1 348 300	90 600	6.7	1 328 000	69 300	5.2	1 220 300	74 800	6.1
	YEAR-TO-DATE	9 882 900	670 500	6.8	10 012 400	692 200	6.9	8 611 000	575 900	6.7

Figure 3-7.

VENDO SERVICE, INC.
OPERATING SUMMARY

LEVEL 6 REPORT
DATE 4/30/69

INDUSTRY DIVISION--100

	CURRENT YEAR - FORECAST			CURRENT YEAR - ACTUAL			PREVIOUS YEAR - ACTUAL		
	SALES	CONT. MARGIN	O/O	SALES	CONT. MARGIN	O/O	SALES	CONT. MARGIN	O/O
110 (L) NORTHEAST AREA									
MONTH	1 348 000	91 000	6.7	1 328 000	69 000	5.2	1 220 000	74 000	6.1
YEAR-TO-DATE	9 883 000	671 000	6.8	10 012 000	692 000	6.9	8 611 000	576 000	6.7
120 EAST AREA									
MONTH	3 042 000	240 000	7.9	2 932 000	203 000	6.9	2 665 000	166 000	6.2
YEAR-TO-DATE	21 678 000	1 699 000	7.8	21 365 000	1 408 000	6.9	19 323 000	1 197 000	6.2
130 NORTH + WEST MIDWEST AREA									
MONTH	3 768 000	303 000	8.0	3 873 000	303 000	7.8	2 979 000	154 000	5.2
YEAR-TO-DATE	26 418 000	1 960 000	7.4	27 641 000	2 128 000	7.7	21 144 000	1 002 000	4.7
140 SOUTH + EAST MIDWEST AREA									
MONTH	3 896 000	320 000	8.2	3 790 000	308 000	8.1	3 301 000	218 000	6.6
YEAR-TO-DATE	28 265 000	2 269 000	8.0	27 812 000	2 475 000	8.9	23 950 000	2 204 000	8.4
150 WEST AREA									
MONTH	2 508 000	192 000	7.7	2 347 000	177 000	7.5	2 501 000	147 000	5.9
YEAR-TO-DATE	18 279 000	1 317 000	7.2	17 389 000	1 128 000	6.5	17 711 000	953 000	5.4
160 SUPPORT GROUP									
MONTH	104 000	34 000	33.2	116 000	75 000	64.1	137 000	70 000	50.8
YEAR-TO-DATE	779 000	243 000	31.2	848 000	351 000	41.4	800 000	308 000	38.5
TOTAL OPERATIONS									
MONTH	14 665 000	1 180 000	8.0	14 386 000	1 134 000	7.9	12 803 000	829 000	6.5
YEAR-TO-DATE	05 302 000	8 159 000	7.7	05 067 000	8 245 000	7.8	91 539 000	6 039 000	6.6
DIVISION OVERHEAD									
MONTH		33 000-	.2		37 000-	.3		31 000-	.2
YEAR-TO-DATE		246 000-	.2		226 000-	.2		216 000-	.2
(M) GRAND TOTAL									
MONTH	14 665 000	1 148 000	7.8	14 386 000	1 097 000	7.6	12 803 000	799 000	6.2
YEAR-TO-DATE	05 302 000	7 913 000	7.5	05 067 000	8 019 000	7.6	91 539 000	5 824 000	6.4

Figure 3-8.

```
                          VENDO SERVICE, INC,              LEVEL 7 REPORT
                          OPERATING SUMMARY                DATE  4/30/69
                                          ALL DIVISIONS

                            CURRENT YEAR - FORECAST      CURRENT YEAR - ACTUAL       PREVIOUS YEAR - ACTUAL
                            SALES  CONT. MARGIN  O/O     SALES  CONT. MARGIN  O/O    SALES  CONT. MARGIN  O/O
```

		CURRENT YEAR - FORECAST			CURRENT YEAR - ACTUAL			PREVIOUS YEAR - ACTUAL		
		SALES	CONT. MARGIN	O/O	SALES	CONT. MARGIN	O/O	SALES	CONT. MARGIN	O/O
100 (M) INDUSTRY DIVISION	MONTH	14 665	1 148	7.8	14 386	1 097	7.6	12 803	799	6.2
	YEAR-TO-DATE	105 302	7 913	7.5	105 067	8 019	7.6	91 539	5 824	6.4
200 INSTITUTIONS DIVISION	MONTH	5 849	396	6.8	5 850	411	7.0	4 746	314	6.6
	YEAR-TO-DATE	43 268	3 056	7.1	44 579	3 224	7.2	35 450	2 464	6.9
300 SERV-O-MAT	MONTH	-0-	1-		8	3	35.4	-0-	1-	
	YEAR-TO-DATE	30	16	52.1	25	19	76.5	-0-	24	
400 NEW ACQUISITIONS	MONTH	147	2	1.1	-0-	-0-		-0-	-0-	
	YEAR-TO-DATE	663	7	1.1	-0-	-0-		-0-	-0-	
TOTAL OPERATIONS	MONTH	20 661	1 545	7.5	20 244	1 511	7.5	17 549	1 112	6.3
	YEAR-TO-DATE	149 233	11 992	8.0	149 671	11 262	7.5	126 989	8 312	6.5
NATIONAL OVERHEAD	MONTH		538-	2.6		929-	4.7		521-	3.0
	YEAR-TO-DATE		4 133-	2.8		4 478-	3.0		3 789-	3.0
GRAND TOTAL	MONTH	20 661	1 003	4.9	20 244	581	2.9	17 550	591	3.4
	YEAR-TO-DATE	149 233	6 845	4.6	149 671	6 784	4.5	126 988	4 522	3.6

Figure 3-9.

NOTE-- OJO ELIMINATED

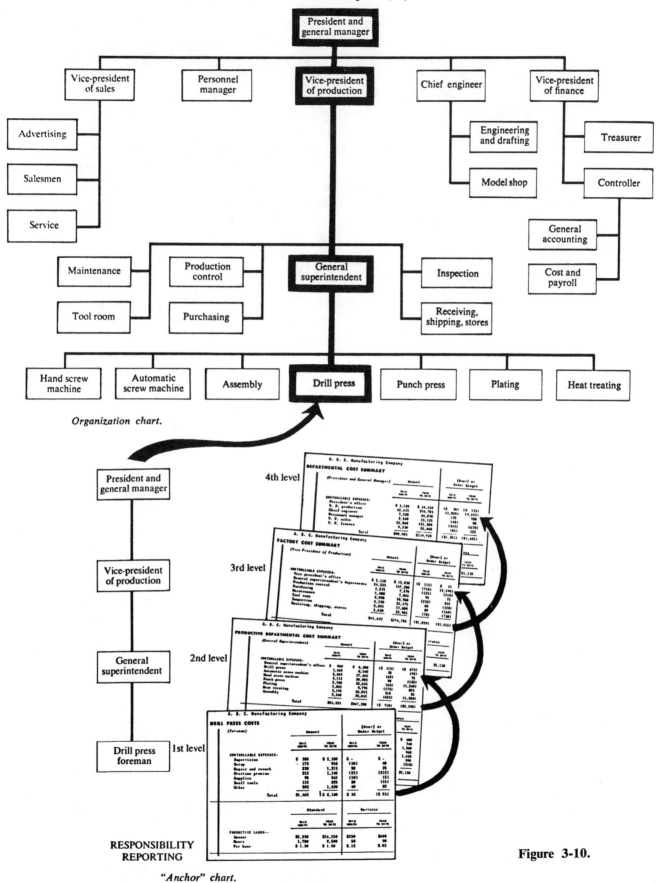

A B C Manufacturing Company

Organization chart.

RESPONSIBILITY
REPORTING

"Anchor" chart.

Figure 3-10.

WHO, WHAT, WHEN: REPORTING TO SPECIFIC
LEVELS OF MANUFACTURING COMPANY MANAGEMENT

Management reports must be designed to fit the organization. Consequently, there is an almost unlimited variety of reports existing among the many companies. A later chapter will present some typical accounting reports to management. Our purpose here is to survey the who, what, and when of reporting to specific levels of management in a manufacturing company. The "how" or techniques of presentation was given in the previous chapters.

Reports to Foremen

The information required by a foreman will vary depending upon his work and areas of responsibility. He will be responsible for supervising and directing the employees in his group, and for seeing that they perform efficiently. He is directly responsible for their morale and their productivity. Day-to-day problems of production are the most important to him, so reports should be prepared weekly or daily so that corrective action may be taken quickly. These reports should show planned performance, actual performance, and variations from plans. Specific information is needed, as well as analyses showing reasons for variances so that the foreman may use these reports for controlling future operations.

Reports to Supervisors

Supervisors may receive copies of the reports issued to the foremen under him, or group summaries of these reports, or both. In addition to or in place of the summaries by processes within his department, the supervisor may receive only a summary statement of variances by foreman responsibilities. In this case he would also receive copies of the detailed reports issued to the foremen. Supervisors have the same responsibilities for efficiency, morale, and productivity as do the foremen, so comparative and analytical periodic reports should be given to him to help him carry out these responsibilities. These would include reports on departmental manufacturing costs and reports on the efficiency of material and labor usage, yield ratios, scrap and wastage.

Reports to Plant Management

Typically plant managers are responsible for production and for cost control, and for inventory control. They would receive copies of the operating reports going to their subordinates, as well as summaries of these and for the whole plant. Since plant managers cannot see and digest everything about operations under their jurisdiction, exception reporting should be used as much as possible. Manufacturing costs and volume statistics should be reported daily or weekly in order to provide for immediate control over operations. Other reports may be devised as desired on material, labor, and overhead efficiency, usage, and yield variances.

Reports to Division Managers and Top Executives

Reporting to top and upper-level management should be directed toward aiding them in performing their managerial functions of planning, organizing, and controlling. As demonstrated above by the pyramid reporting structure, as the level of reporting rises, the coverage broadens but the detail is reduced. The executive should receive only those reports pertaining to the proper administration of his authority and responsibility areas.

Top management may prefer or request only a limited number of key items to follow periodically to keep themselves informed about overall company operations. These key items measure the efficiency and effectiveness of their subordinates—their area of responsibility. Deviations are emphasized and explored; exception reporting is used more extensively than at lower reporting levels, and profit responsibility accounting is relied upon to provide insight into the relationship between planned and actual performance.

Reports to top management levels use a variety of forms: financial schedules and statements; narrative explanations; graphs, charts and other visual aids.

Whatever the form, the reports to a specific executive should be slanted toward his special function, keeping in mind his interest in the whole company. He will be interested in the overall return on investment, operating efficiency of the divisions, coordination of the divisions, and the firm's position in the industry.

General executives will usually require some or all of the following reports, depending upon their level and function, prepared monthly with comparisons and explanatory comment: [2]

1. Summary statement of financial condition
2. Analyses of significant changes in financial condition
3. Statement of cash position
4. Condensed statement of income and expense
5. Statement of income and expense by divisions or product lines
6. Statement accounting for changes in net income
7. Summary of sales by geographical area
8. Summary of volume statistics on sales, orders received, orders unfilled, production, and inventory change
9. Financial and operating ratios, relationships, and trends
10. General measurements of operating efficiency, by divisions
11. Comparison of actual with planned performance
12. Comparison of operations with external indexes of business climate
13. Program and accomplishments in capital expenditures
14. Forecast of following period.

The board of directors, as top executives, are interested in matters similar to those mentioned above. Broad policy matters, general trends of firm operations, competitive performance, and plans for the future are the items usually emphasized in board meetings. Therefore, condensations of the reports listed above are appropriate, on quarterly,

---

[2] Recommended by J. Brooks Heckert and James D. Willson, *Controllership* (2nd ed.; New York: The Ronald Press Co., 1952), p. 543, with some modifications included for our purposes here.

semiannual, and yearly bases. A concise report containing significant items should be prepared, accompanied by written explanations and an oral presentation relating to underlying causes, trends, and relationships.

Special Reports

Periodic reports are useful in systematically controlling operations and planning for the future. But many day-to-day problems arise where the information they contain is not adequate to solve them.

Special reports should be prepared presenting information that is most appropriate in the circumstances. In addition to accounting and cost data, engineering, economic, statistical and other data may be presented in the special reports.

Most special reports concern information relative to alternative choices, among which management must choose the one considered best. These alternatives involve preparing special cost figures, marginal revenue, and other statistics. Only those costs and revenues that will change as a result of the action are pertinent, in most cases.

Reports that compare alternatives figure in the following areas. Special reports here will:

- Aid in establishing general business policies
- Aid in determining pricing policies
- Aid in determining sales policies
- Aid in determining volume policies
- Aid in determining production policies
- Aid in determining capital expenditure policies.

The special costs and other considerations relative to establishing the alternatives in each of these areas are determined by the circumstances existing in the individual firm. Most cost accounting texts give the general details; further elaboration is beyond our present scope.

A representative list of managerial reports of a manufacturing business is given in Figure 3-11.[3]

---

[3] Reproduced with permission, from Adolph Matz, O. J. Curry, and George W. Frank, *Cost Accounting* (4th ed.; Cincinnati: South-Western Publishing Company, 1967), pp. 685–687.

List of Managerial Reports of a Manufacturing Business

Frequency	Name of Report	Sent to	Information Conveyed	Purpose of the Report
Daily	Record of Orders Booked	Sales Manager	Sales by major commodities	To check with sales quotas
Daily	Summary of Billed Sales	Top Management	Dollar value billed to customers	To compare current figures with corresponding figures last month and last year
Daily	Idle Time Report	Production Manager	Analysis of labor tickets regarding idle time	To check and control the cost, the causes, and the location of idle time
Daily	Daily Operating Report	Superintendent	Summary of daily results regarding production, volume, labor, and materials variances	To control specifications and to measure day-by-day performance
Daily	Daily Expense Report	Department Heads	Comparison of variable overhead with budget	To control variable expenses
Daily	Daily Force Report	Department Heads	List of the number of men working in each department	To control allowed number of men according to budget
Daily	Daily Labor Budget	Foremen Supervisors Division Heads	Report on the daily departmental direct and indirect labor cost	To control labor cost, both direct and indirect
Daily	Daily Efficiency Report	Superintendent	Presents standard hours, actual hours, and the rate of efficiency	To assure continuous efficiency and to remedy inefficiencies
Daily	Daily Plant Report	General Manager Executive Vice-president	Presents manufacturing expenses for the plant compared with standards	To measure the performance of the various divisions
Weekly	Bookings and Backlog Report	Sales Manager Production Planning	Summaries of product lines by product groups, regions, and individual territory levels	To guide sales management into selling according to a schedule matched with plant capacity
Weekly	Usage and Waste Report	Production Manager	Summary of physical quantity of materials used against standard quantity allowed	To control proper use of materials and to eliminate excessive waste

Figure 3-11.

Frequency	Name of Report	Sent to	Information Conveyed	Purpose of the Report
Weekly	Direct Labor Report	Production Manager	Summary of actual hours vs. standard hours and their respective costs	To gauge the effect of overtime, of inexperienced labor, of too much time, etc.
Weekly	Departmental Expense Summary	Department Supervisors	List of budget allowances against actual expenses with variances	To control departmental expense
Monthly	Gross Profit Analysis	Vice-presidents in charge of sales and manufacturing	Statement of gross profit by types of outlet and by-products	To indicate gross profit contribution of each outlet and product
Monthly	Analysis of Selling Expenses	Sales Manager	Comparison of budget allowances with actual expenses	To control selling expenses and check variances
Monthly	Materials Price Variance Report	Vice president in charge of operations Purchasing Agent	Comparison of actual materials cost with standard materials price	To show trend of price movement and purchasing agent's efficiency
Monthly	Materials Usage Variance Report	Vice-president in charge of operations Superintendent Foremen	Comparison of actual cost with standard cost in dollar values and percentages	To control actual materials consumption with allowances in standard costs
Monthly	Finished Product Damage Report	Vice-president in charge of operations Foremen	Lists value of good production and value of damages, also percentage of total	To control damages to finished products
Monthly	Performance Report	Foremen Executive Vice-president	States the costs of direct labor and overhead expenses	To point out efficiencies and deficiencies by departments and types of expenses
Monthly	Departmental Budget Report	Foremen	Comparison of actual expenses with budgeted allowances	To control expenses

Figure 3-11 (Continued).

Frequency	Name of Report	Sent to	Information Conveyed	Purpose of the Report
Monthly	Production Cost Statement	Divisional Superintendent	Summaries of actual cost and standard cost with variances	To control major elements of cost and to measure effect of volume
Monthly	Purchasing Report	Purchasing Committee	Comparison of actual purchases, consumption, coverage and inventory figures	To determine the trend and the result of policies decided upon
Monthly	Statement of Operations	President	Result of operations of the month with variances listed	To allow overall view of results
Monthly	Sales Analysis	Sales Manager	Comparison of quotas with actual sales	To control salesmen's activities
Monthly	Returns and Allowances Analysis	Vice-president in charge of operations	List of returns made by customers because of defects	To show the number and the value of returns by causes
Monthly	Income Statement	Top Management	Results of the month	To compare actual results with forecast
Monthly	Balance Sheet	Top Management	Results of the month	To compare actual results with forecast
Monthly	Retained Earnings Statement	Top Management	Results of the month	To compare actual results with forecast
Quarterly	Report on Executive Authorization on Capital Expenditures	Top Management (executive and operating)	Comparison of estimated savings with realized savings	To determine whether contemplated savings because of new facilities were realized
Quarterly	Labor Efficiency Report	Foreman Superintendent	Lists pieceworkers' earnings based on standard hourly rate	To check upon efficiency rate of production per worker
Special	Report of Wage Increases	Top Management	A study of the effect of wage increases on cost elements and inventories	To give management a basis in collective bargaining sessions
Special	Inventory Report	Top Management	A study of slow-moving stock	To reduce inventory cost
Special	Report on Functions of a Department	Top Management	A study of activities carried on in related departments	To control costs in departments and to reduce overlapping activities
Special	Report on Departmental Efficiency	Top Management	A study of a department's efficiency with suggestions for improvement	To reduce costs and to permit greater efficiency

Figure 3-11 (Continued).

4

Creating
Exception
Reports

Business information encompasses all the information relevant to managing an enterprise. The purpose of generating business information is to narrow the areas of uncertainty in decision making. Information technology comprehends determining the information pertinent to managerial decision making, and providing it completely, currently, and accurately. Effective accounting reports to management are a vital part of this information technology. And exception reports are an integral part of the accounting reports package.

Management by exception presupposes an understanding of the functions of management: planning, organizing, directing, staffing, and controlling. In brief, management is defined here as the act of planning goals and organizing resources to obtain those goals. People are involved in all phases of the management functions. People set goals, plan their implementation, organize human and nonhuman resources and make corrections in all these when required for a more efficient organization.

Accountants are involved with all the management functions. They help set goals and help plan their implementation; they measure human effort and the results of that effort; they compare those results to the goals and plans, and establish the degree of effectiveness attained. Reports to management permeate this structure of assistance to all managerial levels. Exception reporting is one facet of this structure.

THE MANAGEMENT BY EXCEPTION CONCEPT

To the definition of management given in the preceding section, a phrase is added. Management is the act of planning goals and organizing resources to attain those goals, *and focusing effort upon unachieved goals.* The ordinary is the achieved goal; the exception is the unachieved goal. This concept finds application in the reporting system in its issuing reports to management only on abnormal or exceptional performance. Normal operations become routine and are assumed. The favorable or unfavorable variance from planned performance becomes significant as a flag demanding managerial attention and action. But the variance is only a symptom; the cause of the variance is the important thing to search out and correct as quickly as possible.

REQUIREMENTS OF AN EFFECTIVE MANAGEMENT BY EXCEPTION REPORTING SYSTEM

There are several requirements which must be fulfilled before the system is effective. These center around setting goals, assigning responsibilities, and setting yardsticks for and evaluating performance.

Written Statement of Broad Goals. Although goals may be established and stated informally and orally, the better practice is to put these down in writing. In this way they become more definite and there is less tendency for operating personnel to forget them. The goals may consist of a number of elements, including profits, share of market, sales revenue, credit worthiness, use of firm resources, treatment of employees, or growth through diversification and product research.

Projected income statements and balance sheets are expressions of net income and financial position goals. From these, yardsticks for measuring deviations may be established, and exception reports compiled.

Formal Definition of Organization Structure. Many businesses operate satisfactorily without ever committing their organization structure to graphic expression on a piece of paper. Others would flounder in inefficiency and overlapping responsibilities if they did not. Understanding the authority and responsibility relationship through a formal definition of the organization structure is a necessary requirement for a hierarchically directed exception reporting system. Such a definition and description of the goals, authority and responsibilities of each manager at each level is a prerequisite for the efficient functioning in any organization of substantial size. But even the very small firms also benefit from such a description.

The accountant must design the exception reporting system using this established organizational structure as his base. This structure is the basis for a "normal" reporting system as well, as was demonstrated in earlier chapters. Reports prepared for a particular person, whether on the exception or the total experience, must take into account his place in the organization.

Assignment of Detailed Goals to Key People. Once the organization structure and its authority-responsibility relationships are established, the elements of the firm-wide goals must be identified with key people. Goal-responsibility must be established. The system of responsibility accounting described earlier in the text expresses this establishment in a set of reports to management.

Certain managers are responsible for certain revenues and costs, others for other elements of operations. For example, the vice-president over production is responsible for producing a certain level of output at a specific level of quality. Given these goals, he is responsible for the costs under his control incurred in attaining these goals. He is responsible for the efficiency of his people and processes. He is responsible in part for the size of the net income produced. Whoever the manager, the details of the goals assigned to him must be defined and understood by him. The accountant must know the goals and responsibilities set in order to adequately report upon achievements.

Definition of Exception Yardsticks and Standards. Probably more important to exception reporting than a written definition of responsibility is the matter of clearly defining what constitutes an exception. There exists no set criterion for what shall be the exception. This is determined by the nature of the business, the level of management reported to, and the recipients' desires as to frequency of the reports.

Setting the exception level is something that must be the result of experiences and experiments within the individual firm. Too-loose standards cause a false sense of security, for performance would be rarely out of the "normal range." Conversely, too-tight standards would cause exceptions to be reported upon small and frequent variation from normal. In any event, a "normal range" of performance must be established as a result of discussions and agreements with the report recipients at each managerial level. Exception reports would then follow these agreements.

The deviations from the normal range, expressed as percentages and/or in terms of dollar or other measurement units, should be supplemented by brief comments on the reasons for the deviations. As we will see in the following sections, other statistical data on operations may be included in the exception report.

Graphically displaying the deviations from standard is very effective in exception reporting. This is demonstrated in Figure 4-1. Normally, the various measures will have different points at which the deviations from the goal become exceptions. This will be illustrated in a later section of this chapter. For our purposes here, however, assume that the 11 items displayed have established for them ± 20% as the "no exception range." Deviations from the goal of more or less than 20% are considered exceptions and should be reported, favorable or unfavorable as the case may be, to management. These 11 items are:

- revenue
- profit
- units sold
- on-time deliveries
- inventories
- order backlog

- fixed costs
- variable costs
- idle time
- machine downtime
- production delays

You will note that the items in the left column have a common characteristic, as do those in the right column. For all the items in the left column, actual performance above

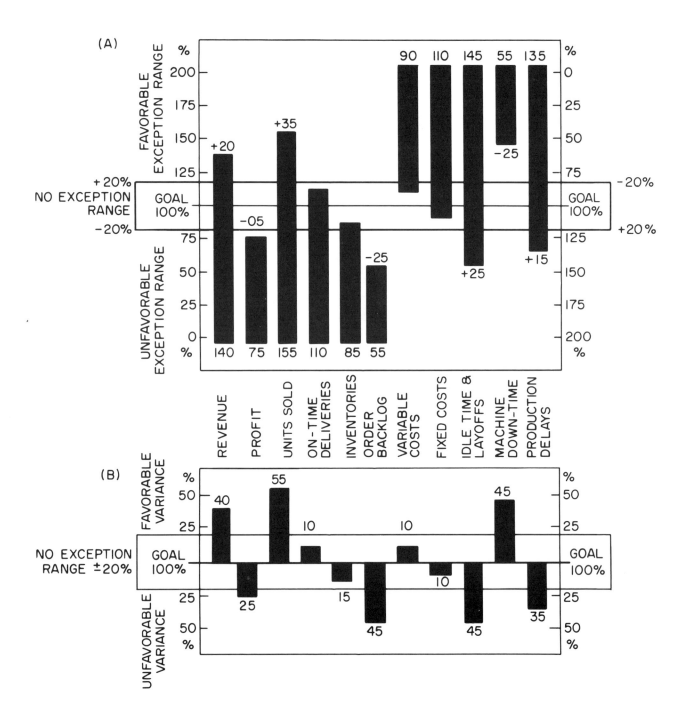

Figure 4-1.

Graphic Display of Performance and Exceptions

the 100% level signifies a favorable variance; below 100%, an unfavorable variance. The opposite is true of those in the right column; actual performance above the 100% standard denotes an unfavorable variance; below 100%, a favorable variance. This is shown on the top portion (A) of Figure 4-1. The items of revenue, units sold and machine downtime are exceptions to be reported, since their actual performance fell outside the ± 20% no exception range into the favorable exception range. Likewise, the items of profit, order backlog, idle time, and production delays are exceptions to be reported, since their actual performance fell outside the no exception range into the unfavorable exception range. Those deviations from the 100% goal falling within the no exception range, on-time deliveries, inventories, variable costs, and fixed costs, need not be reported to management. The figures at the outer end of the bars give the percentage measure of the bar. The figures outside the no exception range signify how much percentage variation from the ± 20% limits the actual experience was. Thus, revenue was 20% above + 20% level, or 40% above the 100% goal. Those bars ending within the no exception range are not considered exceptions and are not emphasized.

The lower half (B) of Figure 4-1 shows essentially the same information. However, here the emphasis is upon the variance itself and its deviation from the 100% goal. The variances are measured from the 100% goal line into the favorable or unfavorable areas, depending upon the nature of the item. The magnitudes of all the variances are shown. This form is slightly easier to read; the reference point (100%) is the same for all items. The item is either above 100% or below 100%; variances above are favorable, variances below are unfavorable.

Observations on Exception Yardsticks. Figure 4-1 leads us to several pertinent observations.

• Exceptions are to be identified as favorable or unfavorable only after careful study. There are two types of goals: minimum and maximum. Exceeding the minimum goal is good; not attaining it is bad. Conversely, exceeding the maximum goal is bad; not attaining it is good. The six items in the left column above (revenue, profit, etc.) are minimum goals. The five items in the right column above (costs, idle time, etc.) are maximum goals; the object is to be as far below 100% as possible. Be specific and accurate in your identification of goals and variances from them.

• Exceptions lie on both sides of the no exception range. Both favorable and unfavorable exceptions should be reported to management. Unattained minimum goals and exceeded maximum goals are unfavorable situations which call for corrective measures. Exceeded minimum goals and unattained maximum goals are favorable, and the persons responsible for this exceptional success should be rewarded.

• The exception reporting system should be so constructed hierarchically that managers at all levels are aware of the broad firm goals as well as the detailed goals for which each is responsible. Further, the reporting system must be so constructed that records are kept of actions taken by the managers and the results achieved. The reporting system must identify the causes and extent of the exceptions, and also report the total actual performance if desired. Only through these means can corrective actions be initiated against unfavorable variances, or commendations be given to those responsible for exceptional favorable variances. The accountant, as information specialist and designer of the exception reporting system, must work with management to determine exactly what information it needs and how the information is best structured for each level.

• In structuring the exception reporting system, the accountant must evaluate the relative merits of speed vs. completeness. Exception reporting, as compared to "full reporting," may take longer to compile and thus cause the information to be obsolete and useless before it is even issued. Most accounting systems are constructed to encompass full recording; full reporting of the results is the easier route in that the information does not have to be so extensively interpreted before being issued to managers as it would have to be in an exception reporting system. But speed of report issuance is not incompatible with exception reporting. Actually, exception reports containing a lesser quantity of (but more useable) information, issued more frequently, are preferable to full reports issued less frequently. Computers, with their capacity for comparisons and analyses, may speed up the exception reporting system.

METHODS AND TECHNIQUES IN REPORTING EXCEPTIONS

Management by exception is an approach that focuses attention on operations and situations which deviate from goals, plans, or normal conditions. With limited managerial time available, it can best be spent on exceptions from the normal, rather than in reviewing normal performance. The reports on operations should be constructed in a manner which draws management's attention to both the good and bad exceptions.

The well-planned reporting system should give each manager the information he needs to make the decisions for which he is responsible. To give him less, causes him to rely on other sources, perhaps inaccurate or irrelevant. To give him more merely consumes his limited time with the reading of superfluous data. There may be some reason to give him more, such as to provide background information on other operations in the expectation of his moving vertically or horizontally in the firm.

Likewise, the well-planned reporting system should give the data the manager needs to control his operations; that is, information on goals and plans, actual performance attained, and deviations from normal and from planned performance.

Full Reports Without Comments

Actually, such reports are not exception reports. They show the goals or budgeted figures and the actual performance achieved. The reader is left to his own interpretive devices to find the dollar (or other measure) difference between the planned and actual figures, and to decide which of these differences merits his special attention. The reader may have informal no exception ranges he may apply to the differences, and therefore use the report as an exception report. But this is an inefficient use of the manager's time when it is the accountant's job to provide the information in the most useful form.

Figure 4-2 shows a comparative statement of monthly cash receipts of revenue. If the statement showed the sources of revenue and the amounts appearing in the two boxed areas, this would be a "full report without comments." It would present the average

	1967-1968 BUDGET ESTIMATE	CURRENT MONTH — AVERAGE ESTIMATE PER MONTH	ACTUAL RECEIPTS FOR NOV 1967	ACTUAL OVER/UNDER ESTIMATE	% OVER/UNDER EST	YEAR TO DATE — ESTIMATE FOR 05 MONTHS	ACTUAL RECEIPTS FOR 05 MONTHS	ACTUAL OVER/UNDER ESTIMATE	% OVER/UNDER EST
SERVICES									
DOCKAGE	1,171,000	97,583	96,815	768-	.8-	487,917	525,633	37,716	7.7
WHARFAGE	4,888,000	407,333	369,801	37,532-	9.2-	2,036,667	1,853,533	183,134-	9.0-
STORAGE	114,000	9,500	2,531	6,969-	73.4-	47,500	34,676	12,824-	27.0- ⟵10%
DEMURRAGE	169,000	14,083	18,478	4,395	31.2	70,417	66,079	4,338-	6.2-
ASSIGN. CHARGES-PRE	116,000	9,667	8,789	878-	9.1-	48,333	49,398	1,065	2.2
ASSIGN. CHARGES-TEM	1,000	83	0	83-	100.0-	417	417	0	100.0-
PILOTAGE	716,000	59,667	72,226	12,559	21.0	298,333	339,622	41,289	13.8
TOTAL SERVICES	7,175,000 *	597,916 *	568,640 *	29,276-*	4.9-*	2,989,584 *	2,868,941 *	120,643-*	4.0-*
RENTALS									
LAND	2,964,000	247,000	211,933	35,067-	14.2-	1,235,000	1,346,836	111,836	9.1
BUILDINGS	65,400	5,450	5,933	483	8.9	27,250	27,574	324	1.2
WHARF AND SHED	191,000	15,917	13,109	2,808-	17.6-	79,583	105,806	26,223	33.0 ⟵15%
WAREHOUSE BLDG. REN	297,000	24,750	42,220	17,470	70.6	123,750	139,599	15,849	12.8
TOTAL RENTALS	3,517,400 *	293,117 *	273,195 *	19,922-*	6.8-*	1,465,583 *	1,619,815 *	154,232 *	10.5 *
SPECIAL									
FEES AND PERMITS	10,000	833	800	33-	4.0-	4,167	4,598	431	10.3
TERMINAL CONCESSION	28,600	2,383	2,214	169-	7.1-	11,917	13,182	1,265	10.6
TERMINAL RAILROADS	35,000	2,917	8,756	5,839	200.2	14,583	17,654	3,071	21.1 ⟵20%
WAREHOUSES	202,000	16,833	46,006	29,173	173.3	84,167	122,112	37,945	45.1 ⟵20%
OIL ROYALTIES	399,000	33,250	28,404	4,846-	14.6-	166,250	152,189	14,061-	8.5-
MISCELLANEOUS	6,000	500	440	60-	12.0-	2,500	2,539	39	1.6
TOTAL SPECIAL	680,600 *	56,716 *	86,620 *	29,904 *	52.7 *	283,584 *	312,274 *	28,690 *	10.1 *
TOTAL REVENUE	11,373,000 **	947,749 **	928,455 **	19,294-**	2.0-**	4,738,751 **	4,801,030 **	62,279 **	1.3 **
NON-REVENUE									
ADVANCED CONSTRUCTI	0	0	0			0	0	0	
SALE OF MATL. AND S	310,000	25,833	16,764	9,069-	35.1-	129,167	132,677	3,510	2.7
MISC. REIMBURSEMENT	25,000	2,083	340	1,743-	83.7-	10,417	9,447	970-	9.3-
MISC. NON-OPERATING	10,000	833	6,258	5,425	651.3	4,167	13,771	9,604	230.5 ⟵20%
INTEREST EARNED	85,000	7,083	0	7,083-	100.0-	35,417	50,986	15,569	44.0 ⟵20%
TOTAL NON-REV.	430,000 *	35,832 *	23,362 *	12,470-*	34.8-*	179,168 *	206,881 *	27,713 *	15.5 *
TOTAL RECEIPTS	11,803,000 **	983,581 **	951,817 **	31,764-**	3.2-**	4,917,919 **	5,007,911 **	89,992 **	1.8 **

Figure 4-2.

monthly budget estimate compared with this month's actual receipts, and the year-to-date estimate and actual receipts. The reader would be left with no comparisons except what he would make on his own. It is fairly obvious that reports limited to this data are not as useful as they could be. Other information is given on the statement to make it more useful; this will be commented upon in the next section.

In addition to being of limited value in terms of usefulness and readability, this type of report has several other disadvantages.

• There is a tendency for the accountant to mass too much data of this type on one page and not interpret it. Even if more data were not added, that given (for example, in the boxed areas in Figure 4-2) is too greatly detailed to be meaningful. The reader would have to mentally or physically calculate the difference for each item. Then he would have to decide which differences merit his attention. The major items needing attention are "buried" among a mass of other figures, making them extremely difficult to identify.

• Because of the mass of data before him that he must interpret, there is a good chance that any formal or informal exception ranges that have been established will not be applied. Most of his time will be used in deciphering the data, leaving little time for interpretation and decision. The accountant should decipher and interpret the information, and present it in a form such that the manager needs only to assimilate it into his collection of decision input facts.

• As a by-product of the prior two disadvantages, the manager may under-react. He is not responsive to the meaning of the statement because he does not understand its meaning. He takes little or misdirected corrective action. He is inefficient in his direction and ineffective in his leadership. This is when the manager operates by the "seat of the pants" method. Certainly he does not manage on the basis of informed judgment.

Full Reports with Comparisons

Figure 4-2 illustrates additional information that may be presented along with the basic planned and actual data. This consists of both dollar and percentage differences between the actual and the estimated.

The dollar and percentage differences between estimated and actual figures for the *current month* do not comprise an exception report. The reader must supply his own criteria to judge whether the differences are within or outside of the no exception range. Yet this form is certainly preferable to having only the boxed data with no differences given.

Full Reports with Comparisons and Exceptions

The extreme right column, the year-to-date percentage over/under estimate figures, does constitute exception reporting. Different percentages are given for the no exception ranges, depending upon the controllability, relative time period involved, and size of the revenue group. Thus, the major source of revenue, services, has a ± 10% no exception range; special revenues are exceptional if they do not fall within its ± 20% no exception range. Within each revenue source group, the exceptional items appear in boxes. With each step made, we have improved the usefulness of the report; where can you make improvements in your reporting system?

Exceptions Only Reported

Exception reporting comprehends both full reporting with attention directed to the exceptions (as described in the prior section) and reports showing only the exceptions. Drawing from the data given in Figure 4-2, we form the following exception report, illustrated in Figure 4-3. Totals for each revenue group are also given so the reader may have a reference point as to the materiality of the exception items. The totals may or may not be within the no exception range; they are still relevant.

At least two disadvantages may be cited for exception-only reporting.

• The manager may over-react because he sees only part of the universe—the exceptions. Maintaining a perspective both of overall operations and of the exceptions relative to the non-exceptions is a problem in this method of reporting. If the manager were presented only with the statement in Figure 4-3, for example, he might spend too much time on the items reported, which in reality are only about half of all revenue sources. The other items may need occasional attention, even if they are normally within the no exception range.

• The second disadvantage stems also from the lack of additional data. Many new automobiles have exception lights instead of full-report gauges to indicate heat, oil pressure, battery discharge, etc. The driver is never quite sure that the lights are working properly. If the reporting system breaks down, the exception is not reported. Managers have similar fears (especially when *all* operations are normal), and sometimes need backup data to be sure the system is working. In the early stages of an exception reporting system's installation, managers may need full reports as backup detail until they gain confidence in the system.

• The third objection sometimes voiced refers to the accuracy of the goal or plan or estimate as a base for comparison. Many times these are carelessly or inaccurately set, and attention is directed to the variances thereby produced, whereas emphasis should be placed on other true and accurate deviations. The accountant must be very careful in establishing and reporting these comparison bases. For example, in Figure 4-2 the comparison base was the simple monthly average of the year's budget estimate. If seasonal variations such as may be caused by weather changes are significant, the monthly comparison base should reflect this, as well as other similar factors.

Management by Exception Hierarchically

If the exception principle is incorporated into the reporting system, it should be effected at each managerial level. The information pertinent to each level would be monitored and the exceptions emphasized. As with "conventional" full reporting, the next higher level of management would be notified if the lower level manager fails to take sufficient action on the exception reports. If corrective action was not taken on unfavorable

MONTHLY CASH RECEIPTS OF REVENUE
EXCEPTION REPORT FOR NOVEMBER, 1967
FISCAL YEAR 1967-1968

SERVICES	NO EXCEPTION RANGE ±10%	CURRENT MONTH OVER/UNDER ACTUAL $	CURRENT MONTH ESTIMATE %	YEAR-TO-DATE OVER/UNDER ACTUAL $	YEAR-TO-DATE ESTIMATE %
STORAGE		6,969 -	73.4 -	12,824 -	27.0 -
DEMURRAGE		4,395	31.2		
ASSIGN. CHGS -TEM.		83 -	100.0 -	417 -	100.0 -
PILOTAGE		12,559	21.0	41,289	13.8
TOTAL		29 276 -	4.9 -	643 -	4.0 -
RENTALS	±15%				
WHARF AND SHED		2,808 -	17.6 -	26 223	33.0
WAREHOUSE		17,470	70.6		
TOTAL		19,922	6.8 -	154,232	10.5
SPECIAL	±20%				
TERMINAL RAILROADS		5,839	200.2	3,071	21.1
WAREHOUSES		29,173	173.3	37,945	45.1
TOTAL		29,904	52.7	28,690	10.1
NON-REVENUE	±20%				
SALE OF MAT'L		9,069 -	35.1 -		
MISC. REIMBURSEMENT		1,743 -	83.7 -		
MISC. NON-OPERATING		5,425	651.3	9,604	230.5
INTEREST EARNED		7,083	100.0 -	15,569	44.0
TOTAL		12,470	34.8 -	27,713	15.5

Figure 4-3.

90

variances, the superior must step in and see that his subordinates do the job. The subordinate would hesitate to have this situation arise very often; he would certainly be out of a job in most firms. The net effect of incorporating the exception principle in the reporting structure is that action is taken when necessary and, most likely, faster.

APPLYING THE EXCEPTION PRINCIPLE IN REPORTING

This pyramid concept of reporting may be applied in exception reporting as well as in "regular" reporting. The following set of reports, beginning at the lowest supervisory level and ending with the president, illustrates the exception principle. This set is based upon the full reports presented for Vendco Service, Inc., in Chapter 3, "Designing and Building an Effective Reporting System," to which the reader should refer.

Figure 4-4 cross-references the full report for each managerial level to the exception report presented in this chapter. Figure 4-4 also states the no exception range allowed for each managerial level. Differences beyond the stated upper and lower limits of the no exception range are considered to be exceptions and are marked with an asterisk (*) on the various managerial reports.

In this set of reports an increasingly larger no exception range was selected as the reports traveled up through the various managerial levels. The difference at reporting level 7 (the president) is more than twice as large as the difference tolerated at level 2. This principle may be applied to any reporting structure and for any item to be reported upon. As examples:

- *Sales of Product A*

Salesman	+ 5%	− 4%
Sales manager	+10%	− 8%
Territory manager	+15%	−12%
Sales V.P.	+20%	−16%
President	+25%	−20%

- *Product A Unit Cost*

Operator	±$0.02
Foreman	±$0.05
Plant manager	±$0.08
Division manager	±$0.12
President	±$0.20

- *Defective Units of A*

Operator	+ 2%	− 1%
Foreman	+ 4%	− 2%
Plant manager	+ 6%	− 4%
Division manager	+ 8%	− 6%
President	+10%	− 8%

- *Output of Product A*

Operator	+ 6%	− 2%
Foreman	+ 8%	− 4%
Plant manager	+12%	− 6%
Division manager	+15%	−10%
President	+20%	−15%

+ means favorable deviation.

− means unfavorable deviation.

Deviations larger than the positive or negative percentages would be considered exceptions deserving managerial attention.

% means percent of change from normal or planned performance.

VENDCO SERVICE, INC.   All Levels
                                        4/30/69

Operating Summary -- Exception Ranges

Figure Cross-Reference		Reporting Level	Item	Limits of Deviations from Forecast (A)			
Full Report	Exception Report			Current Year %		Previous Year (B) %	
3-4	4-5	2	Other Operating Income	.4 +	.2-	(C)	
			Cost of Sales	2.0 +	1.5-	(C)	
			Payroll Costs	3.0 +	1.5-	(C)	
			Other Expenses	3.0 +	1.5-	(C)	
3-5a	4-6a	3	All Sections	2.0 +	1.5-	3.0 +	1.5-
3-5b	4-6b	3	All Companies	2.5 +	2.0-	3.5 +	2.0-
3-6	4-7	4	All Subregions	3.0 +	2.5-	3.5 +	2.5-
3-7	4-8	5	All Regions	3.5 +	3.0-	4.0 +	3.5-
3-8	4-9	6	All Areas	4.0 +	3.5-	4.5 +	4.0-
3-9	4-10	7	All Divisions	4.5 +	4.0-	5.0 +	4.5-

(A) Limits apply both to month and year-to-date figures.
(B) Previous Year Actual compared with Current Year Forecast.
(C) Not calculated.
+   means favorable deviation.
−   means unfavorable deviation.

Figure 4-4.

Wherever there is a goal, or norm, or planned performance, you may apply the principle of exception reporting. Since a goal should exist for every activity, exception reporting should pervade the entire management information system.

Figure 4-5 is the level 2 report which contrasts the forecast and actual performance in terms of percentage of individual cost items to total income. This is done both for the current month of April and for the year to date. The actual percentage is given and the algebraic difference between actual and forecast. Thus, for vending commissions, the actual 0.3% contrasted to the forecast 0.2% (but this figure is omitted from the report)

VENDCO SERVICE, INC.   Level 2 Report
                                                              4/30/69
Operating Summary -- Exception Report

North-Central-Western New York -- 111A-1 -- Industry Div.

	Current Month -- Actual		Year-to-Date -- Actual	
	Actual (A)	Difference (B)	Actual (A)	Difference (B)
Total Sales	100.0	.0	100.0	.0
Other Operating Revenue				
Vending Comm. Receivable	.3	.1+	.3	.1-
Promotion allowances	.2	.1+	.1	.0
Cash discounts	.4	.0	.4	.0
Other Operating Revenue	.6	.4- *	.8	.2+
Total Operating Revenue	1.5	.2- *	1.6	.1-
Total Income	101.5	.2- *	101.6	.1-
Cost of Sales				
Cigarettes and cigars	78.9	1.9- *	78.1	1.1-
Cigarette tax	10.4	100.0- *	1.6	100.0- *
Food through Vend. Mach.	61.7	3.7- *	56.6	8.4+ *
Hot beverages	30.7	1.7- *	32.0	3.0- *
Cold beverages	24.9	.9-	24.6	.6-
Candy, gum, nuts	51.0	1.0+	51.0	1.0+
Milk, juices, ice cream	55.8	3.8- *	53.6	1.6- *
Pastries	68.1	1.9+	69.1	.9+
Losses, matches, sales tax (C)	.2	.1-	.2	.1-
Total Cost of Sales	39.3	2.3- *	39.1	2.1- *
Gross Profit	62.1	2.6-	62.5	2.2-
Payroll Costs (C)	15.6	2.1- *	14.6	.6+
Other Expenses (C)	33.9	3.5- *	31.3	.5+
Total Operating Expenses	49.5	5.6-	46.0	1.8+
① Contribution Margin	12.7	8.1-	16.5	1.2-

(A) Stated as percent of Total Sales.
(B) Difference between Forecasted and Actual, stated as a percent of Total Sales.
(C) Detail omitted in this illustration.
 + means favorable difference.
 - means unfavorable difference.
 * means greater than the acceptable upper or lower limits of the deviations
    from forecasted percentage (see Figure 4-4). Percentages within the boxed
    areas with no asterisk are within the established no exception range.

Figure 4-5.

gives a favorable difference of 0.1%. Favorable is denoted by the plus sign (+); unfavorable, by the minus sign (−). The differences outside the stated (in Figure 4-4) no exception range are noted as exceptions by being marked with an asterisk. The difference columns are boxed for emphasis.

Figure 4-6a, a level 3 report to the manager of the vending service subregion, is cross-referenced to Figure 4-5 by the number ①. This shows that the North-Central-West New York section totals have been carried over from the lower level report. Reports similar to Figure 4-5 would exist for the other two sections (Eastern New York and Southern New York) and their totals likewise would tie in to this Level 3 Operating Summary Exception Report. The line labeled ② would be carried to the Level 4 Operating Summary Exception Report, as would the line labeled ③ in *Figure 4-6b*. This figure shows the cafeteria service subregion operating summary and is also a level 3 report.

The vending service and cafeteria service subregions' totals are carried to the report

```
                       VENDCO SERVICE, INC.                      Level 3 Report
                                                                 4/30/69
                    Operating Summary -- Exception Report

               Vending Service Subregion -- 111A -- Industry Div.


                            Current Year -- Actual      Previous Year -- Actual

                            CM/S % (A)  Difference (B)   CM/S % (A)  Difference (B)

 111A-1   North Central -West New York
    ①        Month              12.7        8.1- *          19.9         .9-
             Year-to-Date       16.5        1.2-            18.2         .5+

 111A-2   Eastern New York
             Month               5.3        6.9- *           7.8        4.4- *
             Year-to-Date        9.8         .4-             8.2        2.0- *

 111A-3   Southern New York
             Month              11.6        3.5+ *          10.4        2.3+
             Year-to-Date       13.0        3.6+ *           9.4         .0

          Total Vending Service
    ②        Month              10.1        3.8- *          13.1         .8-
             Year-to-Date       13.3         .8+            12.4         .1-
```

(A) Percentage of Contribution Margin to sales.
(B) Difference between Actual and Forecasted percentage of (A).
 +   means favorable difference
 -   means unfavorable difference
 *   means greater than the acceptable upper or lower limits of the deviations
     from forecasted percentage (see Figure 4-4). Percentages within the boxed
     areas with no asterisk are within the established no exception range.

Figure 4-6a.

presented in *Figure 4-7*. This is the Operating Summary Exception Report for Region 1—New England. The totals of this report are carried to the next higher report, level 5, the Operating Summary Exception Report for the Northeast Area. These totals are indicated by the number ④ in *Figure 4-8*. This level 5 report also summarizes the performance of the other two regions in the Area.

Figure 4-9 illustrates the operating summary exception report for the whole Industry Division. The Northeast Area totals included therein are cross-referenced by the number ⑤ to the level 5 report; similar summaries would exist for the other areas and the support group listed in this Industry Division Report. The totals of this division report are carried to the uppermost level 7 report, indicated by the number ⑥. The level 7 report, illustrated in *Figure 4-10,* goes to the president and summarizes the performance of the three major operating divisions of the company and a special category entitled "New Acquisitions."

VENDCO SERVICE, INC.   Level 3 Report
                                                                            4/30/69
                Operating Summary -- <u>Exception Report</u>

        Cafeteria Service Subregion -- 111-B -- Industry Div.

	Current Year -- Actual		Previous Year -- Actual	
	CM/S % (A)	Difference (B)	CM/S % (A)	Difference (B)
111B-1 Victor Corporation				
Month	53.6	29.4- *	77.3	5.7- *
Year-to-Date	52.1	30.1- *	75.3	6.9- *
111B-2 Union Manufacturing Co.				
Month	10.0	.0	10.3	.0
Year-to-Date	10.0	.0	9.2	.8-
111B-3 American Industries				
Month	7.5	.9-	9.4	1.0+
Year-to-Date	7.3	1.0-	7.1	1.2-
111B-4 Pacific Corporation				
Month	15.8	9.2- *	28.5	3.5+ *
Year-to-Date	25.6	1.0+	30.6	6.0+ *
111B-5 New Business				
Month	-0-	100.0- *	-0-	100.0- *
Year-to-Date	-0-	100.0- *	-0-	100.0- *
Total Cafeteria Service				
⑤ Month	.8	8.7- *	11.2	1.7+
Year-to-Date	10.1	.8+	9.8	.5+

(A) Percentage of Contribution Margin to sales.
(B) Difference between Actual and Forecasted percentage of (A).
 +   means favorable difference
 -   means unfavorable difference
 *   means greater than the acceptable upper or lower limits of the deviations
     from forecasted percentage (see Figure 4-4). Percentages within the boxed
     areas with no asterisk are within the established no exception range.

Figure 4-6b.

```
                    VENDCO SERVICE, INC.                    Level 4 Report
                                                            4/30/69
                 Operating Summary -- Exception Report

              Region 1 -- New England -- 111 -- Industry Div.
```

	Current Year -- Actual		Previous Year -- Actual	
	CM/S % (A)	Difference (B)	CM/S % (A)	Difference (B)
111-A Total Vending Service				
② Subregion A				
Month	10.1	3.8- *	13.1	.8-
Year-to-Date	13.3	.8+	12.4	.1-
111-B Total Cafeteria Service				
③ Subregion B				
Month	.8	8.7- *	11.2	1.7+
Year-to-Date	10.1	.8+	9.8	.5+
Total Operations				
Month	8.5	4.6- *	12.7	.4-
Year-to-Date	12.7	.8+	11.8	.1-
Regional Overhead				
Month	1.8	.3-	.0	100.0- *
Year-to-Date	1.6	.7-	.0	100.0- *
Grand Total -- Region 1				
④ Month	6.7	4.3- *	12.7	1.7+
Year-to-Date	11.1	1.5+	11.8	2.2+

```
(A)  Percentage of Contribution Margin to sales.
(B)  Difference between Actual and Forecasted percentage of (A).
 +   means favorable difference
 -   means unfavorable difference
 *   means greater than the acceptable upper or lower limits of the deviations
     from forecasted percentage (see Figure 4-4).  Percentages within the boxed
     areas with no asterisk are within the established no exception range.
```

Figure 4-7.

This pyramid structure which was illustrated in the previous Figures could be adapted to any business; we hope you have gleaned the essence and will now be able to improve your own company's reports. We should note that the Figures were complete; exceptions were emphasized by asterisks. An alternative to this presentation would be "pure" exception reports, that is, reports showing only the exception. Differences within the no exception range would not be reported.

OTHER EXAMPLES OF EXCEPTION REPORTING

No one book can set out all the possibilities for exception reporting. Exceptions exist wherever there is a difference between actual performance and the established goal or plan (or other norm). What is needed to search these possibilities out? Creativity.

VENDCO SERVICE, INC.　　　　　Level 5 Report
4/30/69

Operating Summary -- <u>Exception Report</u>

Northeast Area -- 110 -- Industry Division

		Current Year -- Actual		Previous Year -- Actual	
		CM/S % (A)	Difference (B)	CM/S % (A)	Difference (B)
111	Region 1 - New England				
④	Month	6.7	4.3- *	12.7	1.7+
	Year-to-Date	11.1	1.5+	11.8	2.2+
112	Region 2 - Eastern New York				
	Month	2.1	2.8-	.5	4.4- *
	Year-to-Date	2.6	2.5-	2.6	2.5-
113	Region 3 - Western New York				
	Month	7.8	1.4+	10.3	3.9+
	Year-to-Date	8.8	1.4+	10.2	2.8+
	Total Operations				
	Month	5.6	1.4-	7.5	.5+
	Year-to-Date	7.3	.2+	7.8	.7+
	Area Overhead				
	Month	.3	.0	1.4	1.1+
	Year-to-Date	.3	.0	1.2	.9+
	Grand Total -- Area 110				
⑤	Month	5.2	1.5-	6.1	.6-
	Year-to-Date	6.9	.1+	6.7	.1-

(A)　Percentage of Contribution Margin to sales.
(B)　Difference between Actual and Forecasted percentage of (A).
+　　means favorable difference
-　　means unfavorable difference
*　　means greater than the acceptable upper or lower limits of the deviations
　　from forecasted percentage (see Figure 4-4). Percentages within the boxed
　　areas with no asterisk are within the established no exception range.

Figure 4-8.

Imagination. The need to be informed about deviations. The accountant must be at his best here; he must produce meaningful and effective exception reports in addition to the ordinary "full" reports.

Production Scheduling Control. The production of plants or components thereof is usually closely scheduled. This could be in terms of output or flow-through per unit of time (minute, hour, day, week, etc.). A count of the actual production, compared with that scheduled, provides the basis for exception reporting. We might measure on an exception basis the operations behind or ahead of schedule, or the spoiled units. If cost reporting were built into the system, we could measure the deviations from standard of actual material, labor, and variable overhead costs, and of total accumulated costs. The report of actual performance may come from the foreman or a mechanical counter. The latter may be connected on-line to the computer so that the exceptions may be detected as production progresses.

VENDCO SERVICE, INC.
                  Level 6 Report
Operating Summary -- Exception Report   4/30/69

Industry Division

		Current Year -- Actual		Previous Year -- Actual	
		CM/S % (A)	Difference (B)	CM/S % (A)	Difference (B)
110	Northeast Area				
⑤	Month	5.2	1.5-	6.1	.6-
	Year-to-Date	6.9	.1+	6.7	.1-
120	East Area				
	Month	6.9	1.0-	6.2	1.7-
	Year-to-Date	6.9	.9-	6.2	1.6-
130	North & West Midwest Area				
	Month	7.8	.2-	5.2	2.8-
	Year-to-Date	7.7	.3+	4.7	2.7-
140	South & East Midwest Area				
	Month	8.1	.1-	6.6	1.6-
	Year-to-Date	8.9	.9+	8.4	.4+
150	West Area				
	Month	7.5	.2-	5.9	1.8-
	Year-to-Date	6.5	.7-	5.4	1.8-
160	Support Group				
	Month	64.1	30.9+ *	50.8	17.6+ *
	Year-to-Date	41.4	10.2+ *	38.5	7.3+ *
	Total Operations				
	Month	7.9	.1-	6.5	1.5-
	Year-to-Date	7.8	.1+	6.6	1.1-
	Division Overhead				
	Month	.3	.1+	.2	.0
	Year-to-Date	.2	.0	.2	.0
	Grand Total				
⑥	Month	7.6	.2-	6.2	1.6-
	Year-to-Date	7.6	.1+	6.4	1.1-

(A) Percentage of Contribution Margin to sales.
(B) Difference between Actual and Forecasted percentage of (A).
 +   means favorable difference
 -   means unfavorable difference
 *   means greater than the acceptable upper or lower limits of the deviations
     from forecasted percentage (see Figure 4-4). Percentages within the boxed
     areas with no asterisk are within the established no exception range.

Figure 4-9.

Production Efficiency Control. Instead of comparing output against a production schedule, output may be compared with an output standard. This provides a measure of efficiency and thus becomes another basis for exception reporting. Work standards in terms of material, labor and overhead inputs are measured against actual performance to determine deviations from standard. The exceptions so derived and the acceptable tolerances may be structured into meaningful reports to different managerial levels. The foreman's reports show unacceptable deviations from standard by machine or operation; the superintendent's reports, by area; the plant manager, by departments.

	<u>Current Year -- Actual</u>		<u>Previous Year -- Actual</u>	
	CM/S % (A)	Difference (B)	CM/S % (A)	Difference (B)
100 Industry Division ⑥				
Month	7.6	.2-	6.2	1.6-
Year-to-Date	7.6	.1+	6.4	1.1-
200 Institutions Division				
Month	7.0	.2+	6.6	.2-
Year-to-Date	7.2	.1+	6.9	.2-
300 Serv-O-Mat				
Month	35.4	100.0+ *	.0	.0
Year-to-Date	76.5	24.4+ *	.0	.0
400 New Acquisitions				
Month	-0-	100.0- *	.0	100.0- *
Year-to-Date	-0-	100.0- *	.0	100.0- *
Total Operations	7.5	.0	6.3	1.2-
Month	7.5	.5-	6.5	1.5-
Year-to-Date				
National Overhead	4.7	2.1+	3.0	.4+
Month	3.0	.2+	3.0	.2+
Year-to-Date				
Grand Total				
Month	2.9	2.0-	3.4	1.5-
Year-to-Date	4.5	.1-	3.6	1.0-

(A) Percentage of Contribution Margin to sales.
(B) Difference between Actual and Forecasted percentage of (A).
 +   means favorable difference
 -   means unfavorable difference
 *   means greater than the acceptable upper or lower limits of the deviations
     from forecasted percentage (see Figure 4-4). Percentages within the boxed
     areas with no asterisk are within the established no exception range.

Figure 4-10.

Production Quality Control. Quality control through the use of statistics and sampling techniques offers a fertile ground for exception reporting. Statistical quality control selectively samples production and records the results on limit graphs. When significant numbers of samples exceed the established limits, or if there is a similar trend indicated, corrective action is taken to bring the operation back into control. Immediate or quick correction reduces production defects, wasted units and rework costs. Inspection stations record measures of the quality attained, which are then compared with established standards or defect limits. The exception report so generated tells which defect is "out of control" and the starting point for determining the cause of that condition. On-line computer capabilities help reduce the lag time between the out-of-control condition and its correction.

Inventory Condition Control. Inventory condition encompasses both the amount on hand and its usability. Optimum order quantities may be calculated relatively easily, given the availability of certain estimated costs. If on-hand balances of items fall below pre-set order points, the optimum order quantity is determined on the basis of past experience, expected future usage, and estimates of order and storage costs. The exception report is prepared—in this case, the purchase documents.

Inventory usage provides the basis for other exception reports. Excessive usage leads to production bottlenecks and too-frequent purchasing; infrequent usage leads to obsolescence. Exception reports could disclose that there had been no activity for a certain established period or that usage had fallen below a given level, indicating excessive investment in inventory.

Inventory order follow-up provides another area for exception reporting. Orders are specified for delivery at certain times; production scheduling frequently relies on this timetable and delays may prove very costly. Exception reports may be prepared daily on undelivered orders; this concentrates efforts upon the companies proving to be unreliable suppliers and upon finding alternative materials sources if stock-outs are predicted because of the delay. Inventory control is the key to production planning and control; exception reporting is a vital element of this control.

Machine Down-Time Control. Machine down-time may be of two types. The first is that caused by the machine being inoperative for a distinguishable time period. The second is that caused by inefficiencies in the machine resulting in slower or inaccurate operation. Usually this latter type of down-time goes unrecorded. It may be detected, however, by certain counters that record both output and details about the technical functioning of the machine. Summary reports, prepared on an exception basis, could show the machine down-time and causes so that management may take corrective action.

Other Areas. The list of areas of control aided by use of exception reporting is almost limitless. In addition to those described above, here are several other areas:

• Sales control—changes in orders received; excessive stock-outs and back orders; invoice errors; exceptional customer claims and complaints; results of special promotions; exceptional performances by salesmen, territories and product lines; marginal contribution by customer; unfilled and back orders status; order and customer profiles to determine the most profitable; share of market per product line.

• Materials procurement, warehousing, and distribution—exceptional inventory adjustments; excessive inspection delays or inspection rejections; anticipated stock-outs; outstanding purchase commitments; expediting required; unused warehouse space; unusual or persistent claims against shippers; abnormal shipping costs; shipment delays.

• Planning and financial control—unfavorable cash position; unfavorable collection period; delinquency notices sent; payroll changes and turnover; profit center performance; unusual financial position; unusual return on investment in capital projects; variations from forecast and budget; exceptional market and economic trends.

EFFECTS OF EXCEPTION PRINCIPLE UPON REPORTING SYSTEM

The effects of using exception reporting can be minute or far-reaching, depending upon many factors: management's faith in the data accumulation, projection, and reporting system; management's use of the exception reports; the usefulness of the reports themselves; the type of business and the organization structure.

As was stated before, and this point bears repeating, wherever there are standards, actual performance may be compared against them and the exceptions reported. The effects of applying the exception principle in the reporting system are:

- fewer and shorter reports must be read and digested by managers, trouble areas are identified easily, action may be taken quicker;
- greater benefit to the business is obtained through greater control over its operations;
- shorter lag time is required between the ill's occurring and its cure.
- reduced clerical costs, possibly.

Impact of the Computer upon Exception Reporting

The effects of exception reporting listed above are magnified by using the computer. Probably the computer's greatest contribution lies in its ability to make decisions about exceptions, based upon the prior limits established as compared with actual performance. It "decides" first that there is an exception, then measures the degree of variance, then lists this variance on a report. Certain information may be reported in the form of a graph by the computer—again, imagination in constructing *any* report should be the tool by which usefulness is furthered.

Greater speed is also a plus factor for the computer. Being connected on-line with the operation makes the computer even more valuable, for precious time is not lost in preparing man-readable input data.

Last, the great ability of the computer to analyze statistics and to determine statistical and arithmetical deviations has a great impact. More meaningful and difficult comparisons may be made for management's use.

5

Using
Visual Aids
In Reporting

Eighty-five percent of our comprehension, it is said, comes through the visual sense. Accountants should keep this in mind when preparing reports for management. Visual aids, used with oral or written material, enable the recipient to absorb facts much more quickly and to retain information for a longer period of time. Concepts and relationships which are difficult to communicate verbally are often quite adaptable to visual aids.

Quantified data is often confusing, even overwhelming, when presented in narrative or tabular form. Visual aids, particularly graphs and charts, are excellent media for communicating numerical values. Verbal presentations tend to give the reader parts of the picture which he must put together in his mind. Visual aids afford to the reader the possibility of grasping the whole picture at once.

The proper use of visual aids speeds the learning process by as much as 50%, enabling the group to cover more material in the same time period. Visual aids attract and hold the recipients' attention. They provide a frame of reference which both the speaker and the audience may use in reaching a meeting of the minds. The use of visual aids should be considered where complex concepts or extensive quantified data is to be presented. This would include most situations where the accountant is called upon to present information.

Types of Visual Aids

Visual aids are identified as technical or presentation aids. Technical visual aids are submitted in support of written material. Such aids can have considerable detail because the reader may take time to absorb the material and can refer back to it as needed. Presentation visual aids are used to enhance oral presentations. These aids generally require simplicity and visibility. This chapter is concerned primarily with presentation visual aids. Technical visual aids, as far as the accountant is concerned, consist mostly of graphs. These will be discussed in Chapter 6.

Blackboards, magnetic or adhesive boards, flip charts and overhead and opaque projections are the principal visual aids discussed in this chapter. There are many types of visual aids such as motion pictures and slides which do not fit within the accountant's time limits for report preparation. Our aim is to discuss only those visual aids which can be prepared today for tomorrow's meeting.

When preparing visual aids keep in mind the proper aid for the audience. Do not spend a great amount of money to prepare visual aids for the new "Cost Cutting Committee" just established by the President. There are a number of requirements that all presentation visual aids must meet:

- The aid must be seen from all parts of the room.
- The aid must be capable of being understood within 60 seconds.
- Each aid should be direct, factual, and meaningful.
- One, and only one, principal idea should be presented on each aid.
- No more data than is absolutely necessary should be included in the aid.
- The accompanying oral presentation should supply the necessary details.

Oral Presentations

Oral presentations involving quantified data deserve some comment here. Figures confuse people. Numbers take longer to absorb and are often not remembered accurately. The hearer will recall that the profit for the West Coast Division was "eight" but whether it was $8,000 or $80,000 he is not sure. Extra care must be taken when using figures orally. Rounding is indispensable. Do not say "Two million, nine hundred and thirty two thousand, nine hundred and twenty one dollars and eighty two cents." Instead, say "Two million, nine" or "Just under three million." If exact figures are important, then they should be supplied to the group in written form.

It is a good idea to prepare a written digest of the important points of the presentation, or at least the important figures. The written hand-out material is best held until after the presentation. Otherwise, the group will read ahead and not pay attention to what the speaker is saying. The written material can be in considerably greater detail than the oral presentation but there must be a definite link between figures given orally and those contained in the written information.

There are two schools of thought regarding the proper use of visual aids in connection with an oral presentation. One school holds that, as the name "aid" implies, visual aids should be secondary to the material presented orally. Visual aids are developed to clarify or illustrate specific points. They are removed from sight when they have served their purpose so that the group will not be distracted from what the speaker has to say.

The other school holds that visual "aids" should be the basic communications media with the oral presentation used to enlarge upon and explain the "aid." Each central point is represented by a visual aid and the speaker builds his discussion around the visual representation. The audience is encouraged to focus its attention on the visual aid and is often supplied an 8½" x 11" copy on which to make notes regarding the speaker's supplementary information.

CHALKBOARDS

Perhaps the most widely used visual aid is the chalkboard. For years, boards which could be written on and erased were called blackboards. However, with so many different eye-ease colors now available such devices are more properly called chalkboards. Not only has the color of the board changed but the chalk now comes in many different colors.

Most chalkboards are attached to a wall which reduces their flexibility as a visual aid. A wall is needed to support the heavy board and to absorb the firm pressure which must be exerted to write legibly with chalk. There are several good portable chalkboards on the market. While portable chalkboards are not as sturdy as wall mounted boards, they do have certain advantages. The speaker does not have to worry about whether a board will be available; he can bring his own. Prior to the presentation, faint outlines of the chart to be drawn can be sketched or memory jogging notes placed on the margin of the board. This is difficult when others also use the chalkboard, however.

A portable chalkboard in use is shown in Figure 5-1. The chalkboard is supported by a well-constructed easel which provides a firm support for the writer. Both the chalkboard and easel can be folded and easily carried under one arm.

**Figure 5-1. Folding Chalkboard on Portable Easel.
Courtesy of Oravisual Company, Inc.**

Advantages and Disadvantages of Chalkboards

As a visual aid, the chalkboard's chief advantages are its flexibility and the low cost of preparing the aid. Most other visual aids must be prepared beforehand and there is no opportunity for the speaker to improvise. He cannot illustrate or emphasize a point which occurs to him while speaking. Chalkboards allow the speaker to expand and clarify complex points as needed based on the audience's reactions to the oral presentation. The only cost involved, after the initial outlay, is for chalk and erasers.

The disadvantages of chalkboards are their untidy appearance, illegibility, and general informality. Very few of us are able to write neatly and evenly on a chalkboard and, at the same time, speak about the subject. The speaker tends to write as fast as he speaks. As a result, the audience often cannot read what has been written.

There are two possible solutions to illegibility and untidiness. Slow down and print instead of write. Step back and see if you can read what you have written. If you can't, how do you expect the audience to read it? The audience would rather wait a few seconds and be able to read what has been written.

Another solution is to have the aids drawn out on the board beforehand. This is often neither possible nor desirable. Chalkboards are not usually large enough to hold more than one aid at a time. Therefore, only the first illustration used can be drawn in advance. Also, having more than one illustration before the audience at the same time is a poor presentation technique.

Predrawing illustrations eliminates one of the most important benefits of chalkboards. This is the ability to let the audience see the drawing unfold as the speaker develops his presentation. A diagram or a chart is easier to understand if the audience sees it develop as opposed to having the completed work suddenly thrust before the group.

The flexibility and informality of chalkboards often lull the speaker into a false sense of competence. Many speakers rely on their ability to improvise visual aids on chalkboards as they speak. As a result, they do not plan the visual aid portion of their presentation. Unless you are an outstanding speaker, you cannot afford to wait for the proper illustration to occur to you. You must plan ahead.

Plan Your Visual Aid

Diagrams, drawings, charts and even figures placed on a chalkboard should have been thought out prior to the presentation. Their usefulness and relevance to the central subject should be evaluated. Does this aid add to the objective of the presentation, or does it detract from it? Complex diagrams and charts should be drawn beforehand in light chalk. Pencil should not be used for this purpose because of possible damage to the chalkboard. To place a small complex drawing on a chalkboard, divide the original into squares. Then divide the chalkboard in a similar manner. Now the original drawing can be reproduced in correct proportion.

In addition to diagrams and charts, chalkboards are useful in emphasizing important points as they are presented. Technical terms and definitions can be written on the chalkboard to avoid possible misunderstanding. More importantly, numbers can be written out to reduce the confusion which always accompanies oral presentation of quantified data. By placing key figures or ideas on the chalkboard, the speaker and the audience have a mutual frame of reference.

As with any visual aid, the speaker using chalkboards must be certain that all necessary tools are available and in usable condition. There is nothing so distracting as to find that last night the janitor erased the carefully drawn diagram you prepared yesterday for today's meeting. Chalk, erasers and a pointer should be on the rack below the chalkboard. Rulers, stencils and other required items should be nearby. Don't distract from your presentation by stopping to search for materials while you are talking.

Prior to your presentation view the chalkboard you are going to use from the audience's vantage point. Does the light cause a glare on the board? Is there an object, often your lectern, which obstructs the view? Can the colored chalk you planned to use be seen on that particular color of board? Write something on the board. Then, go to the back and sides of the room. Can you easily read what you have written?

Keep the Illustration Simple

Possibly the most important point in any presentation visual aid is to keep it simple. This is doubly true with the chalkboard. Lay out what you want to write on the board. Is it crowded? Will it be necessary to write smaller at the bottom of the board for lack of space? The fewer the points and the neater and more legible they are the better and longer lasting the impression will be. Be certain you spell the words correctly. Some people, usually including your supervisor, can't get past a misspelled word in a presentation. And, you will not be able to blame the error on the transcription as with typed material.

Even though you use a chalkboard, do not talk to it. Talk to the audience. Stand to one side and use a pointer when referring to items on the board. A skillful speaker will stand in a half-front position which faces both the audience and the board. Try not to turn your back to the audience while writing on the board. If you must turn from the audience, stop talking until you have finished the drawing.

Erase an exhibit when you are through with it. If you do not, your audience will fail to follow you to your next point. They are still on the previous point represented by the visual aid. When the meeting is concluded, erase the chalkboard completely. This is not only a courtesy to the next user but prevents possible misunderstanding based on incomplete data observed by passersby.

FLANNELBOARD

Flannelboard has been used as a visual aid for over 60 years. During this period, flannelboard materials and techniques have improved steadily. But flannelboard's image with businessmen has not improved. Flannelboard was first used by missionaries in Asia and Africa as a portable, inexpensive, colorful and highly visible means of communication. These early flannelboards were crude and clumsy to use. As a result, they were slow to gain favor as a business visual aid.

Today's flannelboard is a far cry from its ancestors. Properly used, flannelboard can be a sophisticated, effective aid in oral presentations. A number of major companies and the U.S. Government are using flannelboard for employee training, project control and public relations. One company uses flannelboard to show foremen how the responsibility reporting and control system affects them and their work.

Flannelboards consist of chemically treated flannel stretched over a board which can vary in size from 1' x 1' to 10' x 10'; most are about 4' x 5'. Nylon flock is attached to the back of drawings, pictures, words, letters, and phrases. When placed on the flannel the flock adheres firmly to the board.

Ordinarily, the entire visual aid is laid out in advance. Each word, phrase or picture is on a separate backing. As the speaker begins his presentation he places the indivdual components on the flannelboard one by one. Thus, the speaker builds his visual aid as he progresses through the oral presentation. At the end of the presentation the board presents an excellent tool for summarization. The principal advantage of the flannelboard is this capability of providing progressive disclosure of ideas and concepts.

Other advantages are the low cost and ease of preparing materials for the flannelboard. Materials can be purchased at any stationery store and scissors is the only tool needed. Yet, unlike the chalkboard, the flannelboard presents a formal, neat and colorful visual aid.

How to Prepare Flannelboard Visual Aids

Accountants using flannelboard as a visual aid will use more words, phrases and numbers than they will pictures and diagrams. In the past, lettering was done laboriously by hand. Today, there are any number of methods available to prepare words and figures for visual aids.

Typically, letters and numbers are applied on a backing by a dry transfer process as follows. A sheet of transfer letters or numbers can be purchased at most stationery supply stores. The desired character is placed on flocked backing and rubbed firmly. The sheet is lifted away and the letter remains. If an error has been made it can be corrected easily and quickly. Words and phrases can be prepared by clerical personnel in a very short time. The dry transfer process does not have some of the disadvantages of ink or paint methods and can be done quickly.

A complete line of symbols are available in addition to letters and numbers. Arrows, stars and cartoon figures can be purchased. Using these materials, a professional visual aid can be prepared. Dry transfer figures are available in any size up to two inches which is large enough to be clearly visible in most meetings. The dry transfer technique is also useful in preparing flip charts and cards and other visual aids.

Flannelboards are particularly advantageous for accountants with little experience in oral presentations. The symbols can be used as an outline of the presentation. The speaker can glance at the next exhibit and begin his discussion. At the appropriate time he can easily slip it on the flannelboard with no break in the presentation. The problem of what to do with the hands is solved by having objects to pick up and attach to one board.

How to Use Flannelboard

Flannelboard should not be used with very large audiences. As a rule, if you need a microphone the group is too large or too far away for effective use of the flannelboard. Flannelboard, like other presentation visual aids, should not be used to convey detailed information. Only the highlights can be effectively presented, supplemented by the oral presentation or an accompanying written explanation.

The room where the flannelboard is to be used should be inspected prior to the presentation. Most important is a sturdy table or easel on which to place the board. A flimsy support can distract the audience and unnerve the speaker. Remove distracting background objects as well as any physical barriers between you and the audience.

There are certain actions or mannerisms which should be avoided in using flannelboard visual aids. Do not use the symbols to gesture while you speak. When you are ready for the next point pick up the related symbol, glance at it and place firmly on the board. If you hold the symbol in your hand too long the audience will learn what it says before you are ready for them to.

Be sure that the symbols are in the order you will use them. Check this twice. Even a good speaker can be thrown off by symbols out of order. Have before you only those symbols you will use. It is distracting to see a speaker pick up a symbol, look at it, and then discard it. The audience wonders what was omitted.

Speakers have a tendency to move through flannelboard presentations too fast. The audience does not have time to absorb the last symbol before the next one is presented. One problem may be that there are too many symbols. Does each symbol represent a central thought? If so, you may be trying to cover too much.

As with any visual aid, don't block the audience's view. Place the symbols on the board and step back. Use a pointer to refer to the board. One exception may be when you want the audience to forget the board for a moment. In this instance you may step forward and in front of the board thus forcing the audience's attention away from the exhibit.

MAGNETIC BOARDS

Somewhat akin to flannelboard are visual aids using magnetized materials. A wide variety of letters, numbers, words and symbols can be attached to magnetized boards. Flexible, colored strips of plastic can be magnetized and attached to the boards. Thus, lines, curves and diagrams can be illustrated on magnetic boards.

The most common use of magnetic boards is for production scheduling and control. However, some companies effectively use this technique for financial presentations to top management. Most of the visual aids are in graphic forms. Graphic representations of cash flow, sales, and profits over a specified period are constructed by using flexible plastic strips and letters and numbers. Each month the prior periods are shifted one space by moving the plastic strips and the monthly captions. The new period data is shown by a new plastic strip. The use of magnetic visual aids in this manner makes a very colorful and effective presentation.

Magnetic boards can be used to develop an illustration step by step by adding items to the board as they are discussed. Finally, the complete picture emerges. Review is easy; just refer to the board. Generally, magnetic boards are not as flexible as flannelboard and the symbols are more difficult to prepare. Magnetic boards should be considered when other visual aids are inadequate for the speaker's needs.

FLIP CHARTS

One of the most widely used visual aids is the flip chart. Flip charts are easily made, readily portable, and can greatly increase the speaker's ability to clarify complex concepts. Flip charts are frequently used to enumerate the salient points of a presentation. The speaker can use such a chart as an outline. If necessary, detail notes can be made in light pencil on each chart. Ordinarily the speaker does not need any material other than the chart.

Flip charts are pads of paper, about 2' x 2' in size, which can be mounted on an easel. The material to be displayed is placed on successive charts. As the presentation progresses, the speaker folds the first page over to reveal the next page and so on through the entire set. A flip chart in use in a conference environment is shown in Figure 5-2.

The paper used in flip charts should be of good quality to withstand repeated use. The charts should be stored and carried in flat form. Rolled charts will be difficult to work with because they tend to curl when placed on the easel. Facing and backing sheets should be provided to protect the material used in the presentation.

Figure 5-2. Flip Chart on Multiuse Easel.
Courtesy of Oravisual Company, Inc.

How to Prepare Flip Charts

Flip chart visual aids should be kept simple in detail and contain a minimum of words. Complete sentences are not always necessary. Omit words which are not absolutely vital to comprehend the meaning. Use plain, simple letters and drawings. Avoid elaborate art work.

Overcrowding should be avoided at all costs. Use clear, large, bold, uncluttered letters and drawings. The audience should be able to comprehend the meaning of the entire chart in less than a minute. The speaker should carefully plan the material to be presented keeping in mind that he is much more familiar with the subject matter and may not recognize excessive detail.

Color should be used sparingly and to good effect. Color is best used to highlight important points. Indiscriminate use of color distracts from a flip chart. No more than three colors should be used on one series of charts. Two colors are frequently sufficient.

Numerous drawings and illustrative diagrams can be used very effectively with predominately alphanumeric material. These aids should not dominate the chart but should help capture and hold the audience's attention. The illustrations must be relevant and compatible with the meaning of the chart.

Flip charts can be lettered by freehand methods, stencil, or by pressure sensitive and dry transfer methods. There is such a variety of pressure sensitive and dry transfer material available that this method is to be preferred in preparing professional visual aids. Letters, numbers and symbols can be purchased in many sizes, colors and shapes. Using these materials, inexperienced clerical personnel are able to quickly prepare flip charts which may be presented to top management.

Flip Chart Examples

Elements of a flip chart are shown in Figure 5-3. This chart was used to aid and support an oral presentation to middle managers relative to a proposed new inventory control system. Only four of eight charts are shown. The first chart, indicating the topic of the presentation, is exposed to the audience as they enter the meeting room. The second chart (on right side of page 112) is exposed as the speaker begins his presentation. It tells what "COINS" means, a *Co*ordinated *In*ventory *S*ystem, and sets forth certain broad objectives.

The next chart (page 113, left) presents the objectives in more detail. The last chart (p. 113, right) was also the final one in the presentation. It reviews what has been presented in the first seven charts. Note that two charts have drawings which help attract and maintain audience attention. Two colors in addition to black letters were used in the original charts.

Card charts are a variation of flip charts. Each illustration is prepared on separate pieces of firm cardboard about 3' x 4' in size. The cards are placed on an easel. As the speaker progresses through the presentation he removes the first and then successive cards. Often speakers are confused as to how to dispose of used cards and this detracts from their presentations. Flip charts are preferred over card charts by most speakers because of easier handling.

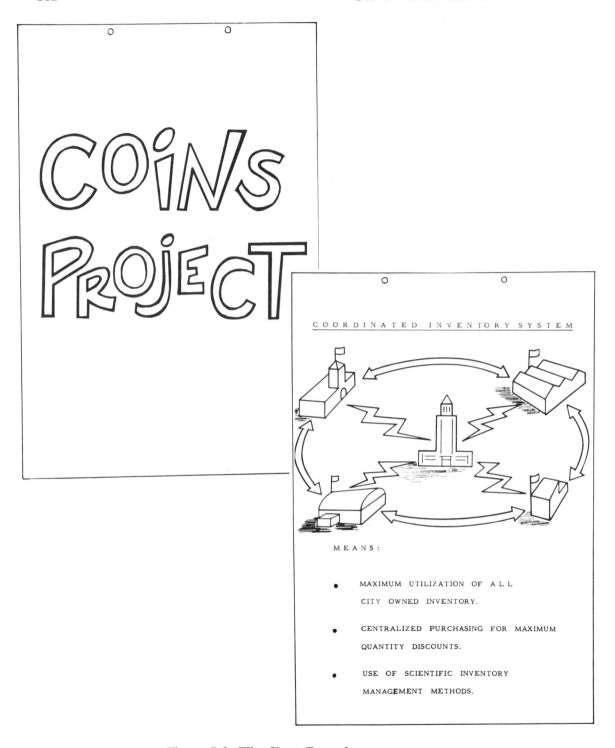

Figure 5-3. Flip Chart Examples.
Courtesy of City of Los Angeles.

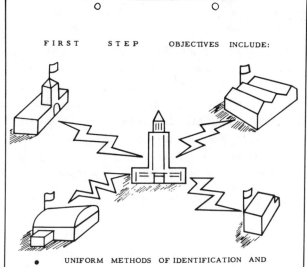

FIRST STEP OBJECTIVES INCLUDE:

- UNIFORM METHODS OF IDENTIFICATION AND PROCESSING OF INVENTORY.

- STANDARD REPORT INFORMATION FOR OPERATING AND CONTROL FUNCTIONS.

- A CENTRAL INFORMATION POINT FOR ALL STOCK STATUS DATA.

- HISTORICAL INFORMATION FOR USE WITH SCIENTIFIC INVENTORY METHODS.

REVIEW OF BENEFITS

- UNIFORM IDENTIFICATION.

- UNIFORM PROCESSING.

- MECHANIZED PROCESSING.

- COMPATIBLE WITH CENTRAL PURCHASING.

- COMPATIBLE WITH SCIENTIFIC INVENTORY MANAGEMENT

OPAQUE PROJECTION

The opaque projector is one of the most useful visual aid devices available. Through the use of light reflecting mirrors and lenses, opaque projectors are able to project on a screen images of objects, materials and written matter, all in natural color. Reports, charts or graphs which are on paper can be easily displayed to an audience. This device can be used to good advantage by accountants to present quantified data to small groups.

Opaque projectors can project any image where the original is no larger than 10″ x 10″. Ordinary 8½″ x 11″ paper can be handled easily because of the one inch margin provided on most written material. A large screen, preferably 6′ x 6′, is recommended for use with opaque projectors.

Features of Opaque Projectors

The principal advantage of opaque projectors is that almost any material the accountant works with can be displayed without an intermediary process. For example, the page of a book can be projected on the screen by placing the open page under the lens. No preliminary processing is necessary. No special materials are needed.

The disadvantages of opaque projectors are that they must be operated from the back of the room and, for best results, the room should be darkened. By having the speaker at the rear of his audience much of the effectiveness of oral presentations is lost. The audience tends to be less attentive when the speaker is out of view.

There is considerable audience irritation when the room must be darkened. They tend to lose interest fast. This seems to be particularly so with businessmen. If the lights must be turned on and off throughout the presentation, a certain disorientation occurs on the part of the audience. These disadvantages can be overcome by a good, strong speaker who is able to hold the audience's attention under adverse environmental circumstances.

Most opaque projectors are equipped with a light pen which allows the speaker to draw attention to certain features of the projected image. Material can be fed into the projector in a continuous roll or each item separately. The continuous roll requires that the material be in scroll form which is somewhat inconvenient. Material to be projected is inserted into the rear of the machine which is shown in Figure 5-4. The platen can be raised or lowered to hold the object firmly in place. Usually, some adjustment is necessary to focus the image. Most modern projectors run cool enough to prevent scorching the exhibited material. This was a serious problem with earlier opaque projectors.

Planning for Opaque Projection

The ease with which materials can be projected causes many speakers to overlook the important planning aspect of visual aids in connection with opaque projectors. Users tend to place whatever material they have in the projector without regard to its usefulness. Although almost any material *can* be projected, opaque visual aids should be specially prepared for each presentation. The usual 8½″ x 11″ document has far too much data on it to be an effective visual aid. Few people have the inclination to absorb a detailed cost accounting report which has been flashed on the screen.

Figure 5-4. Opaque Projector.
Courtesy of American Optical Corporation.

The first step in planning opaque projection visual aids is to write down the important points, figures or charts in your presentation. Then, decide which points should logically be presented together. An assistant can then draw or type the necessary information on 8½″ x 11″ paper. The speaker should use the visual aids as he practices his presentation so he feels comfortable with the material.

Before the meeting begins the speaker should inspect the room. Is the projector working? Turn it on to be certain. Does the screen need adjustment? When the lights are turned off is the projector power off also? Finally, are the exhibits in the proper order for presentation? It is disconcerting to find that your notes refer to one aid while the audience is viewing another.

Sometimes you can use an assistant to advantage when operating opaque projectors. While you stand near the front of the room the assistant can insert the material and operate the light pen. This involves close coordination between the speaker and assistant. It also takes another man away from his work.

OVERHEAD PROJECTORS

One of the most popular visual aid devices is the overhead projector. Specially prepared material up to 10″ x 10″ in size can be projected clearly in a lighted room. Overhead projectors come in a variety of sizes; one model can be folded into a small, narrow case and carried from place to place. A screen is not mandatory. Any wall in pastel color will suffice. However, a 70″ x 70″ screen is desirable with most overhead projectors.

Advantages of Overhead Projectors

The popularity of the overhead projector stems in part from the fact that the equipment can be operated from the front of the room. The speaker faces the audience while the material is projected on a screen behind him. He can maintain eye contact during the entire presentation. He can observe the audience's reaction and adjust his discussion accordingly. The speaker thus exercises more control over the audience than he can with opaque projectors which are operated from the rear of the room.

Another advantage of the overhead projector is that it can be used in a fully lighted room and still project clear images. The speaker can write and erase on the illustration while he is talking. A variety of special techniques such as progressive disclosure, overlays, and "strip tease" can be effectively used. The overhead projector is the most versatile visual aid which can be utilized by the accountant on reasonably short notice.

The major disadvantages of overhead projectors are the processes involved in preparing material for presentation. Unlike opaque projectors, overhead devices require a specially prepared transparency. Most office equipment manufacturers sell a machine which can make transparencies for their overhead projectors. Some of these machines are quite inexpensive. The more expensive ones are used for regular reproduction work as well as to make transparencies.

Most material for overhead projectors is prepared by placing the desired information on an ordinary piece of 8½″ x 11″ paper. The paper is then passed through a machine which makes a transparency. At this point any color shown on the original is lost. The transparency is usually in black and white. However, by using colored pens or pencils or special dry transfer materials, color can be applied to the transparency. One manufacturer sells transparent paper which gives a colored background with white letters. Adding color is particularly desirable when working with graphic material.

Using Overhead Projectors

The exhibits are placed in the proper order near the projector. The speaker faces the audience and places the first exhibit on the projector with the top pointing toward the audience. By glancing downward the speaker can see exactly what is being projected behind him on the screen. Figure 5-5 shows an overhead projector in use. The speaker may use a pointer to call attention to significant items on the transparency, or he may write directly on the transparency with a special pencil. The image will be projected onto the screen.

When using overhead projectors, the speaker often sits at the side of the machine. If he stands, some part of the audience may not be able to see the screen. In smaller groups, with careful planning, the screen can be placed in a position where the speaker is able to stand or move about without obstructing the view.

One of the disadvantages of the chalkboard is that the speaker has to turn his back on the audience while writing on the board. Using a blank transparency and a special pencil, the speaker can face the audience as he writes. The projector displays on the screen what he has written. The image is quite bright and clear, erasing is easy and eye contact has not been lost.

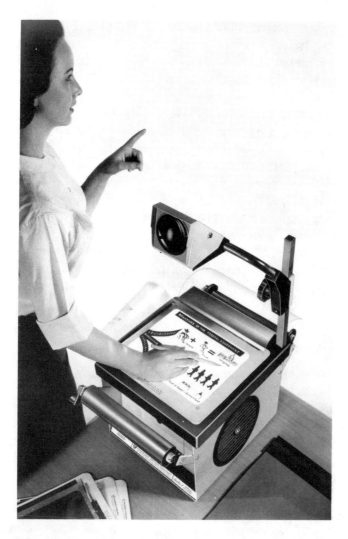

Figure 5-5. Overhead Projector.
Courtesy of American Optical Corporation.

An excellent use of overhead projectors is to develop or unfold presentations by the use of overlays. This is particularly useful when complex concepts are involved which, if thrust before the audience in complete detail, would overwhelm the viewer. A simple outline can be prepared on one transparency. Another transparency is prepared for the next level of detail and so on. The transparencies are hinged together so that the speaker may expose the first exhibit and explain it to the audience. Then he lays the next exhibit over the first. The audience is thus able to absorb complex presentations in simple steps. The speaker in Figure 5-5 is using the overlay process, an important feature of overhead projection.

Progressive Disclosure Technique

Another useful technique in working with overhead projection is progressive disclosure. A number of important points or figures are placed on one transparency. An opaque material, cardboard perhaps, is placed over the transparency. As the speaker proceeds through his presentation, he slides the opaque material down thus uncovering each point in succession. In this manner, the speaker can control the exposure of the material to the audience.

Figure 5-6 illustrates the use of the progressive disclosure technique. If the complete aid (at bottom in Figure 5-6) were exposed initially, the audience would be overpowered. Instead, only the title (at the top) is projected on the screen. After preliminary and introductory remarks, the first of three major categories is exposed by sliding the opaque shield down two inches (second part). The speaker discusses this point and then moves the shield again so that the second major category is exposed (third part). Finally, the shield is removed completely and the third category discussed. The audience, having been exposed by degrees, now understands the entire aid.

A variation of this technique is the "strip tease." After the material to be presented has been transferred to a transparency, opaque strips are mounted over each word, sentence, or concept as desired. The contents of the transparency are revealed on the screen as the strips are removed during the presentation.

Planning for Overhead Projection

An effective visual aid is simple and easy to comprehend. While an overhead projection transparency can be made of almost any data or drawings on paper, such material seldom meets the criteria for effective visual aids. Good overhead projection visual aids are usually designed for each presentation.

Plan what you want projected. Write big or use a typewriter with large characters. Do not put more than ten lines on one exhibit. Each line should not have more than six or seven words. Remember, the visual aids should be in broadbrush, and supplemented by the oral presentation.

Pressure sensitive materials can be used to prepare a professional visual aid. Pressure sensitive refers to letters, numbers or symbols which adhere to cellophane or acetate and are heat resistant. Much more variety can be introduced by using these materials. Not only is there a number of sizes and shapes, but these materials come in a variety of colors.

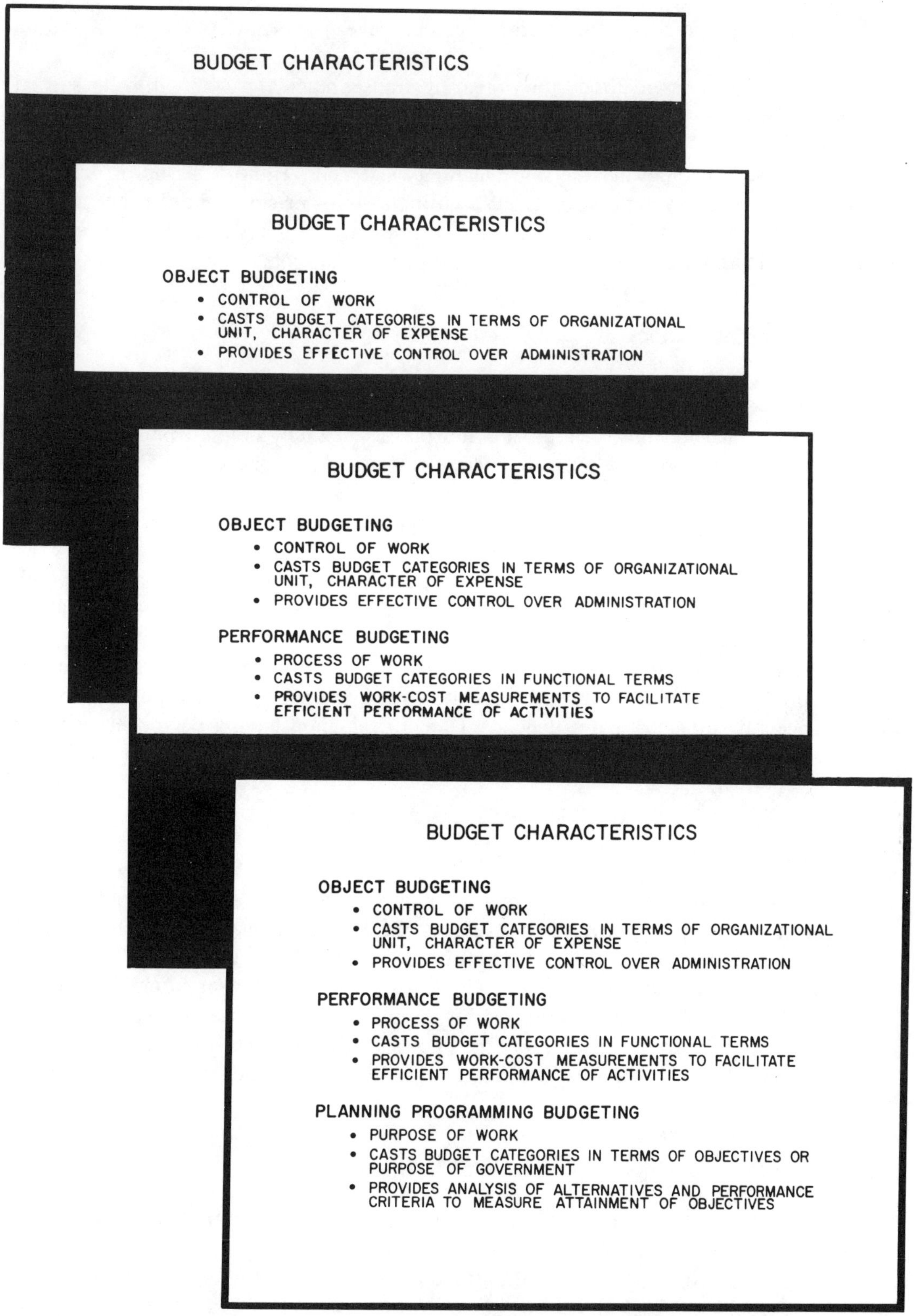

BUDGET CHARACTERISTICS

BUDGET CHARACTERISTICS

OBJECT BUDGETING
- CONTROL OF WORK
- CASTS BUDGET CATEGORIES IN TERMS OF ORGANIZATIONAL UNIT, CHARACTER OF EXPENSE
- PROVIDES EFFECTIVE CONTROL OVER ADMINISTRATION

BUDGET CHARACTERISTICS

OBJECT BUDGETING
- CONTROL OF WORK
- CASTS BUDGET CATEGORIES IN TERMS OF ORGANIZATIONAL UNIT, CHARACTER OF EXPENSE
- PROVIDES EFFECTIVE CONTROL OVER ADMINISTRATION

PERFORMANCE BUDGETING
- PROCESS OF WORK
- CASTS BUDGET CATEGORIES IN FUNCTIONAL TERMS
- PROVIDES WORK-COST MEASUREMENTS TO FACILITATE EFFICIENT PERFORMANCE OF ACTIVITIES

BUDGET CHARACTERISTICS

OBJECT BUDGETING
- CONTROL OF WORK
- CASTS BUDGET CATEGORIES IN TERMS OF ORGANIZATIONAL UNIT, CHARACTER OF EXPENSE
- PROVIDES EFFECTIVE CONTROL OVER ADMINISTRATION

PERFORMANCE BUDGETING
- PROCESS OF WORK
- CASTS BUDGET CATEGORIES IN FUNCTIONAL TERMS
- PROVIDES WORK-COST MEASUREMENTS TO FACILITATE EFFICIENT PERFORMANCE OF ACTIVITIES

PLANNING PROGRAMMING BUDGETING
- PURPOSE OF WORK
- CASTS BUDGET CATEGORIES IN TERMS OF OBJECTIVES OR PURPOSE OF GOVERNMENT
- PROVIDES ANALYSIS OF ALTERNATIVES AND PERFORMANCE CRITERIA TO MEASURE ATTAINMENT OF OBJECTIVES

Figure 5-6. Progressive Disclosure Technique.
Courtesy of Peat, Marwick, Livingston & Co.

Transparencies prepared by this method do not have to be passed through a special process.

There are also other methods for preparing transparencies without utilizing special equipment for preprocessing. By using a special carbon and clear acetate, effective visual aids may be prepared for direct use on the overhead projector. Typewritten transparencies can be prepared in somewhat the same manner as stencils. Hand lettering or drawings can be added to the typewritten material by using a stylus or sharp, hard pencil. Visual aids can be prepared completely by hand although the use of typewritten and/or pressure sensitive letters and numbers results in a more professional job.

Add Color to Projections

Color is a very useful tool in visual aids, and almost all users of overhead projectors are willing to expend extra effort to obtain color in transparencies. Color can be added: (1) by special acetate foils, cellophane, and plastics; (2) by colored paints, inks and pencils; and (3) by pressure sensitive materials. Easiest to work with are the pressure sensitive materials which come in many shapes and colors. Charts and graphs can be prepared in beautiful colors by using this technique. The effective use of inks, paints and pencils depends on the type of transparent material used. Colored pencil will not write on some slick materials. Also, colored inks and paint are often difficult to apply to smooth surfaces. Consult your local supplier as to which coloring techniques are compatible with your transparencies.

Color may also be added to overhead visual aids by the diazo process. While this method produces excellent transparencies, it is somewhat complicated. The use of the diazo process by the accountant depends a great deal upon having personnel available who know how to prepare transparencies and upon the time limit within which the material is needed.

Example of Overhead Projection Visual Aids

Figure 5-7 shows four charts taken from a set of visual aids used in support of an oral presentation. Using the overhead projector, the charts are displayed in three colors: red, green and yellow all on a black background. The first sheet (upper left, Figure 5-7) is the facing. The second sheet (upper right) is an "outline of presentation" which also serves as the speaker's notes. A graph is presented in the next chart (lower left). This illustration is done with overlays so that the line "FEDERAL" appears first. Then, either the "STATE & LOCAL" or the "STATE" can be displayed. Each line is in a different color.

The final sheet (lower right) contains a great deal of information—too much to be absorbed at once by the audience. Using overlays, the "INTERCITY TRANSPORT" section is exposed first. Then, all of "TRANSPORTATION" is shown. Finally the entire chart is projected. The audience is better able to understand the complete chart because it was exposed piecemeal.

The overhead projector as a visual aid is quite effective. If the equipment is already available in your organization, you ought to know how to use it. If such equipment is not

PLANNING PROGRAMMING, BUDGETING SYSTEM

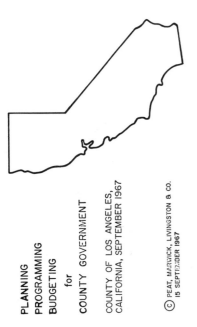

**Figure 5-7. Examples of Overhead Projection Sheets.
Courtesy of Peat, Marwick, Livingston & Co.**

now available, any one of a number of manufacturers would be happy to demonstrate their product to you. For the accountant who must make many oral presentations of detailed or quantified data, the overhead projector is an invaluable aid.

6

Graphic
Reporting
Techniques

The proper use of graphs and charts can do more to aid in the presentation of quantified information than any other single technique. Numerical data in graphic form is much easier to explain, interpret and analyze than the same figures in tabular form. By using points, lines, areas and other geometric forms, the comparison of values, the discernment of trends and the understanding of relationships is facilitated.

The usefulness of graphs can be easily demonstrated by reference to Figure 6-1. The objective of this exhibit is to show that, while bonding capacity has increased steadily, bonds outstanding have held even or actually decreased. This fact can be grasped in a moment by glancing at the chart. Considerably longer time is required to assimilate the numerical data in Figure 6-1 and arrive at the same conclusion.

Graphs and charts are more interesting and appealing and are remembered longer than tabular material. Two hours or two days from now the chart in Figure 6-1 will still be in the mind's eye, but the figures will be forgotten. The reader's time is saved when numerical data is presented in graphic form. Discussion is thus stimulated. A word of caution is in order, however. The improper use of graphs can easily result in misunderstanding and lead to erroneous conclusions. The maker of a graph has a responsibility to accurately portray the underlying numerical data.

Types of Graphs

The accountant ordinarily deals with three basic types of graphs when reporting to management. The most common is the line graph, followed by column and bar charts. There are numerous variations to each of these basic types. Two other types of graphs which are sometimes found in management reports are the pie chart and the surface

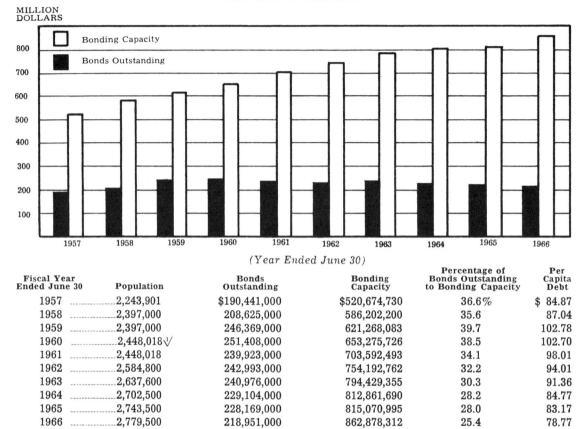

RELATIONSHIP BETWEEN BONDS OUTSTANDING
AND BONDING CAPACITY

1956-1957 to 1965-1966

MILLION
DOLLARS

□ Bonding Capacity

■ Bonds Outstanding

(Year Ended June 30)

Fiscal Year Ended June 30	Population	Bonds Outstanding	Bonding Capacity	Percentage of Bonds Outstanding to Bonding Capacity	Per Capita Debt
1957	2,243,901	$190,441,000	$520,674,730	36.6%	$ 84.87
1958	2,397,000	208,625,000	586,202,200	35.6	87.04
1959	2,397,000	246,369,000	621,268,083	39.7	102.78
1960	2,448,018	251,408,000	653,275,726	38.5	102.70
1961	2,448,018	239,923,000	703,592,493	34.1	98.01
1962	2,584,800	242,993,000	754,192,762	32.2	94.01
1963	2,637,600	240,976,000	794,429,355	30.3	91.36
1964	2,702,500	229,104,000	812,861,690	28.2	84.77
1965	2,743,500	228,169,000	815,070,995	28.0	83.17
1966	2,779,500	218,951,000	862,878,312	25.4	78.77

**Figure 6-1. Column Chart Showing Trends and Relationships.
Courtesy Los Angeles City Controller's Office.**

chart. All these graph types are discussed in this chapter. Other graphic forms commonly seen but seldom used by accountants are pictorial and map charts.

COMMON GRAPH CHARACTERISTICS

There are certain conventions which apply to the preparation of all types of graphs. First, always keep the intended audience in mind. A technically oriented audience will be affronted by an oversimplified graph. They expect some substance. Similarly, someone who has been working with the data presented will quickly digest the overview and demand more detail.

The size and proportions of the graph and of the letters and symbols thereon depend upon how the material is to be presented. Many graphs are used to aid in oral presentations. They should be large, colorful and simple. Ordinarily, they will not be reproduced. Other graphs are prepared in support of a narrative report. More detail can be added to this type. If they are to be reproduced in quantity, color cannot be used economically.

Graph Titles

All graphs should have a title which is placed at the top of the exhibit. The purpose of the title is to tell what the data is, what it applies to and the period covered. An example would be "GROSS NATIONAL PRODUCT, UNITED STATES, 1950–1970." This title succinctly satisfies all three requirements. It is not necessary to begin a title with "CHART SHOWING. . . ." The title should be in the largest letters used on the chart. Ordinarily, the title is in all capitals.

Subtitles should be avoided whenever possible and where used should be limited to a very few words. Other information above the chart proper should be curtailed. Most explanatory information is better placed at the bottom of the chart or graph.

Body of the Graph

The body or grid portion of the graph should be rectangular in the proportion of five horizontal units to three vertical units. On most charts, equal amounts must be represented by equal lengths on the respective scale. One important exception to this rule is logarithmic graphs.

Purchased graph paper has too many grid lines for attractive presentation of most business information. Seldom are more than ten horizontal or vertical grid lines needed to establish relative values. Less than four is considered too few. Values are ordinarily shown for each grid line. Values for the grid lines crossing the vertical axis (horizontal lines) are placed on both the right and left of the graph. Values for the lines crossing the horizontal axis are placed only at the bottom of the grid.

Explanatory Information

The key is one of the most important parts of any graph or chart. The key explains the meaning of lines, bars and columns on the graph. Ordinarily the key is found in a conspicuous location at the bottom of the chart. Again, as few words as possible are used.

Accountants ordinarily do not need to state the source of graphic data. If the source is stated it should be in the far right corner at the bottom of the graph. Lengthy footnotes should be avoided if at all possible. Destroying the usefulness of a graph by too much verbiage is a common error.

GRAPHS ILLUSTRATED

Arithmetic Line Graph

The best known and most widely used graph is the line chart or graph. A line graph is made by plotting one or more series of figures on a grid. The successive plotted points are joined by lines known as a "curve."

The line graph is used almost exclusively to portray time series in such a way that trends can be identified. The emphasis is on movement or direction rather than absolute amounts. The line graph cannot be effectively used where only a few values are available. Neither is the line graph the best type of chart to show difference in values or amounts on different dates. Other graphic media should be considered in these situations or where the movement or trend is very irregular.

Figure 6-2 illustrates the principle of the line graph. Where more than one value is plotted as in Figure 6-2 the respective curves must be clearly differentiated. The use of color is an obvious solution. However, many charts must be reproduced by methods which eliminate color. Therefore, dashes, dots, or other patterns should be used to differentiate between lines. The meaning of each curve is explained in the key found at the bottom of the graph.

By convention the horizontal grid on a line graph represents time and the vertical grid, the amount of value. Usually, the vertical grid represents only one value series. However, in some circumstances it is permissible to show one value series on the left side and another on the right. An example might be where a division's sales were plotted against the left grid and the total company sales against the right. In this manner trends indicated by each line can be easily compared even though total company sales are ten times those of the division. The use of multiple value scales is subject to great misinterpretation and should be avoided.

Ordinarily, the vertical value series begins with zero at the bottom of the grid. Sometimes it is desirable to show negative values. In this instance the zero grid line should be clearly marked in bold ruling. All negative values on the scale must be preceded by a minus sign.

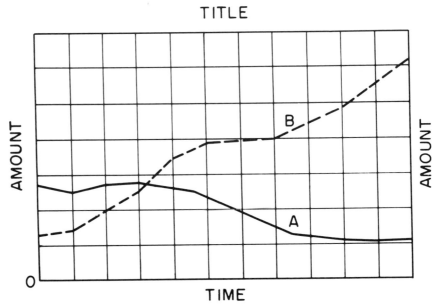

Figure 6-2. Line Graph.

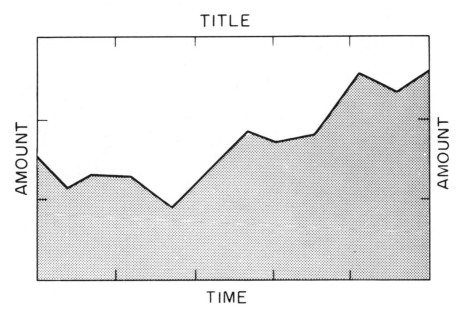

Figure 6-3. Surface Line Chart.

Surface Charts

Surface charts are another form of the line graph. First, a series is plotted as with a line graph. Then the area under the curve is shaded. Figure 6-3 shows a simple surface chart. This is called a surface line chart. Another variation is the staircase surface chart which is really a column chart with the columns connected. Column charts will be discussed subsequently.

Simple surface charts are not widely used as they offer little advantage over line charts. However, multiple surface charts can be very effective in showing total values and the component parts simultaneously. Figure 6-4 illustrates the multiple surface chart. Total sales are represented by the top line. The three products making up total sales are shown by first plotting Product C. Then, Product B is plotted using the Product C curve as base or zero. Product A is plotted on top of B in the same manner. Then the areas between the curves are shaded or crosshatched to differentiate between each product.

Instead of a key, the name of each segment is shown on the face of the multiple surface chart. No more than five components may be effectively shown on a multiple surface chart. Three components result in the most appealing charts.

The most important component, not necessarily the largest, should be plotted first. Readers can easily compare the trend line of the bottom component to the total movement whereas the trend line of subsequent components is distorted by the fact that they rest on the first curve plotted. When preparing surface charts for persons unaccustomed to reading graphs be sure that they do not take the top curve of each component as the value of that item. Emphasize that the value is the difference within the crosshatched areas of each component.

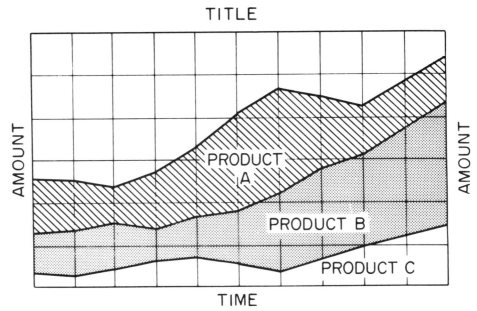

Figure 6-4. Multiple Surface Chart.

One-Hundred Percent Surface Chart

The one-hundred percent surface chart attempts to show the changes in the relative proportion of the total represented by each component over a period of time. Data is in percent. No absolute values are shown.

After the actual figures of each component have been translated into a percent of the total, they are plotted in the same manner as multiple surface charts. The problem with charts of this type is that the reader has no absolute figures to form a frame of reference. To overcome this deficiency one-hundred percent charts are usually used in conjunction with other graphs which do present absolute values. Figure 6-5 shows a one-hundred percent chart.

An interesting variation of the surface chart is the silhouette chart. Such charts are used to show the difference between two values. Figure 6-6 illustrates this principle. The income and contract cost figures are both plotted from the zero base line. The area between the two curves is shaded and labeled "profit." Since this is presumably the most important value shown by this particular chart, it is properly emphasized. The reader could not overlook it.

Semilogarithmic Graphs

The semilogarithmic graph is an excellent tool for depicting proportional and percentage relationships. By plotting absolute figures on a specially drawn grid the resultant curve indicates the rate of increase or decrease. To show the same information on an arithmetic grid, two charts would be required. One chart would be used to show absolute

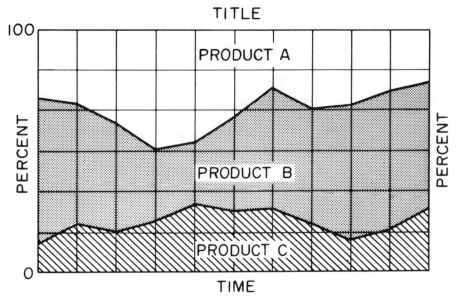

Figure 6-5. One Hundred Percent Surface Chart.

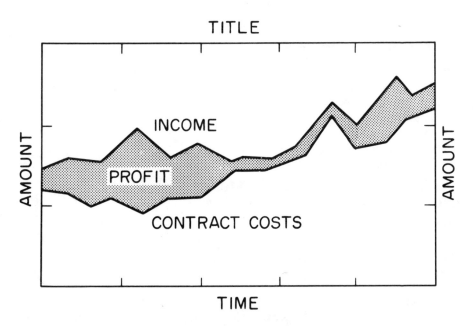

Figure 6-6. Silhouette Chart.

values. The absolute values must then be converted into percentages and plotted on the second chart to show the rate of change. Since managers are often more interested in maintaining rates of growth or change, the semilogarithmic is an excellent reporting tool.

In Figure 6-7 the semilogarithmic graph is compared with the arithmetic graph. The value of 100 increased by 50% each period is plotted on both graphs. The respective values, 100, 150, 225, 337, 506 and 759 can be read from either graph. However, the curve on the arithmetic graph (left) seems to indicate that the rate of progression is increasing because the angle becomes steeper with each new value. The semilogarithmic graph (right) curve is a straight line thereby accurately showing a steady rate of increase of 50% per year.

From Figure 6-7 it is obvious that the semilogarithmic graph differs considerably in appearance from the arithmetic graph. The vertical axis is ruled logarithmically which is characterized by the continued narrowing of the spaces on the grid. The horizontal axis is ruled arithmetically, thus the name semilogarithmic. Complete logarithmic graphs with both axes ruled logarithmically are used by engineers but are seldom seen in business communications.

Another unique feature of semilogarithmic graphs is that there is no zero base line. The logarithm of zero cannot be plotted. Therefore, the base line must always begin with a positive value. A multiple of 10 is by far the most convenient base for a semilogarithmic graph.

Semilogarithmic graphs can be used effectively to compare the rate of change in two or more value series which differ greatly in absolute amounts. For instance, the rate of change in the population of the State of California can be compared to the rate of change in a city of about 50,000 people. This is accomplished by using semilogarithmic graphs with tiers or decks. A very large arithmetic graph would be needed to show the same information and the small city data would be hardly noticeable.

Semilogarithmic Graphs Illustrated

A salary dispute involving engineering personnel in a large company serves to illustrate the use of semilogarithmic charts. The engineers confronted the manager of industrial relations with the arithmetic graph shown on the left in Figure 6-8. Supporting this graph was the following data:

	President's Salary	Average Salary of Engineer	Difference
1964	$50,000	$10,000	$40,000
1965	55,000	11,000	44,000
1966	60,000	13,500	46,500
1967	65,000	15,000	50,000
1968	70,000	17,500	52,500
1969	80,000	20,000	60,000

The engineers particularly objected to the 1969 increase of $10,000 in the President's salary, contending that it was excessive. They used the arithmetic graph to show how the President's salary was rising much faster than that of the average engineer.

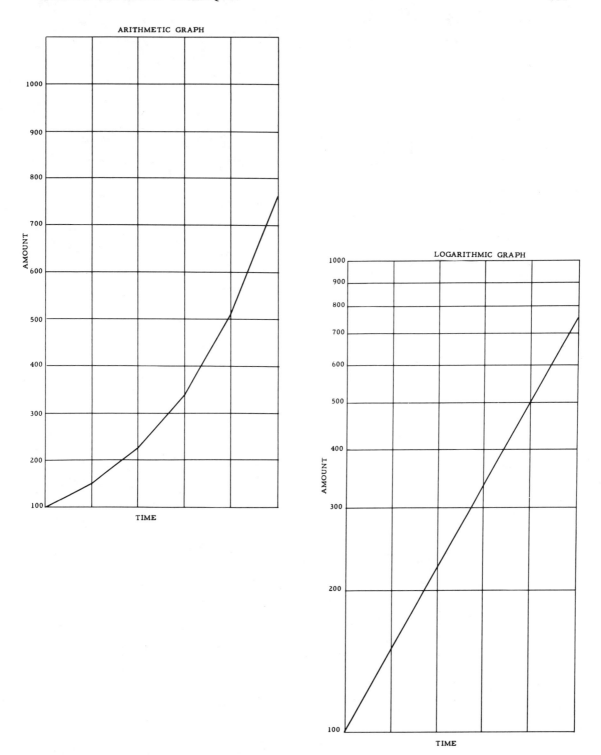

Figure 6-7. Arithmetic and Logarithmic Graphs Compared.

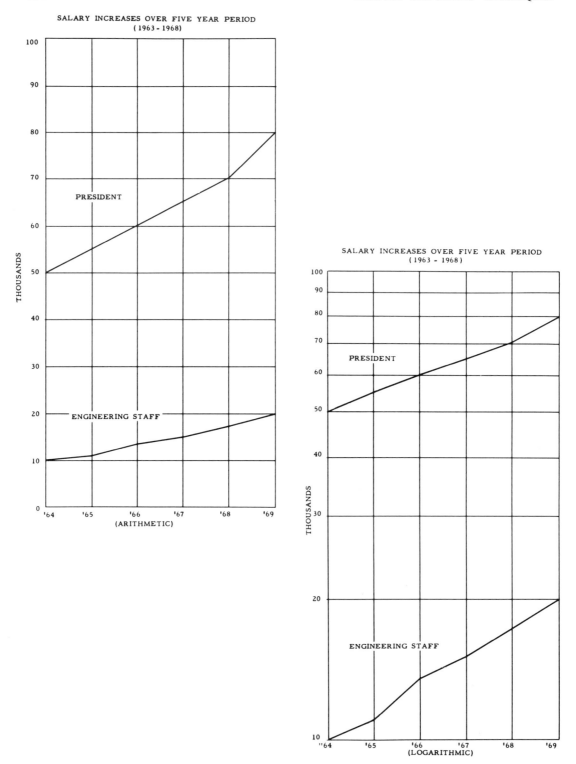

Figure 6-8. Two Series Contrasted on Arithmetic and Logarithmic Graphs.

The manager of industrial relations countered with the semilogarithmic graph in Figure 6-8. He also presented the following tabulation:

	RATE OF INCREASE	
	President	*Engineers*
1965	10%	10%
1966	9%	23%
1967	8%	11%
1968	7%	17%
1969	14%	14%

Referring to the semilogarithmic chart the manager of industrial relations pointed out that the engineers' salaries were increasing at a more rapid rate than was the President's as evidenced by the steepness of the respective curves. This exchange of charts and data did not resolve the issue. However, it does point out the differences between semilogarithmic graphs and common arithmetic graphs.

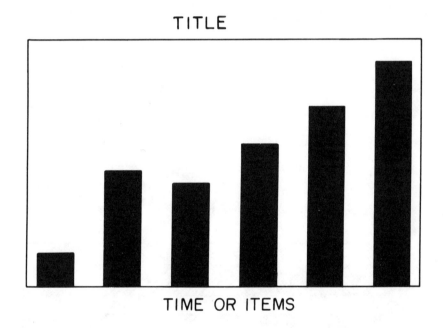

Figure 6-9. Column Chart.

Bar and Column Charts

While the arithmetic line graph is preferred by most technically oriented people, the bar or column chart is more acceptable to lay persons. The two types of charts differ only in that the bars are arranged vertically in a column chart and horizontally in a bar chart. Figure 6-9 shows a simple column chart. The bar chart is shown in Figure 6-10. Column charts or bar charts are used to compare the relative magnitude of comparable items or parts of a total.

Figure 6-10. Bar Chart.

Column charts can also be used to show trends or movement in a time series similar to the function performed by the line graph. Bar charts are not used for time series. Figure 6-1 is a multiple column chart which shows the movement of two values over a period of time. The emphasis in this chart is not only on trends but also on the relationship of the two values at different times.

The simple bar chart is used exclusively to show the relative magnitude of different items at any given time. It is usually used where there are a large number of values to be shown. The large value is always placed at the top and the other items arranged in descending order.

Bar and Column Chart Variations

The simple bar and column charts and the multiple column chart are the most common types used by accountants. However, there are a number of variations which

Figure 6-11. One Hundred Percent Bar Chart.

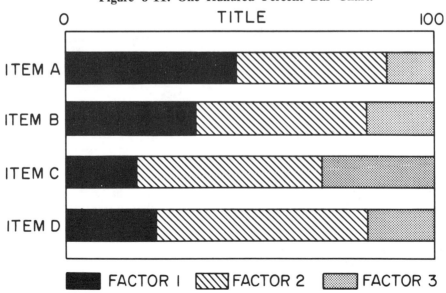

can be used effectively in certain circumstances. Figure 6-11 shows a one-hundred percent bar chart. In this instance a column chart could be used just as satisfactorily. One-hundred percent charts are used to show the percentage of the total represented by each factor.

If the primary objective in Figure 6-11 had been to show the value of each item in relation to the other items, then a segmented column or bar chart would have been used. Using this technique, both the totals and the components are shown in absolute figures.

Figure 6-12 is a net deviation chart. Net deviation charts show both positive and negative values usually involving a time series. The most frequent use of net deviation charts is to show profit and loss data. Gross deviation charts are sometimes found which extend both above and below the zero base line. Gross deviation charts are not often used by accountants.

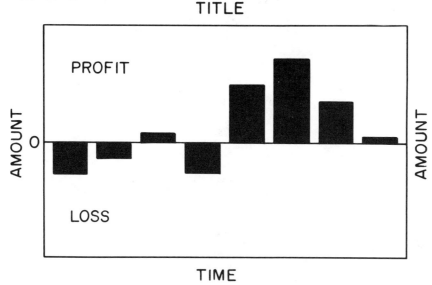

Figure 6-12. Net Deviation Chart.

Another useful variation of bar and column charts is the paired bar chart shown in Figure 6-13. The paired bar chart is the best possible method to compare, component by component, two or more items. This presentation is superior to the component bar chart if the comparison of components in absolute figures is more important than the comparison of totals.

Pie Charts

Pie charts are popular with many persons involved with the communication of business data. Such charts are used to compare components as a percent of a total value or amount. Thus, pie charts are quite similar in use to component bar charts.

A pie chart is presented in Figure 6-14. Customarily, the components are arranged

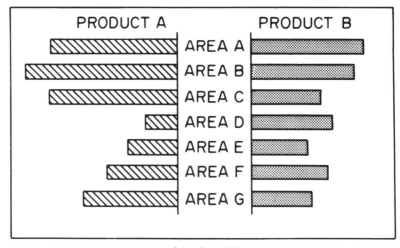

Figure 6-13. Paired Bar Chart.

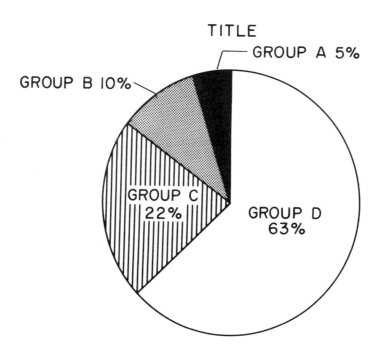

Figure 6-14. Pie Chart.

THE BUDGET DOLLAR

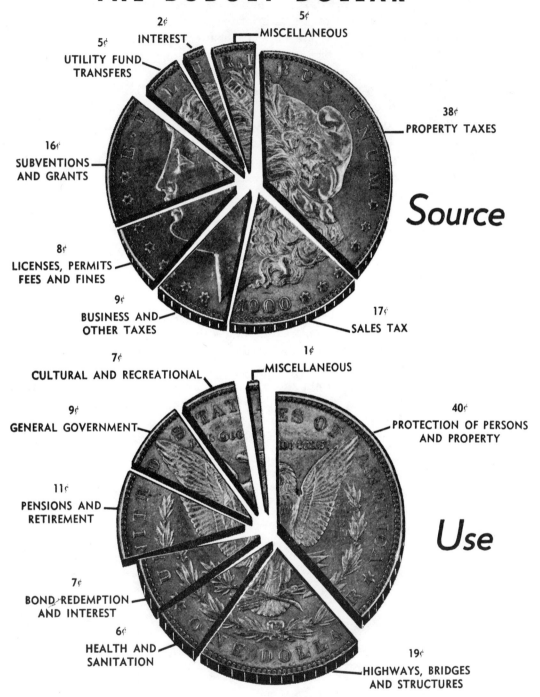

Figure 6-15. Illustrated Use of Pie Charts.
Courtesy Los Angeles City Controller's Office.

in descending order, clockwise, starting from the top of the circle. Each section or component should be carefully labeled. If possible, the label should be within the area itself. Otherwise, place the label near the related portion of the pie and connect the two with an arrow. Percentages should be shown directly below the label.

No more than five components should be shown on a pie chart. It is too difficult to differentiate between the various items when a larger number is shown. Pie charts are best used where one or two components dwarf the remainder. If all the components are nearly the same size, the pie chart is ineffective; a component bar chart should be used.

Perhaps the best and most common use of pie charts is illustrated in Figure 6-15. The source of the tax dollar in cents is shown in the top pie and the use of the tax dollar in the lower pie. By using cents instead of percent, the meaning of the chart is much easier to grasp. Note that there is no relationship between the components in the top chart and those in the bottom chart. Only the totals can be compared, i.e., "Use" must equal "Source."

COMMON GRAPH ERRORS

There are some common errors in graphic presentation which should be avoided lest the reader be confused or misled. One frequent error is to attempt too much in one chart. Ordinarily, only three or at most four values should be shown on one line graph. Where these curves tend often to intersect and generally show no relationship, as in Figure 6-16, the reader is unable to attach any meaning to the graph. If a number of such curves must be presented on a single graph, color should be used to differentiate between values. The overlay technique described in the chapter on visual aids is an excellent method of presenting such data.

There are two common errors with bar charts. Often the crosshatching on segmented

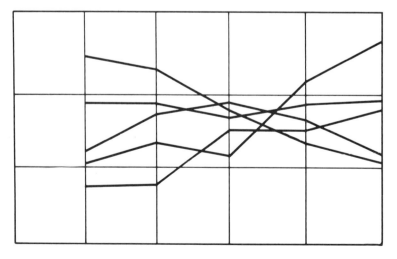

Figure 6-16. Ineffective Line Graph.

bars is incompatible. Figure 6-17 illustrates this point. Also, some chart makers attempt to show differences in value in two dimensions, also as in Figure 6-17. This is incorrect. Only one dimension should be used to show a single value. If two values are represented by a single bar, then width can be used. However, few chart makers are successful at using bars in this manner.

Starting bar or column charts at a base other than zero is poor practice usually identified with unethical operators. The accountant should never do this. Sometimes it is necessary to begin at zero base and then cut a segment from all bars. The omitted segment is indicated by two parallel sawtooth lines. However, to remove a segment from only one bar, as in Figure 6-18, is absolutely unacceptable.

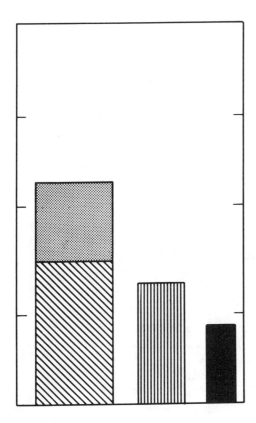

Figure 6-17.
Column Chart Errors.

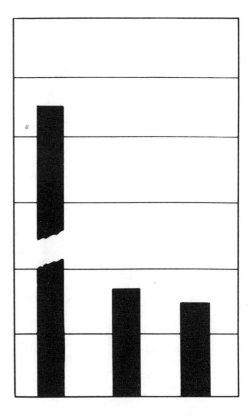

Figure 6-18.
Column Chart Improperly Segmented.

EXAMPLE OF GRAPHIC REPORTING

This section discusses how a major corporation uses graphic forms for management reporting. The graph and charts shown are factual reproductions except that the figures have been altered. Quarterly, top management receives a loose leaf, 8½″ x 11″ status report containing all the information needed to plan and control the company.

Graphs are the basic documents in the status report, but each graph is supplemented by tabular and narrative data. While the graphs are well done, the material presented as backup consists of photostat copies of tabulations prepared in pencil. Not only does this save time and the cost of typing but the reader is naturally drawn to the more formal graph and away from the handwritten detail.

All the basic types of graphs used by the company are shown in Figures 6-19 through 6-25. Only one example of each chart form is shown. Fourteen charts and graphs are used in the entire report.

Figure 6-19. Budgeted and Actual Sales.

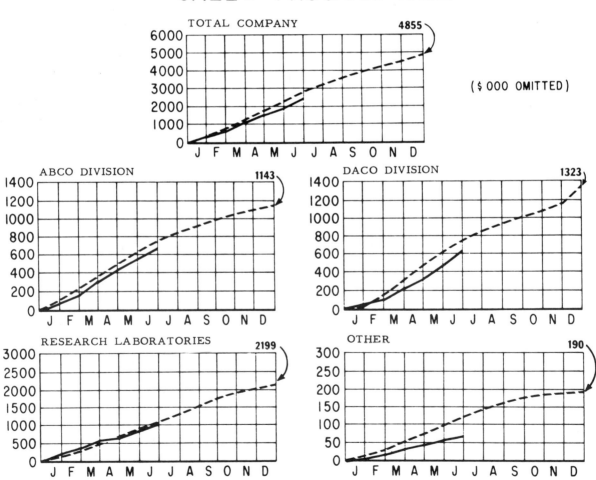

Figure 6-19 shows projected sales for the various segments of the company and for the organization as a whole (dash lines). Against this budgeted figure actual sales for the first six months (solid lines) are plotted. Management can tell at a glance which segment of the company is in trouble. Note that the key has been omitted. All readers are presumed to know that dash lines represent budgeted figures unless otherwise indicated.

Combination of Graphs

Sales are broken down by region in Figure 6-20. Particularly noteworthy is the use of both line graphs and column charts. The line graphs compare actual sales for the current year to budgeted sales whereas the column charts show a five year history.

Sales, profit after tax and percent to sales are shown in Figure 6-21. The most interesting aspect of these charts is the six-year history and three-year projection shown by bar columns. The projection is made for two different forecast assumptions. Note that the line graph and column chart are on the same scale as should be the case.

The graph in Figure 6-22 uses columns to show prior figures and projections for next year. Figure 6-23 uses a single dot to show future goals but presents the past year in a line chart. Note that almost all graphs show monthly figures together with year-to-date and usually have prior year data and future projections.

Information regarding the company's investment base is presented in Figure 6-23. The reader must be careful in interpreting this set of graphs. The vertical grid rulings for each category appear to be equal. Measurement will disclose that this is not quite so. Much more important is the fact that different values have been assigned to the vertical scales on similar size charts shown as a set.

	Grid Ratio	Numerical Ratio
Net Working Capital	2	5
Capital Equipment	3	5
Real Property	3	10
Other	3	1

Perhaps most readers of this report would realize that as of January 1, 1968 "other" is only 1/30 of "Real Property." However, a casual glance at the chart would lead one to conclude that "other" is ⅓ of "Real Property." This is quite a difference.

Component Column Chart

Figure 6-24 is interesting because of the way component or multiple columns are used. Three values are shown here, total accounts receivable, billed accounts, and unbilled accounts. Most chart makers would have placed the unbilled column on top of the billed column. However, by presenting the two parts of total accounts receivable side by side the reader can visually compare the relative position of billed and unbilled. Should unbilled accounts exceed billed accounts, it would be noticed immediately. This

SALES ($ MILLIONS)

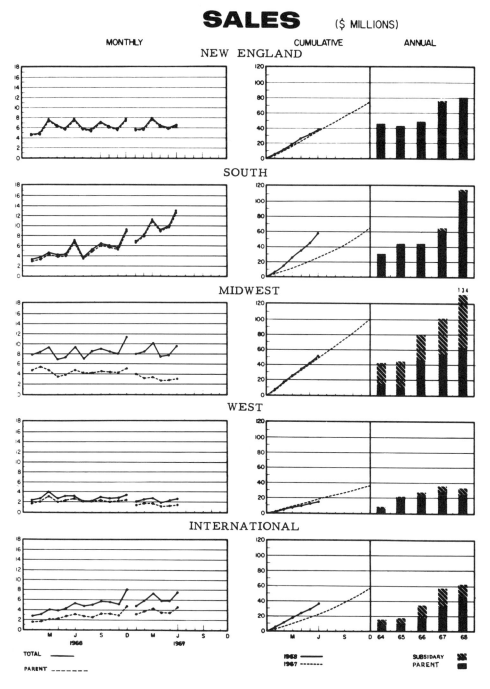

Figure 6-20. Sales by Region.

142

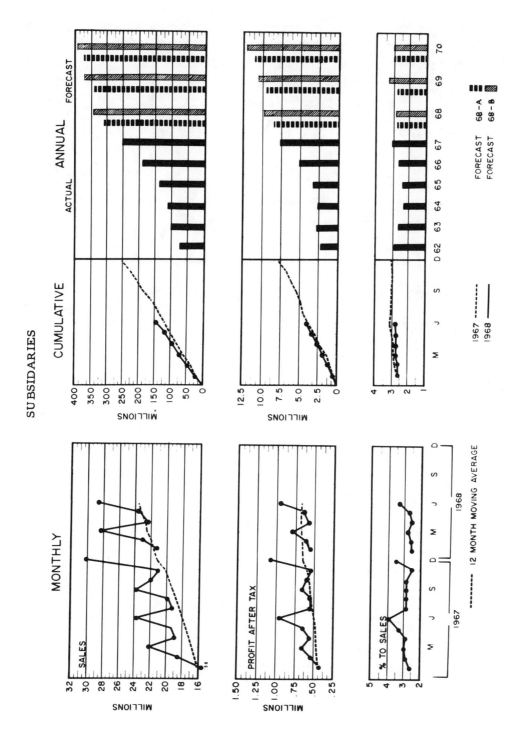

Figure 6-21. Sales, Profit After Tax and Percent to Sales.

143

CONTRACT RESULTS

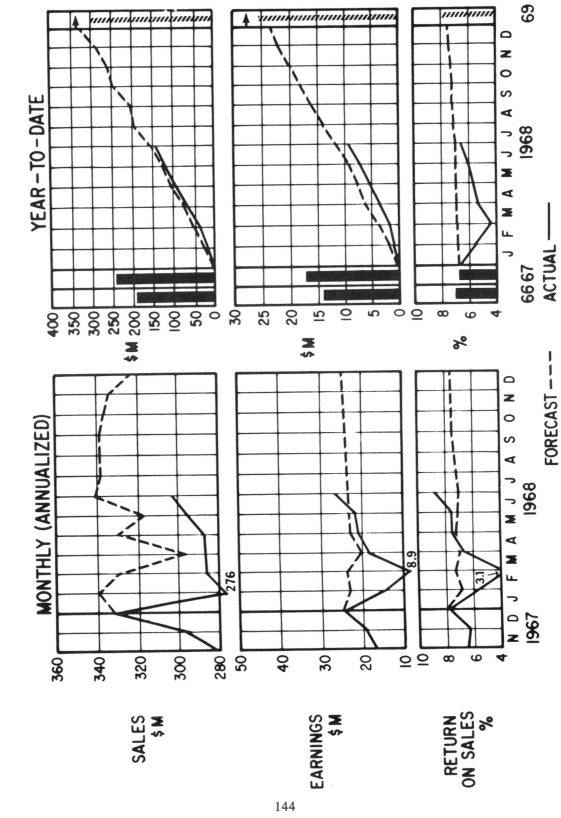

Figure 6-22. Sales, Earnings and Return on Sales.

144

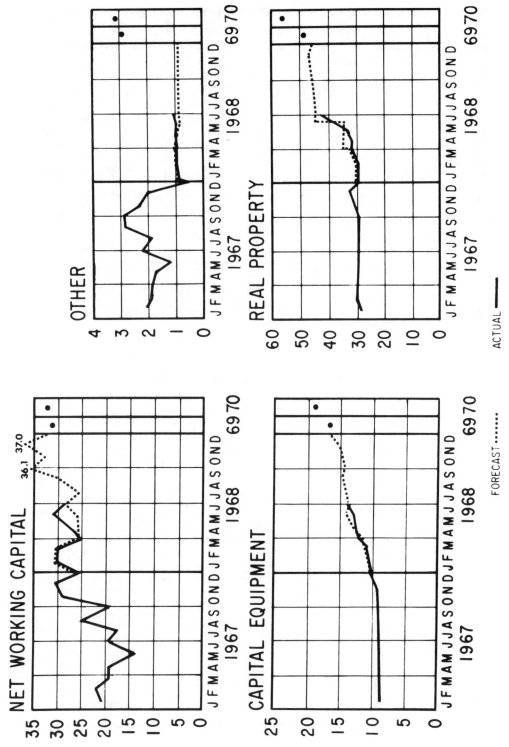

Figure 6-23. Investment Base Data.

145

ACCOUNTS RECEIVABLE

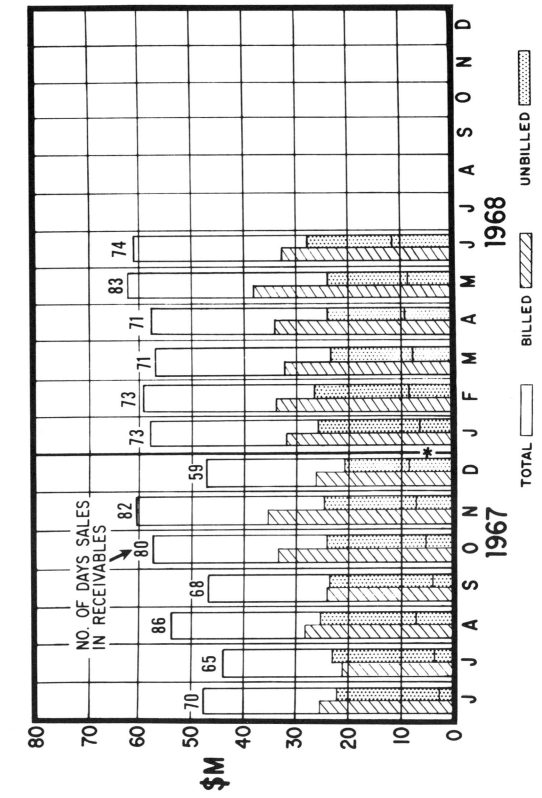

Figure 6-24. Accounts Receivable.

146

INDIRECT EXPENSE - 19

ENGINEERING POOL

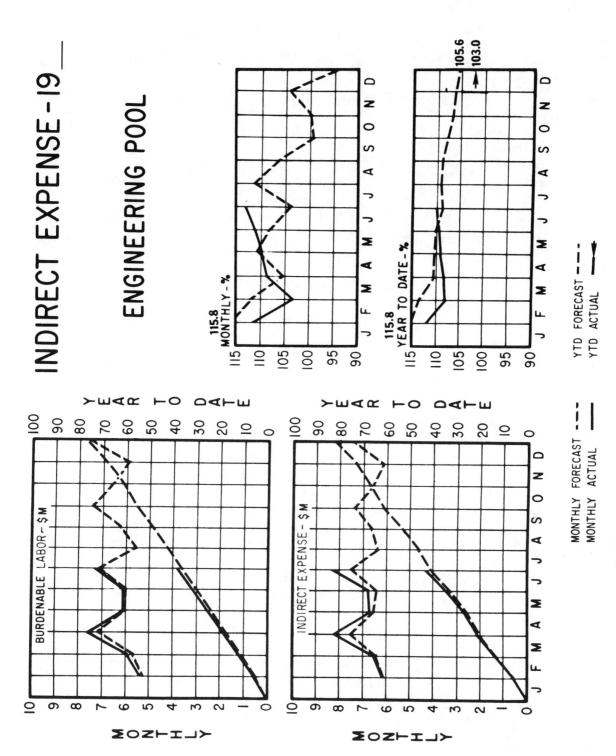

MONTHLY FORECAST – – –
MONTHLY ACTUAL ——

YTD FORECAST – – –
YTD ACTUAL ——➤

Figure 6-25. Indirect Expense, Monthly and Year to Date.

relationship would not be so readily discernible if one column were placed on top of the other.

The technique of two scales on a single grid is used in Figure 6-25. The left scale represents monthly values and the right, yearly values. This is the best possible use of the dual scale technique. However, this method can be very misleading under other circumstances and should be used carefully.

Taken as a whole, the group of graphs and charts presented here represents an excellent use of graphic reporting. These graphs are presented as a set to top management at least quarterly. If the manager requires additional details, tabulations are enclosed directly behind the related graph. After using the set for a period of time the manager is quite familiar with the meaning of each graph.

HOW TO PREPARE GRAPHS

There are three basic processes by which graphic exhibits can be prepared, freehand, mechanical and dry transfer. The use of the freehand method requires the services of an experienced draftsman. These talents are not often available to the accountant particularly on short notice. However, if a draftsman skilled in chart making is available, use him.

Often it is possible to find someone in the accounting organization who can draw charts well enough but has difficulty in lettering. There are various mechanical lettering devices on the market which are relatively easy to use. The Leroy and Wrico systems are the best known and can be seen at most drafting supply outlets.

Another efficient lettering device is the VariTyper. Using typewriter-like equipment, letters, words or phrases can be prepared in any reasonable size or style. By an additional process letters can be produced in color. The words or phrases can be fixed to the chart by an adhesive material.

Some lettering can be done by ordinary typewriter for graphs to be used in overhead projection or reproduced on ordinary copying equipment. The primary disadvantage of typewriter lettering is that all letters are the same size. Most graphic exhibits require different size letters as well as bold print to add proper emphasis.

Dry Transfer Method

The most rapidly growing method for preparing graphic material is with the various dry transfer processes. Border lines, crosshatching, bars, and lettering can all be produced by this method. Border lines, bars and crosshatching all come in convenient tape-style dispensers. Letters are purchased in sheets. All are available in a wide range of styles, sizes and colors. Simple burnishing is all that is required to place these materials on any dry surface.

The principal advantage of the dry transfer method is that no special skill is required. One of the office personnel can easily learn to use the process. There is a greater variety of styles and symbols available in dry transfer than any other method. Finally, the dry transfer method produces better looking, more colorful graphs in less time than other methods.

The set of graphs shown in Figures 6-19 through 6-25 is prepared by two processes. The basic format continues from year to year. Therefore, the outline of the grids, scales and much of the lettering is done by commercial printing equipment. Each quarter a clerk plots the curves on each graph and adds whatever lettering is necessary. Then the graph is reproduced on ordinary office copying machines and placed in a booklet for top management's review.

7

Reproduction, Distribution and Control of Reports

Seven steps are involved in the proper development and control of reports:

- Authorization
- Design
- Preparation
- Reproduction
- Distribution
- Retention
- Review

For the most part this book is concerned with the design and preparation phases. This is as it should be because the effectiveness of a reporting system is directly proportional to the skill and ingenuity which go into design and preparation. The remaining aspects of reporting, called housekeeping functions, also deserve some attention.

The seven steps outlined above apply to most formal reporting systems. However, in small and some medium-size companies the housekeeping functions are implicit as opposed to being set forth as a formal procedure. The organization is sufficiently small so that everyone knows who can authorize a report, who can receive confidential information, or how long a report is to be retained.

Larger organizations are faced with a different situation. The quantity of data available and the number of people who need this data to carry on their work increase rapidly as the organization grows. There is no longer a personal relationship between the custodian of data and the user of information. Requests for information multiply. Duplication of reports occurs. One-time requests for information become part of the regular reporting system. Reports are continued long after their usefulness has ended.

151

Report Control Program

When these inefficiencies creep into the reporting system, it becomes advantageous to establish formal procedures for authorizing, reproducing and distributing information in the form of reports. The point at which an organization needs a report control program varies, of course, but such a program should definitely be considered when the company begins to store data in a computer. The use of a computer actually makes it easier to control reports because of the single information source.

The first step in establishing control over reports is to make this function the responsibility of a specific individual or group. Usually the systems and procedures unit or its equivalent is given this responsibility. The systems group ordinarily is involved in the design of all reports even though it may work closely with or even at the direction of the user department. The systems group acts as a clearing house for information and reports and is, therefore, the logical unit to administer a report control program.

Many companies require that any new function such as a report control program be formally inaugurated or "mandated." A statement similar to the one shown below is often issued.

DIRECTIVE NO.: 82-68
RE: COMPANY REPORTS
EFFECTIVE: 6/1/—

An information analysis and report control program is hereby established. This program will:

—Provide all levels of management with the information needed for carrying out their assigned responsibilities;

—Provide all reports required by persons or organizations outside of the company;

—Prevent unnecessary duplication of information and proliferation of reports and determine the most economical and efficient means of preparing reports.

This responsibility is assigned to the Information Systems Unit which will:

—Establish reporting standards;

—Devise and maintain a system of information control;

—Review and approve all requests for establishing, changing, or discontinuing reports;

—Develop new methods of presenting information to management.

REPORT CATALOGUE

The first step in instituting a report control program is to establish a catalogue of existing reports. This catalogue should contain all formal, continuing company reports which relate to quantitative measurements. This would include the many external and historical reports produced in most companies as well as internal management reports.

The purpose of the catalogue is to indicate what information is now being supplied and to whom, and to spotlight duplication of information and reports. Each report is listed by number in the catalogue. The frequency of issue, the distribution schedule, a description of the contents, and the disposal data are shown. Catalogue entries may appear as follows:

- *Report No. 5501*—Major Contract Analysis

  Description: Booked Sales (per accounting inputs) vs. Report of work accomplished, sales for month and year-to-date by Major Contract, Division and Total Company.

  Frequency: Monthly

  Distribution Level: Business & Resource Planning Personnel supporting top level management.

  Controls: Available only to Finance Planning & Control Personnel with need to know upon approval by supervision—maintained in secured files.

  Disposition: Retained as permanent record in active department files for 2 years— to company data retention center after that.

- *Report No. 6300*—Sales Acquisition Costs

  Description: Analysis by category, program or product line of costs incurred in preparation of proposals and bids for additional contracts.

  Frequency: Monthly (on a year-to-date basis)

  Distribution Level: Middle & Top Level Management and their support personnel.

  Controls: Distributed only to prescribed individuals on approval of section supervisor—maintained in secured files.

  Disposition: Active files for 2 years. Data retention center thereafter.

A more comprehensive entry in a report catalogue is shown in Figure 7-1. All entries are supported by an up-to-date copy of the report which is on file in the report control unit. The completion of a report catalogue is a major step toward establishing control over company reports.

Report Numbering

Reports which are listed in the catalogue should be assigned a number in accordance with an established coding system. A report coding system should have the following characteristics:

- Flexibility to allow for expansion of categories and additional entries.
- Easy recognition and identification by persons working with only segments of the system.
- Simplicity of construction to include the least possible number of digits or characters.
- Efficient operation for machine processing.

There are a number of sophisticated numbering or coding systems in use. However, most companies continue to use a simple combination of letters and numbers. The letters designate the broad category such as a department. Numbers are assigned in sequence

1. TITLE OF REPORT: Company Status Report

2. PURPOSE OF REPORT: To provide an operations oriented analysis geared to current planning, which provides a basis for timely date-based management decisions. This emphasizes early identification of deviations on other planning elements, and recommendations for minimizing the impact of undesirable events. Key data concerning long term outlook and long term goals is used as a frame-work for near term decisions.

The Annual Presentation is a review of established goals and strategy. This is a ten year plan, concentrating on defining the goals and strategies of the total company, product line, business mix, acquisitions, foreign/domestic mix and other. It defines the basis, such as, environmental assumptions, product line contribution, and other considerations.

The review also covers:

A. Policies and goals for organizationally implementing strategy throughout the company - product line development, general capability development, planning, market/mission area studies.

B. Expected business results - projections of sales expenditures, business mix, and profitability.

C. What are the alternatives (for each product line) - comparison of probable resource requirements, business results, risks?

C. What are the probable consequences of these alternatives on the company character?

The Semi-Annual Presentation relates progress to the company plan.

Questions, such as:

1. Are we achieving what we expected - product line, diversification, penetration of foreign market, other - noting accomplishments or failures that are significant to the company's long range plan?

2. Are there significant changes in the external environment from what we expected - potential business threats, potential new areas of business opportunity, major program rephrasing, major governmental budgeting changes, etc?

3. Are there other factors that have affected progress?

4. What are the near term management decisions that will be required over the next 6 months, which will have a significant affect on long term results?

-2-

5. And Finally, a review of planned management actions of the last 6 months affecting long term results.

The Quarterly Presentation is a comparison of near term plans with actual performance on a total company basis. Emphasis is on short-term results of deviations from plans, the effect of the deviations on other planning elements, and recommendations for minimizing the impact of undesirable events.

The Monthly Presentation is a presentation by the Division General Managers who compare their actual performance with Near Term Plans with reference to the progress toward long range goals.

Each General Manager presents the comparisons once each quarter and reports the probable results of significant deviations and planned actions.

3. FREQUENCY & METHOD OF PRESENTATION: The analysis is distributed in report form on a monthly basis. This is followed by two (2) meetings with key middle/management personnel for review and discussion.

Finally, a meeting of top & middle management takes place for a complete review in viewgraph/35mm slide format which includes further statistical support and recommendations in light of current events.

4. CONTROL OF DISTRIBUTION: A listing of key management personnel concerned with the data is submitted to top management for approval and addition/changes, etc.

5. PHYSICAL DISPOSITION: Monthly reports are retained indefinitely as a source for research and other historical usage. 35mm slides are stored and controlled for ready access.

Figure 7-1. Comprehensive Report Catalogue Entry.

or in some logical manner to all reports of that department. For example "IS-320" would represent a report which is concerned with the Information Systems unit.

Because of cost accounting requirements most companies have assigned numbers to the various departments and work units. In this situation the number code is usually substituted for letters in designating the department. Thus "IS-320" becomes "180-320."

A report coding system may also indicate the number of copies prepared, date last revised, or level of security of information. To put all of this information in one code will result in an unwieldy system. The designer must decide what information is most important to his system.

REPORT AUTHORITY

After control is established by developing a complete, well documented catalogue of existing reports, a procedure must be devised for instituting new reports. The purpose of such a procedure is to prevent needless proliferation of reports and duplication of information, and to control the cost of preparing reports.

In establishing procedures for authorizing reports, a distinction must be made between continuing reports and one-time or demand reports which are needed immediately. The system must not delay getting the necessary information before the manager. Therefore, demand reports should be expedited, with only a check to be sure that the required information is not already available. Paper work, if necessary at all, should follow the preparation of the report.

Requests for a regular, continuing report should be handled according to an established review procedure. Figure 7-2 illustrates a form which can be used by operating managers to request information which they need in carrying out their responsibilities. A description of the information required and why it is needed are provided by the intended user. He is also asked to place a value on the information. While this is often difficult for the user to do, he is in a better position than anyone else to place a dollar value on information he needs.

The completed request for a report is forwarded to the unit in charge of the report control program where it is assigned to a staff man. The first step is to determine if the information is available in an existing report. If not, the analyst must find out if the basic, underlying data is being recorded at present and in what form. Can it be made available to the manager within the time restraints and what will be the cost? The staff analyst will have considerable contact with the "customer" as he makes his investigation.

Once the technical questions have been answered and the cost of the report established, the request is approved by the head of report control. The user is notified of the cost which will be charged to his account. Failure to charge for reports would result in the information processing unit being swamped with requests. Even with charging back the costs of reports, a system of priorities must be established to determine which request is processed first.

The report authorization process ought not to be so involved that legitimate requests for information are discouraged. The user-customer should be relieved of as much paper

NORTHWEST CRYOGENICS

REQUEST FOR CONTINUING REPORT

REQUESTED BY: TITLE:

DEPARTMENT: PHONE:

SHORT TITLE OF REPORT (SUGGESTED):

INFORMATION DESIRED (Use additional page if necessary):

PURPOSE OR USE OF INFORMATION:

REPORTS TO BE REPLACED IF ANY:

VALUE OF INFORMATION (Estimateif necessary):

WHEN NEEDED:_____   HOW OFTEN NEEDED_____

TO BE COMPLETED BY INFORMATION SYSTEMS

Development Costs: Continuing Cost:

No. Copies: No. Pages: Due Date:

Report No. Assigned: How to be Reproduced:

APPROVED: DATE: W/O No.:   Assigned to:

Figure 7-2. Request for Report.

work as possible. The burden of handling requests for information should rest with the report control group which was established for this purpose.

REPORT DESIGN

The design of accounting reports for management has been discussed and illustrated at length in preceding chapters. Certain generalizations, however, can be made regarding report design. A fundamental premise is that good report design begins at the time the underlying data is recorded and continues throughout the entire collection, summarizing, and interpretation process. Information cannot be synthesized from data which is not available.

Reports should indicate trends. Past figures and budgeted figures should be compared against actual amounts in such a way that the reader can readily see in which direction the operation is going.

Reports should evaluate results. A need for management intervention should be apparent from reading the report. Unusual circumstances which would tend to distort results should be noted.

Reports should reflect responsibility. A good reporting system focuses on the organization chart and shows how well each manager used the resources placed at his disposal. Each report should be part of a total reporting system. It should develop accountability for the operations of the company from the first-line supervisors up to the president.

Reports should be timely, complete, accurate and easily read. The accountant must use all resources at his command, from typewriters to visual aids to electronic computers, to meet these requirements. Reports should be simple yet present all the information needed to evaluate the situation and prescribe indicated action.

REPORT PREPARATION

Report preparation was also discussed in preceding chapters. Most reports today are prepared by two basic processes. In one process the information is developed from underlying data by manual methods. The information is then either presented in the original handwritten form or retyped for better appearance and readability. Although most members of higher management will not accept handwritten financial reports, one large electronics firm submits a majority (excluding those prepared by computer) of its reports in this format. Typed or handwritten reports may be prepared on custom forms or on stock paper.

The second process involves the use of tabulating equipment or electronic computers. Underlying data is massaged by machine and, for the most part, printed directly on custom forms or stock paper. The report is prepared in accordance with instructions in an internal machine program or from a wired board.

Too much reliance on computers can lead to trouble in the event of machine malfunction. Where computers are used extensively to prepare management reports, have provisions been made for backup facilities? If a typewriter breaks down, another is usually available. Many companies do not have computers with duplicate characteristics. Does the data processing unit have plans for preparing important management reports elsewhere in case of a breakdown?

REPORT REPRODUCTION

The method by which a report is to be reproduced will affect its design and preparation as well as its cost. The accountant should be aware of the various reproduction and copying techniques available. This section discusses some of the more widely used methods. Ordinarily, report reproducing requirements are only one of the factors involved in a company's decision to acquire reproduction or copying equipment. Often the accountant must work with whatever facilities are available.

Reproduction Methods

Offset printing is perhaps the most useful report reproduction technique at the accountant's disposal. Many companies have offset printing equipment which can be used for reproducing high quality, readable financial reports. This method is a relatively low cost process which will accept a combination of type faces, bold line rulings, shading and other techniques useful in producing eye-appealing reports. Offset masters are commonly made from special stencils prepared on a typewriter. A machine is available which will automatically make offset masters from any printed or typed document, thus reducing the time and cost of using offset printing. Offset printing is becoming the principal method of office reproduction for quality reports.

Mimeographing is a relatively high volume, low cost duplicating process. The process operates from a stencil which is usually "cut" by a typewriter with the ribbon shifted out of position. Stencils can also be cut by tabulating printers and can be drawn or written on by hand. Offset printing, where available, has displaced mimeograph equipment because of the higher quality finished product.

Ditto processing is a widely used, low cost method for duplicating reports. Ditto equipment and supplies are much less expensive than other reproduction techniques. The chief disadvantage of ditto is the low quality of reproduction. The usual purple copy is not well accepted by managers. Black, red and other colors are available but the readability is low.

Copying Methods

Electrostatic copiers are the most rapidly growing method of copying documents including reports. This is primarily because of a variation of the electrostatic process called xerograph which has swept the country recently. Xerography uses ordinary paper in the copying process. Images are formed on a revolving drum coated with selenium. These images are then transferred to regular bond paper. Some electrostatic processes do require special paper while others use liquid. Good copies may be obtained from electrostatic copiers. However, the equipment tends to require more than the average amount of maintenance. Electrostatic copiers are generally clean and easy to use, and are by far the largest sellers today.

Thermal processes have the advantages of (1) not using chemicals, (2) being simple and fast to operate, and (3) requiring minimum maintenance. However, copies can become brittle with age and excessive handling or darken if exposed to heat. Also, documents which have no metallic content cannot be copied.

Dual spectrum processes result in excellent reproductions. Their chief advantage is that copies may be made of pages in books or other bound volumes. This process uses two special papers and the equipment requires more than the usual amount of maintenance.

Dye transfer processes are most economical when more than four copies are needed. Dye transfer is basically a simplified photo process. Wet chemicals are used and a trained operator is required. The cost of a single copy is comparatively high.

Diffusion transfer processes make sharp, high contrast copies and the equipment is relatively inexpensive. It is a wet chemical process and copies must be dried after they emerge from the machine. Often the transfer sheet and finished copy must be pulled apart. A trained operator is ordinarily required.

Reproduction Costs

The cost of using the various reproduction and copying processes varies widely, depending primarily on the number of copies made monthly or yearly. For example, the cost of using copying machines on a per copy basis ranges from 5¢–45¢ at low volume usage (1,000 per month) to 1.3¢–5.2¢ at high volume usage (50,000 per month). The variances in cost at a given volume are largely a function of the quality of the product.

Assuming that a copy machine and reproducing equipment (offset) are both available, certain cost economy rules of thumb apply. From one to fifteen duplicates should be made on copying equipment. For more than fifteen copies, offset masters should be prepared. On new material, from one to six copies could be prepared by using carbon paper in the original typing.

REPORT DISTRIBUTION

Report distribution involves deciding who will receive reports and how and when they will receive them. These decisions are made at the time the report is instituted and become a part of the reporting system.

Who Should Receive Reports

There are two schools of thought regarding who should receive reports. One holds that anyone who wants a report should have it. It is maintained that reproduction costs are minor in relation to the cost of recording and handling data and of preparing the first copy of the report.

The other school takes the position that only those who can demonstrate that they need the information to carry out their responsibilities should have a report. It is maintained that most managers feel an obligation to read the reports which they receive. Thus, valuable time may be devoted to matters which do not directly affect the manager's responsibilities.

The authors support the latter view. If the reporting system is well designed, each report focuses on the resources assigned to each manager and his use of these resources. Generally, few others need this information. The individual manager's supervisor will need a summary of the important activities under his overall jurisdiction. Ordinarily, however, the supervisor does not require all the detail available to his subordinate managers. A supervisor who insists on seeing the details has less than complete faith in the abilities of his subordinates, and is not operating as a manager.

Determining who shall receive copies of a report should be based on a definite "need to know." Even this criterion involves subjective considerations which cannot be expressly stated. However, establishing a policy covering the distribution of information and reports is a valuable aid in guiding those charged with designing and preparing reports.

Distribution Cover Sheet

Some organizations provide a cover sheet for each management report. In addition to the name of the report and the period covered, the cover sheet lists the persons who receive copies. Higher management then knows who is receiving the report, and also distribution is facilitated.

In some instances, the cover sheet summarizes the information in the report and indicates any important problems or action required. Information about the retention period and date for renewing the report is also found on distribution cover sheets. The cover sheet in Figure 7-3 is a composite of a number of forms in use today.

Some organizations have found it necessary to verify that all those who are scheduled to receive a report actually do. In one company a system has been designed which requires that each report recipient initial a card when he gets the report. A check-off system is provided so that an undelivered report comes to the attention of the accounting department in time to supply another copy. Ordinarily, such elaborate systems are not necessary to assure delivery of reports.

Deliver Reports Promptly

Report timeliness depends on recording and massaging the underlying data promptly. These factors are incorporated into the system at the time it is designed. There is one other, perhaps mundane, but nevertheless often overlooked aspect to report timeliness. This involves procedures for reviewing and editing reports after they are produced and prompt delivery to the user.

One company designed a management reporting system which depended on the mail service for delivery of reports. These reports, which were prepared at a central data processing facility, were an important part of operations. The system was installed in July and worked well until winter weather tied up transportation in the Northeastern states. When the reports and even more important to the employees, the payroll checks, were held up, chaos reigned. Such conditions should be thought out beforehand.

Procedures should be established to deliver reports to the user as soon as they are produced. Don't leave the reports lying around the data processing room. It may be necessary to work accountants in the early morning hours to review and edit reports produced by data processing during the night. The regular company messenger service may be too slow for report delivery. Check this out. If management reports are worth producing, they are worth delivering on time.

Report Security

Internal management reports must not be made available to persons outside of the

REPRODUCTION, DISTRIBUTION AND CONTROL OF REPORTS

NORTHWEST CRYOGENICS

INDIRECT EXPENSE POOLS
ANALYSIS BY COST CENTER

Year to Date
As of June 30, 19_____

Distribution

Complete Sets

G. O. Brown
P. D. Beckman
A. S. Matson

Partial as Indicated

	Pages
C. L. Marvin	3-10
T. J. Allen - E. C. White	11-15
L. M. Hunt	11-20
D. W. Jensen - G. B. Niel	16-20
H. K. Bertram - R. A. Williams	21
D. T. Smith	22
P. A. Fong - A. P. High	
H. Y. Beatty	23
R. G. Tamaru	10-25

Prepared by
Information Systems
Operating Reports Section
Report No. 6521

Approved November
Destroy on Receipt of Next Report

Figure 7-3. Cover Sheet for Report.

company unless specifically authorized by higher management. This is perhaps the most widespread and uniform rule in connection with the distribution of reports. All employees should be instructed that requests from outsiders for reports and information must be cleared far up in the organization. Undoubtedly the need to safeguard confidential data requires such controls. Also, a good internal reporting system is, in itself, a competitive tool which most managements seek to protect.

REPORT RETENTION

The retention schedule for reports must be closely coordinated with the company's records management program. A decision as to how long a report should be kept depends on the retention schedule of the underlying data and related documents. Several guidebooks are available which set out retention programs.

Legal considerations are the controlling factor in company-wide records retention programs. Ordinarily, internal management reports are not concerned with legal requirements. However, the many external or historical reports which are part of the total reporting system do have legal implications. The company's legal department must be consulted in establishing a report retention schedule.

The report catalogue is an excellent place to start in establishing a report retention schedule. All reports and the data contained therein are described in the catalogue. A retention period should be established for each existing report, and for new reports at the time they are authorized. The date when the report may be destroyed should be noted on each recipient's copy. If ten file copies have been prepared, nine could be destroyed after a reasonable length of time and the tenth placed in a central file. Where the pyramid approach to reporting systems has been used, only the basic or lowest level report need be retained. However, many companies follow the practice of preparing one extra copy of all reports and sending it directly to a central file.

Most managers disregard last month's report when the new one arrives. Other managers pride themselves on keeping every report they ever received. Not only do these reports occupy space and become possible fire hazards, they also take the time of the manager who periodically peruses his file of stale reports looking for "interesting" information. Keep the manager looking into the future rather than into the past, by providing a report destruction timetable and insisting it be followed.

REPORT REVIEW

Even after a catalogue of reports has been developed and a system of authorizing new reports established, the reporting system does not operate indefinitely without proper review and evaluation. Conditions change and reports become obsolete. Personnel and organizational changes cause imbalances in the reporting system. Duplication occurs despite good report control procedures. A system of reviewing the usefulness of reports on a periodic basis should be established.

Many organizations require that every major report be reviewed at the end of a specified time, usually a year. The authority to produce the report is set to expire in twelve months and unless renewed, the report will be discontinued. Automatically stopping reports can lead to serious operational and interpersonal problems, however.

Before a continuing report is dropped, a positive review of its usefulness should be made. Ordinarily this is done by a questionnaire to all those on the distribution list. This questionnaire should accompany the report at the next distribution. In this manner the manager has the report before him and can better answer questions as to its usefulness. Figure 7-4 is a questionnaire which can be used in the report review process.

NORTHWEST CRYOGENICS

REPORT REVIEW

TO: DATE:

FROM: Information Systems

        Each year all company reports are reviewed to determine
whether they should be modified, discontinued or continued as is.
Your answers to the following questions and supplementary comments
will help determine what should be done with this report.

REPORT (ATTACHED): (Name)_____ No.:_____

PRODUCED: (Daily, Monthly, Yearly)   ANNUAL COST:_____

FROM YOUR STANDPOINT THIS REPORT IS:

    Vital ( )   Desirable ( )   Not Necessary ( )

REPORT NEEDS:

    Additional Information ( )   Less Information ( )
    Is Too Late for Action ( )

COMMENTS:

SIGNED:_____   DATE:_____

DEPARTMENT:_____

When complete return to ANNEX 8-339

Figure 7-4. Report Survey Form.

8

Computer
Prepared
Reports

Report preparation methods have gone far beyond pen, pencil and typewriter. The majority of reports in large companies today are prepared on electronic computers or off-line tabulating equipment. Therefore, any consideration of reporting systems must include a discussion of the methods and techniques used in making available to management computer stored information.

This and the next two chapters discuss ways in which the accountant can improve the usefulness of computer prepared reports. This chapter will be concerned primarily with how to improve the appearance and readability of conventional computer reports. Chapter 9 deals with one of the most difficult problems involved in computer reporting: How to satisfy management's need for "demand" or unscheduled reports. Chapter 10 will be concerned with three relatively new reporting media—the cathode ray tube, graphic displays, and computer connected microfilm systems. These will be discussed with illustrations as to how they are being used in computer reporting systems.

THE COMPUTER REVOLUTION

The computer has brought about a new dimension in information handling and communication. In the past management could not get enough data. Now management is inundated by the data which is made available. More and more, computers are being used to collect, classify, analyze and print out data. High speed printers are devoted to printing, often in an unstructured format, all the data in the file. There is, typically, little selectivity and no synthesis applied to computer stored data before it is printed out.

The trend in the preparation of reports by computer is, however, moving toward the predigestion of data and its automatic conversion into information. Computers are well able to select, summarize, sample, and classify data. As a matter of fact the computer was designed primarily for the internal manipulation of data. These machines were built to make mathematical computations requiring a small amount of input, a great amount of computations, and a small output. Thus the computer's basic limitation is input and output flexibility and speed. The increased use of computers for business applications has placed pressure on the manufacturers to develop peripheral devices to speed communication with the outside world.

Computer Output

Computers today communicate with persons primarily through high speed printers. Many computer printers can operate at up to 2,000 lines per minute, printing numeric only; 1,000 lines per minute, printing alphanumeric. More typically, printers move at somewhere around 600 to 800 lines per minute. Even at this rate, 16 pages of 66 lines per page can be printed in 15 minutes.

The primary method of printing is the use of a chain containing 50 to 60 characters. Chains with up to 120 characters are available. Usually chains with extra characters are used to print graphic or special output and are quite slow in relation to standard chains. One manufacturer offers 20 different chains for use on its printers. Chains on most computers may be changed with little difficulty.

Most computer printers encountered by the average accountant are quite limited as to format. The typical printer can print only uppercase letters, numbers and a few special symbols. It cannot print true lines. Printers are much slower than the computer itself and excessive printing often results in delaying the central processor.

Computer Paper

Paper used on high speed computer printers is fan folded and can be fed into the machine in one continuous stream. Computers ordinarily print six or fewer lines per inch, although it is not unusual to see eight lines per inch. Almost any size, color and shading is available. However, it is advisable to limit computer forms to two or three sizes. The most common sizes are 8½" x 11" and 14⅞" x 11".

Computer paper is classified by weight. If a firm, standup ledger card is desired, 24 lb. paper should be used. Ordinarily, when one to four copies are desired, the first copy is 16 lb. and the other 13. When five to eight copies are used, all should be 13 lb. If over eight copies are needed, then tissue type paper should be used. Practically speaking, with most high speed printers, only four copies can be prepared which will be acceptable for presentation to management. Of course, this varies by printer and quality of paper.

Paper is also specified by grade. The number of years the report is to be retained is a good method for determining grade:

Retention	Grade
1 to 5 years	100% sulfite
6 to 12 years	50% sulfite, 50% rag
Over 16 years	100% rag

Since it is almost always necessary to have more than one copy of a report, paper is available in as many copies as desired. Because carbon varies from manufacturer to manufacturer, it is best to obtain a sample and run it on the computer before purchasing large quantities. It is the accountant's responsibility to determine that all carbon copies can be read.

Paper can be purchased with horizontal or vertical shadings. Because of printing difficulties vertical shading is not found very often even on custom forms. Ordinarily, paper will have horizontal lines or shaded bands at a certain specified number per inch. Often six lines per inch with every other line shaded is used. Shading in this manner allows the reader to easily follow a line across the entire page, even if the form is crowded with data.

REPORTS FROM COMPUTER PRINTERS

Stock Forms

Computer reports are prepared on either stock or custom forms. When stock paper is used, the computer must print any headings and lines required by the report. Most computer printers cannot print a true line. It is fairly unusual for a computer to print vertical lines. There are also severe font limitations to most computer printers. Despite these deficiencies, the use of stock as opposed to custom forms is increasing.

There are major benefits to using stock forms. First, stock forms are less expensive to buy and to store. Less storage space is needed because there are not as many different forms. Delivery on stock forms is much faster than on custom forms. Also, the computer can go from report to report without the necessity of changing paper. One of the most important benefits of stock forms is that the report format may be changed by merely changing the computer program. Therefore, it is not necessary to discard large quantities of preprinted forms when reports are altered.

The most obvious disadvantage of stock forms is the limited format. It is not possible to effectively use lines and boxes to emphasize or spotlight certain information. The computer wastes time printing the headings on page after page. Headings are frequently abbreviated and often unintelligible. There are also some programming problems in having the computer print its own forms. And, finally, there never seems to be enough explanatory information supplied on reports using stock forms.

Typical Computer Reports

A review of representative reports prepared on computers gives one the impression that the person designing the report has as his primary objective the conservation of paper stock. Every possible printing space is used to get as much data on every page as is mechanically possible. The computer spews out unanalyzed, unstructured and too-detailed data. Such a report overwhelms its prospective reader. It causes him to work on getting the information he wants when he should be concentrating upon using the information. It is not unusual to find printouts, which are called reports, 6″ high with little or no reference data, few if any headings, and no more than three or four subtotals. Such

STORE 82

	TOTAL	O/O	NURSERYGDN	O/O	HDWHOMERP	O/O	LUMBLDGSUP	O/O
SALES	121425.17	100.00	52821.32	100.00	38321.92	100.00	30281.93	100.00
COSTSALES	68820.83	56.68	27223.52	51.53	22061.83	57.56	19535.48	64.51
GROSSPRFT	52604.34	43.32	25597.80	48.47	16260.09	42.44	10746.45	35.49
EXPENSES								
EXECUTIVE	2575.00	2.12	1250.00	2.36	800.00	2.08	525.00	1.73
ACCT REC	915.51	0.75	481.18	0.91	282.22	0.73	152.11	0.50
CREDIT DP	493.59	0.41	188.44	0.35	183.33	0.47	121.82	0.40
ACCT PAY	553.99	0.46	201.21	0.38	171.77	0.44	181.01	0.60
ADJUSTMT	274.97	0.23	133.31	0.25	88.89	0.23	52.77	0.17
FRINGE BF	1109.81	0.91	482.21	0.91	343.82	0.89	283.78	0.93
INSURANCE	153.33	0.13	92.11	0.17	38.41	0.10	22.81	0.07
ALTERATON	1333.41	1.10	321.99	0.60	211.21	0.55	800.21	2.64
RENT	5750.00	4.74	2500.00	4.73	1750.00	4.56	1500.00	4.95
TAXES	552.51	0.46	177.92	0.33	193.38	0.50	181.21	0.60
L/H/P	523.33	0.43	199.31	0.37	172.81	0.45	151.21	0.49
DEPRECIAT	506.69	0.42	220.00	0.41	164.82	0.43	121.87	0.40
PROM ADVT	2765.88	2.28	982.00	1.99	1001.88	2.61	782.00	2.58
MAIL ADVT	909.76	0.75	333.34	0.63	288.21	0.75	288.21	0.95
DISPLAYS	591.64	0.49	310.25	0.58	192.11	0.50	89.28	0.29
DEPT ADMN	4374.00	3.60	1800.00	3.40	1492.00	3.89	1082.00	3.57
PURCH SAL	2165.97	1.78	982.88	1.86	682.21	1.63	500.88	1.65
RECEIVING	418.58	0.34	161.78	0.30	156.52	0.41	100.28	0.33
INV COST	652.26	0.54	288.78	0.54	211.27	0.55	152.21	0.50
SALES SAL	14632.74	12.05	5821.18	11.02	4829.28	12.72	3982.28	13.15
SHIP SUPP	710.36	0.59	318.89	0.60	210.26	0.54	181.21	0.59
DRIVERSAL	2124.77	1.75	1082.21	2.04	521.28	1.36	521.28	1.52
TRK DEPR	204.00	0.17	102.00	0.19	51.00	0.13	51.00	0.16
TRK OPER	168.00	0.14	84.00	0.15	42.00	0.10	42.00	0.13
TOTAL EXP	44460.10	36.62	18514.99	35.07	14078.68	36.74	11866.43	39.19
NET PRFT	8144.24	6.71	7082.81	13.40	2181.41	5.69	1119.98CR	3.69

Figure 8-1. Typical Computer Prepared Report.

168

#35-13 (1/3)

To: MR. BRENTON

HALLWOOD CENTER STORE
INCOME AND EXPENSE BY DEPARTMENT

STORE 82

4 WEEK PERIOD ENDING JUNE 28

	TOTAL	O/O	NURSERYGDN	O/O	HDWHOMERP	O/O	LUMBLDG.SUP	O/O
SALES	$ 121425.17	100.00	$ 52821.32	100.00	$ 38321.92	100.00	$ 30281.93	100.00 ①
COSTSALES	68820.83	56.68	27223.52	51.53	22061.83	57.56	19535.48	64.51
GROSSPRFT	52604.34	43.32	25597.80	48.47	16260.09	42.44	10746.45	35.49 ②
EXPENSES								
EXECUTIVE	2575.00	2.12	1250.00	2.36	800.00	2.08	525.00	1.73
ACCT REC	915.51	0.75	481.18	0.91	282.22	0.73	152.11	0.50
CREDIT DP	493.59	0.41	188.44	0.35	183.33	0.47	121.82	0.40
ACCT PAY	553.99	0.46	201.21	0.38	171.77	0.44	181.01	0.60
ADJUSTMT	274.97	0.23	133.31	0.25	88.89	0.23	52.77	0.17
FRINGE BF	1109.81	0.91	482.21	0.91	343.82	0.89	283.78	0.93
INSURANCE	153.33	0.13	92.11	0.17	38.41	0.10	22.81	0.07
ALTERATON	1333.41	1.10	321.99	0.60	211.21	0.55	800.21 ②	2.64
RENT	5750.00	4.74	2500.00	4.73	1750.00	4.56	1500.00	4.95
TAXES	552.51	0.46	177.92	0.33	193.38	0.50	181.21	0.60
L/H/P	523.33	0.43	199.31	0.37	172.81	0.45	151.21	0.49
DEPRECIAT	506.69	0.42	220.00	0.41	164.82	0.43	121.87	0.40
PROM ADVT	2765.88	2.28	982.00	1.99	1001.88	2.61	782.00	2.58
MAIL ADVT	909.76	0.75	333.34	0.63	288.21	0.75	288.21	0.95
DISPLAYS	591.64	0.49	310.25	0.58	192.11	0.50	89.28	0.29
DEPT ADMN	4374.00	3.60	1800.00	3.40	1492.00	3.89	1082.00	3.57
PURCH SAL	2165.97	1.78	982.88	1.86	682.21	1.63	500.88	1.65
RECEIVING	418.58	0.34	161.78	0.30	156.52	0.41	100.28	0.33
INV COST	652.26	0.54	288.78	0.54	211.27	0.55	152.21	0.50
SALES SAL	14632.74	12.05	5821.18	11.02	4829.28	12.72	3982.28	13.15
SHIP SUPP	710.36	0.59	318.89	0.60	210.26	0.54	181.21	0.59
DRIVERSAL	2124.77	1.75	1082.21	2.04	521.28	1.36	521.28	1.52
TRK DEPR	204.00	0.17	102.00	0.19	51.00	0.13	51.00	0.16
TRK OPER	168.00	0.14	84.00	0.15	42.00	0.10	42.00	0.13
TOTAL EXP	44460.10	36.62	18514.99	35.07	14078.68	36.74	11866.43	39.19
NET PRFT	$ 8144.24	6.71	$ 7082.81	13.40	$ 2181.41	5.69	$ 1119.98CR	3.69

1. WE BUDGETED THIS ITEM AT 37.2%

2. REPAIR OF DAMAGE CAUSED BY VANDALISM

Figure 8-2. Edited Computer Report.

169

a report is of limited value to the manager and does no credit to the accountant responsible for its preparation.

In Figure 8-1, a typical computer report is shown. This report itself is not fully representative in that it is one page long rather than many pages. Note that the report contains a number of abbreviations which are difficult to understand. All in all, it does not present an attractive appearance because of the amount of data shown on the single page. Another deficiency is the fact that the form is not properly identified as to what it is, and for what period it was prepared. The date that the report was prepared is not shown, dollar signs are omitted, and there is no underlining. The percentages are carried to two decimal places and one is forced to wonder as to the value of this detail. Also, cents are included which could easily be omitted in such a report. Perhaps the most serious deficiency of all is that the report does not compare actual figures reported with either budgeted or prior periods. The one thing that can be said for this report is that it was easy to prepare. It certainly is not easy to use.

Manual Editing of Computer Reports

It is the responsibility of the accountant to improve to the extent possible the appearance and usefulness of reports prepared by the computer. Significant improvements may be made without changing the basic format of the report. Before any report leaves the accounting office it should be reviewed, edited, and approved by some responsible individual.

In Figure 8-2 the same report as shown in Figure 8-1 is used to demonstrate the value of editing. Editing can be done by a rubber stamp, or better, by a marking pencil. First, and most important, the report must be identified as to what it concerns and what period is covered. In this instance, the report is titled "Income and Expense by Department" and covers the four week period ending June 28. The report has a number assigned to it and indicates the date that it was prepared. The date of preparation is most important because, frequently, errors or additional information is discovered which requires subsequent reprints of the report. Should this occur, all previous runs should be located and destroyed. There is nothing more confusing than to have in one's possession two reports for the same period and not to know which is correct.

In the report of Figure 8-2, the name of the person who is to receive the report is written in the upper left-hand corner. Dollar signs and underlining have been added. The most important contribution of the editing process is that certain figures have been spotlighted for the attention of management. Two notes have been made which will help the manager understand the significance of the emphasized figures.

In dealing with a lengthy report, it is not always possible for the accountant to follow all of the editing techniques suggested above. With such reports, a summary should be prepared by computer or typewriter which is placed on top of the report. An index should also be prepared if the report is quite lengthy. The summary and the index should call attention to any items in the body of the report which deserve the manager's attention. Tabs should be used in the body of the report which tie in to the index and show the location of subtotals or of items requiring attention.

Computer Synthesis and Reports

The suggestions made in the preceding section for improving computer prepared reports can be instituted immediately by the accountant and do not require reprogramming of the computer. However, even extensive editing and review cannot make up for basically poor design techniques often encountered in computer reports. In these instances the best solution is to develop standards for computer prepared reports to be followed by data processing analysts and programmers.

The accountant should be responsible for establishing guidelines for report design. By sitting down with the systems design and programming personnel, he can develop attractive, clear, concise computer reports. In almost all cases, it is well worth the extra effort although the computer programmer may not always agree with this. But then he does not have to explain poorly designed, excessively cramped reports to management. The accountant does.

Figure 8-3 depicts essentially the same report shown in Figures 8-1 and 8-2 but with extensive reworking. This report was prepared entirely by computer. The first thing that comes to the reader's attention is the liberal spacing of the report making it initially more acceptable. This particular report is printed on the back side of stock paper to eliminate the distracting effect of four-to-the-inch lining. All necessary identification information is printed by the computer. Abbreviations and symbols are explained in the upper right-hand corner. In addition to the report number and the date, the number of copies of this report is also shown in the upper left-hand corner. Headings are clear and completely understandable. The greatest improvement in this report over Figure 8-1 is that actual percentages are compared to budgeted figures. Using this technique and the asterisks to denote deviations from standard, the store manager's attention is automatically called to problem areas. This report also eliminates excessive detail by dropping the cents and one decimal point in the percentage calculations. Dollar signs and underlining are also inserted by the computer.

Some detail has been omitted which appeared in Figure 8-1. At first it is often desirable to submit backup data for a summarized report. As soon as the manager becomes familiar with the new report, his reliance on the detail backup will diminish and it can be discontinued.

The report shown in Figure 8-4 is the same data found in 8-3 except that it has been recast to separate direct controllable expenses chargeable to specific departments from costs which are not under the control of the department managers. As was discussed elsewhere, this is a desirable improvement from the standpoint of controlling operations and fixing responsibility within the company.

Custom Forms

There is no doubt that good forms design is a great help in communicating information clearly. The flexibility of preprinted forms makes it much easier to add emphasis and to focus the reader's attention on important aspects of the report. Such reports are generally more attractive and more acceptable to the manager.

REPORT NO. 35-13 (7/3)
COPIES. 4
THIS COPY TO.

HALLWOOD CENTER STORE NO. 82
INCOME AND EXPENSE BY DEPARTMENT
4 WEEK PERIOD ENDING JUNE 28

BDT = BUDGETED COST AND PROFIT AS O/O SALES

**=10 O/O OVER BUDGET
*=20 O/O UNDER BUDGET

	TOTAL			NURSERY AND GARDEN			HARDWARE AND HOME			LUMBER AND BUILDING		
	AMOUNT	ACTUAL PERCENT	BDT	AMOUNT	ACTUAL PERCENT	BDT	AMOUNT	ACTUAL PERCENT	BDT	AMOUNT	ACTUAL PERCENT	BDT
SALES................	$121 423	100		$52 821	100		$38 321	100		$30 281	100	
COST OF SALES........	68 820	56.7	55	27 223	51.5	50	22 062	57.6	55	19 535	64.5	63
GROSS PROFIT ON SALES......	52 603	43.3	45	25 598	48.5	50	16 259	42.4	45	10 746	35.5	37
EXPENSES.												
ADMINISTRATION...........	6 076	5.0	5	2 828	5.4	5	1 908	5.0	5	1 340	4.4	5
FACILITIES...........	8 670	7.1	7	3 419	6.4	7	2 494	6.5	7	2 757	9.1	6**
SALES PROMOTION..........	8 641	7.1	7	3 426	6.5	7	2 974	7.8	7	2 241	7.4	7
PURCHASING............	3 236	2.7	4*	1 433	2.7	4*	1 050	2.7	4*	753	2.5	2**
SELLING...............	15 342	12.6	13	6 140	11.6	14	5 039	13.1	13	4 163	13.7	10**
DELIVERY..............	2 497	2.1	3*	1 269	2.4	3*	614	1.6	2*	614	2.0	2
TOTAL EXPENSES........	44 462	36.6	39	18 515	35.0	40	14 079	36.7	38	11 868	39.5	32**
PROFIT................	9 263			$ 7 083	13.5	10	$ 2 180	5.7	5			
LOSS..................	1 122									$ 1 122		
NET PROFIT............	$ 8 141	6.7	6								4.0	

172

Figure 8-3. Redesigned Computer Report on Stock Paper.

COPIES. 4

THIS COPY TO.

HALLWOOD CENTER STORE NO. 82

DEPARTMENTAL CONTRIBUTION TO INCOME
INCOME STATEMENT

4 WEEK PERIOD ENDING JUNE 28

BDT = BUDGETED COST
AND PROFIT AS O/O SALES

**=10 O/O OVER BUDGET
*=20 O/O UNDER BUDGET

	TOTAL COMPANY			NURSERY AND GARDEN			HARDWARE AND HOME			LUMBER AND BUILDING		
	AMOUNT	ACTUAL	PERCENT BDT	AMOUNT	ACTUAL	PERCENT BDT	AMOUNT	ACTUAL	PERCENT BDT	AMOUNT	ACTUAL	PERCENT BDT
SALES	$121 423	100		$52 821	100		$38 321	100		$30 281	100	
COST OF SALES	68 820	56.7	55	27 223	51.5	50	22 062	57.6	55	19 535	64.5	63
GROSS PROFIT ON SALES	52 603	43.3	45	25 598	48.5	50	16 259	42.4	45	10 746	35.5	37
DIRECT DEPARTMENTAL COSTS.												
ADMINISTRATION	-0-			-0-			-0-			-0-		
FACILITIES	7 920	6.5	6	3 051	5.8	6	2 625	6.9	6**	2 244	7.4	6**
SALES PROMOTION	8 641	7.1	7	3 426	6.5	7	2 974	7.8	7	2 241	7.4	7
PURCHASING	-0-			-0-			-0-			-0-		
SELLING	10 130	8.3	10	4 621	8.7	11	3 095	8.1	4	2 414	8.0	12
DELIVERY	2 497	2.1	3*	1 269	2.4	3*	614	1.6	2*	614	2.0	2
TOTAL DIRECT COSTS	29 188	24.0	26	12 367	23.4	27	9 308	24.3	19	7 513	24.8	27
CONTRIBUTION—BY DEPARTMENT	23 415	19.3	19	$13 231	25.0	23	$6 951	18.1	26*	$3 233	10.7	10
INDIRECT COSTS.												
ADMINISTRATION	6 076	5.0	5									
FACILITIES	750	0.6	1*									
SALES PROMOTION	-0-											
PURCHASING	3 236	2.7	4*									
SELLING	5 212	4.3	3**									
DELIVERY	-0-											
TOTAL INDIRECT COSTS	15 274	12.6	13									
NET PROFIT	$ 8 141	6.7	6									

Figure 8-4. Contribution to Income Report.

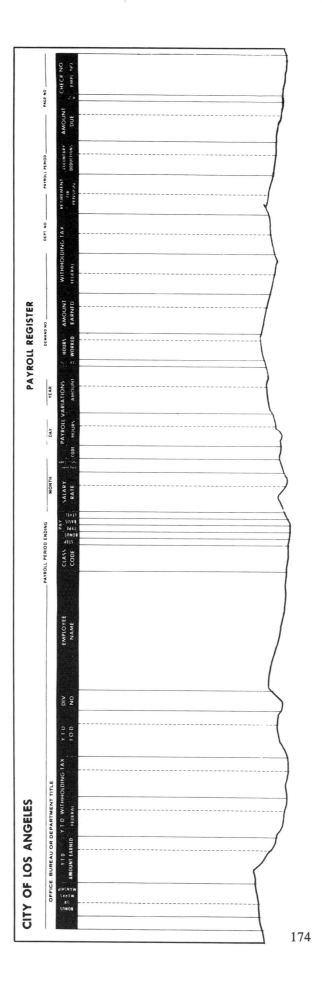

Figure 8-5. Use of White on Black Printing.
Courtesy City of Los Angeles.

174

CARD CODES

CLASS	JVI	CC AORD DE	TYPE OF DOCUMENT AND TRANSACTION
4		15	Internal Demand
9		15	Cash Demand Transfer Credit
3		17	Cash Deposit
5		36	Checks Paid
1		37	Correction Decrease Cash Demand
1		39	Cash Demand
2		47	Correction Decrease Internal Demand
2		49	Internal Demand
7		87	Coupon Adjustment
7		89	Coupons
7		97	Bond Adjustment
7		99	Bonds
8		47	Correction Decrease Cash Demand Transfer
8		49	Cash Demand Transfer

Journal Voucher - Credit

CLASS	JVI	CC	TYPE OF DOCUMENT AND TRANSACTION
6	01	27	Budget Allocation (Receiving Fund)
6	02	27	Add. Appropriation (Receiving Fund)
6	12	27	Adj of Add Approp (Receiving Fund)
6	13	27	Adj of Budget Alloc (Receiving Fund)
6	20	27	Transfer of Funds (Receiving Fund)
6	21	27	Transfer Received from Reserve Fund
6	22	27	Loans Received from Reserve Fund
6	23	27	Reserve Fund Receipt of Repayment of Loan
3	35	27	Adjustment Decrease of Cash Deposit
5	39	27	Adj. Increase of Demands/Checks Paid
3	45	27	Adjustment Increase of Cash Deposit
4	55	27	Adjustment Decrease Internal Demand Dep.
9	55	27	Adj Decr of Cash Dem Transfer Credit
6	63	27	Trans Adj Canc Prior Yr Dem (Recvng Fund)
4	65	27	Adjustment Increase Internal Demand Dep.
9	65	27	Adj Incr of Cash Dem Transfer Credit
6	69	27	Canc of Prior Year Demand
6	74	27	Trans Adj Canc Prior Yr Dem (Dsbrsg Fund)
6	78	27	Reinstatement of Prior Year Canc

Journal Voucher - Debit

CLASS	JVI	CC	TYPE OF DOCUMENT AND TRANSACTION
6	02	29	Adj of Add Approp (Disbursing Fund)
6	03	29	Adj of Budg Alloc (Disbursing Fund)
6	11	29	Budget Allocation (Disbursing Fund)
6	12	29	Add Appropriation (Disbursing Fund)
6	30	29	Transfer of Funds (Disbursing Fund)
6	31	29	Transfer fr Reserve Fund to Another Fund
6	32	29	Loans by Reserve Fund to Another Fund
6	33	29	Repayment of Loans to Reserve Fund
1	35	29	Adjustment Increase Cash Demand
5	38	29	Adj Decrease of

Column headers (form body): MO | DAY | YR | VENDOR NAME OR DESCRIPTION | CLASS | JVI | CARD CODE | DOCUMENT NUMBER

Figure 8-6. Use of Codes on Report Form. Courtesy City of Los Angeles.

175

Custom forms cost more. But keep in mind that the cost of paper is only about 4% of the total cost of preparing a report. Often by increasing the cost to, say, 8%, it is possible to increase the usability of a report by as much as 50%. The first step in purchasing custom forms is to find a reliable supplier. Their staff can be of great assistance in forms design and in guiding the purchaser away from certain pitfalls. Some important factors to keep in mind in purchasing custom forms are the limitations of bursting and deleaving equipment, binding and filing equipment, and copy and duplicating equipment. Do not buy a form that cannot be processed by your existing equipment.

Forms Design

Forms should be arranged for the convenience of a reader and not the computer. However, watch out for sloppy forms design which wastes machine time. To the extent possible, all forms should be standardized throughout the company. The form number, the company name and the date and other common information should be located in the same portion of the report. As it becomes necessary to modify reports, do not change any more information than is necessary. Readers become familiar with a certain format and are irritated when it is deviated from unnecessarily. On the other hand, when major changes are made in a report, it is a good idea to alter the entire format so that the reader knows that he cannot compare this report with previous reports.

Study the objectives of the report before beginning the actual design. Do not make report forms overly complicated. Forms should be kept simple by the judicious use of boxes, rulings and borders. These techniques should be used to add emphasis and to help distinguish between items. Alternating between heavy and faint lines can be used very effectively. Avoid the excessive use of gimmicks such as stars, elaborate art work, and arrows. But use these techniques where they can be effective. In designing forms, use the layout sheets supplied by form suppliers which have computer print positions marked off. This will give a fair idea of how the final form will be spaced on the paper.

Color in custom made forms should be used sparingly and for a purpose. The usual color scheme is, of course, black ink on white paper. Very effective use can be made by reversing this and using white ink on black as shown in Figure 8-5. Other colors cost considerably more but this should not be a deterrent if color can be used effectively. The most common use of color is to make each copy a different pastel shade which will denote the distribution of the report.

It is desirable to preprint as much data as possible on custom forms. This is one of the major advantages over stock paper. Column headings can be printed in much smaller print than if they were printed on the computer. Notice how many print positions would be required if the computer had to print out the headings in Figure 8-5. Sufficient room should be allowed on reports for signatures, for handwritten items and for remarks by executives. While computer printers use 1/6″ and 1/8″, spacing arrangements for handwriting must be at least 1/3″.

Another significant advantage of custom forms is that it is possible to use short carbon or spot carbon to omit the printing of the same information on all copies. This can be a very useful technique where certain information is restricted as to its distribution.

It is frequently impossible to avoid the use of abbreviations and codes in reports.

DEPARTMENTAL EXPENSES

Mo. Yr. ____/____

Dept. _____ Dept. Name _____

Account No.	Account Name	Current Month			Year-To-Date			Remarks
		Actual	Budget	Variance	Actual	Budget	Variance	

Figure 8-7. Use of Custom Forms for Reports. Courtesy Philip Hano Company.

177

FC	No.	Date								
FC	0121	12-23-66		PREV BALANCE						77.77 77.77
FC	0129	12-30-66		PREV BALANCE				8.0 8.0		77.77 77.77
FC	0130	12-30-66		PREV BALANCE						
FC	0132	12-30-66		PREV BALANCE				11.5 11.5		77.77 77.77
FC	0133	12-30-66		PREV BALANCE				7.0 7.0		77.77 77.77
FC	0134	12-30-66		PREV BALANCE		030	R13	8.0	31.5	55.55 77.77
FC	0134	01-07-67	9999			030	R13	2.0		55.55
FC	0134	01-09-67	9999			030	R13	8.0		55.55
FC	0134	01-09-67	9999			060	R13	8.0		55.55
FC	0134	01-09-67	9999			030	R13	.5		55.55
FC	0134	01-10-67	9999			060	R13	1.5		55.55
FC	0134	01-10-67	9999			020	R13	1.5		55.55
FC	0134	01-10-67	9999			030	R13	4.0		55.55
FC	0134	01-11-67	9999		0412		R24	41.5		55.55
FC	0135	12-30-66		PREV BALANCE					73.0	77.77
FC	0135			PREV BALANCE				21.0 21.0		77.77 77.77
FC	0136	12-30-66		PREV BALANCE				5.0 5.0		77.77 77.77
FC	0137	12-30-66		PREV BALANCE						
FC	0138	12-30-66		PREV BALANCE				10.5 10.5		77.77 77.77
FC	0144	01-06-67		PREV BALANCE						
FC	0145	01-06-67		PREV BALANCE						
FC	0146	01-06-67		PREV BALANCE						
FC	0147	01-06-67		PREV BALANCE				5.5		77.77

Figure 8-8. Computer Report Without Headings or Lines.
Courtesy Zerox Corporation.

178

WORK ORDER ANALYSIS — DATE 2/10/67 — PAGE 2

XEROX CORPORATION

PROD. CODE	WORK ORDER	DATE	EMPL NO.	ENTRY	MACH. CODE	OPER. CODE	JOB CODE	TEMP. CODE	ELAPSED HOURS CURRENT	ELAPSED HOURS TO DATE	LABOR COST CURRENT	LABOR COST TO DATE
FC	0121	12-23-66		PREV BALANCE								77.77
FC	0129	12-30-66		PREV BALANCE						8.0		77.77
FC	0130	12-30-66		PREV BALANCE						8.0		77.77
FC	0132	12-30-66		PREV BALANCE						11.5		77.77
FC										11.5		77.77
FC	0133	12-30-66		PREV BALANCE						7.0		77.77
FC										7.0		77.77
FC	0134	12-30-66		PREV BALANCE	0412					31.5		77.77
FC	0134	01-07-67	9999			030	R13		8.0		55.55	
FC	0134	01-09-67	9999			030	R13		2.0		55.55	
FC	0134	01-09-67	9999			030	R13		8.0		55.55	
FC	0134	01-09-67	9999			060	R13		8.0		55.55	
FC	0134	01-10-67	9999			030	R13		.5		55.55	
FC	0134	01-10-67	9999			060	R13		1.5		55.55	
FC	0134	01-10-67	9999			020	R13		1.5		55.55	
FC	0134	01-11-67	9999			030	R24		4.0		55.55	
FC			9999						41.5	73.0	55.55	
FC	0135	12-30-66		PREV BALANCE						21.0		77.77
FC										21.0		77.77
FC	0136	12-30-66		PREV BALANCE						5.0		77.77
FC										5.0		77.77
FC	0137	12-30-66		PREV BALANCE								
FC	0138	12-30-66		PREV BALANCE						10.5		77.77
FC										10.5		77.77
FC	0144	01-06-67		PREV BALANCE								
FC	0145	01-06-67		PREV BALANCE								
FC	0146	01-06-67		PREV BALANCE								
FC	0147	01-06-67		PREV BALANCE						5.5		77.77

Figure 8-9. Size Reduced and Headings and Lines Added by Overlay. Courtesy Zerox Corporation.

Figure 8-6 shows a report which makes extensive use of codes and has the codes printed with their meaning to the left of the report. A report involving complicated codes should never be prepared without an index of this type.

Figure 8-7 is an example of a well designed report form which effectively uses vertical shading and dark and light lines to set off information. The headings and captions are easily read and a space is provided for remarks by the recipient. The report form is not complicated nor is it overburdened with special characters. (Certain identification data has been removed at the request of the supplier.) Other report formats may call for more sophisticated forms design.

Pros and Cons of Custom Report Forms

Custom forms generally look better and command more attention of the reader. They permit emphasis and spotlighting of certain important items. Captions and headings are neat and readable; there are fewer abbreviations. It is actually possible to place more information on a well designed custom form than on a well designed form using stock paper. Programming is somewhat easier using custom forms and the supplier will often do your forms design work for you. In large quantities, custom forms are not too much more expensive than stock paper. However, in quantities of fewer than 5,000, custom forms are quite expensive.

As to disadvantages, in addition to increased cost, custom forms require more storage space and more setup time on the computer. Usually, there is a long lead time when purchasing custom forms. When a report is changed, all related forms are made obsolete. This can be a real deterrent to the use of custom report forms.

REPRODUCTION OF COMPUTER REPORTS

There are certain problems in preparing computer reports for management use. It is difficult to print enough clear copies for proper distribution. Very few managers will accept a report that is past the fourth copy. There is, no doubt, an ego problem involved in handing a manager a copy of a report when someone else has received the original. Often additional computer runs are required to duplicate reports. Also, computer reports with a number of copies require deleaving and bursting. Finally, large 15″ x 11″ forms are difficult to handle.

Xerox is marketing a duplicating machine which can aid in eliminating these problems. This machine, known as the 2400-IV, will accept the original of computer reports directly from the printer, reduce the report to 8½″ x 11″ size and collate the product ready for binding. Forty copies per minute can be made. A report printed on 15″ x 11″ continuous fan fold paper can be produced into 20 sheets of a 60 page report, 8½″ x 11″ size, within a half-hour period. Extra copies can be made of summary pages or other specified pages.

Another advantage of this particular process is that transparent overlays may be used to convert reports prepared on stock paper to custom form reports. Figure 8-8 shows the original copy of a computer run without headings, lines, or boxes. Figure 8-9 is the same report processed through the reproducing equipment with the use of an overlay. The dramatic improvement in quality can well be worth the cost of this equipment. At the present time there is only one manufacturer marketing this type of equipment. Undoubtedly there will be other machines appearing on the market soon.

BINDING OF COMPUTER REPORTS

The way in which computer reports are bound can influence their usefulness. The proper binding of reports should take into consideration who will be using it and how they will be using it. The size and type of binding should be standardized. Binders for computer reports can be purchased in any size but are, of course, less expensive for the standard size. Binders are either hard back or flexible back, depending upon the desires of the user. Computer reports are usually bound at the top or at the left side. If top binding is selected, no bursting of continuous form paper is necessary.

Top management should be supplied with reports in loose-leaf form so that the new reports may be easily added by assistants and old reports removed so that great bulk does not accumulate. Binders present an excellent opportunity to use colors. Certain types of reports, such as sales reports, may be bound in the same color binders or the reports of each division may be bound in different colors. Whether or not color is used, each binder should have on its face a label indicating the nature of the report.

All binders should use tabs to separate reports by period or by department or whatever reasonable division is called for. Because most computer paper is not of high quality, it has a tendency to tear easily. Therefore, insert sheets should be used and tabs attached to them. Reports for different time periods are sometimes printed on different colored paper making it easier for the manager to find the period desired.

9

Time-Responsive or "Demand" Computer Reports

Before the XYZ Corporation automated its records the Sales Manager received, 15 days after it was needed, a report on sales by district and by sub-district. There was little detail involved in the report. It was frequently inadequate for the Sales Manager's purposes. He could, however, supplement the report by a call to the bookkeeping department. To be sure, fulfilling the request meant a certain amount of scurrying around, but within a matter of hours the information he desired was placed on his desk.

Then the XYZ Corporation automated its records. On the third day of the month, the Sales Manager receives a four-inch thick report of the detail of all sales in all the districts. He is, for the time being, quite pleased. One day he decides that he needs additional information on which to make an important decision. His phone call to the bookkeeping department is transferred to the data processing section. Within a few minutes, a young man from the systems and programming section arrives in his office with a three page form to be completed. During the interview, the Sales Manager is questioned very carefully as to why he needs the report, what he is going to do with it, and whether he will ever need the report again. The young man leaves. Two days later the Sales Manager receives a form requiring his signature which states that he has requested a special computer report, that the cost of the report will be $2,000 and that it will be delivered to him within three weeks. The Sales Manager quite understandably develops a negative attitude toward "automated" reporting systems.

The hypothetical situation described above is more the rule than the exception in most companies which use computers. Operating people become frustrated at their inability to get reasonably quick answers to questions. They tend to develop their own "unofficial" system which is more responsive to their needs. As a result the cost of record keeping in the organization increases substantially.

183

Reason for Inflexibility in Computer Reports

Computer systems are designed only after a careful analysis of known information needs. However, once the system has been programmed and is operational it is extremely difficult to produce special or demand reports. On the other hand, managers are simply not able to predict in advance what information they will need in the future. For example, for the purpose of making some personnel transfers, the Vice President–Marketing wants to know the sales figures for the last twelve months for the four Southwestern states. He wants this information by salesmen ranked according to the percentage of quota achieved, age, and length of time with the company. The Vice President could not, nor should he be expected to, have anticipated that he would need this information at the time the system was designed.

The most serious, persistent and difficult problem in dealing with computers is how to inject flexibility and timeliness into the reporting system. Everyone, from the president to the foreman, is machine paced in the sense that he must wait for regular scheduled reports. It is the responsibility of the accountant to design a system for producing unpredictable, "demand" reports which are needed by management to operate the enterprise. The fact that the data is on computers does not negate the accountant's responsibility.

This chapter discusses what steps are necessary to provide computer reports which are time responsive. The material is, of necessity, somewhat technical and involves certain computer systems concepts. Mastery of this chapter is, however, a requisite for the accountant who wishes to improve computer reporting in his organization.

Information Retrieval

The problem from a management reporting standpoint is how to make data stored within the computer responsive to the manager's demands for information. To state the problem another way: how can we get information out of the computer on a timely, efficient manner? How to get information out is dependent entirely upon how data was put into the computer. Thus, the design of such a system begins at the planning of the entire computer system and involves file establishment and file maintenance as well as a retrieval system. Information retrieval is the name given to this process.

The term "information retrieval" is used here in a somewhat different context than is ordinarily the case. Typically, information retrieval is an automatic library function of searching for and retrieving reference material for a given profession or field. Information retrieval systems are under development for the legal, medical, and scientific fields. Used here, information retrieval has to do with the ability of managers to have quick access to operating data on a flexible, as needed, basis.

Computer Files

Files are the key to computer based systems and to information retrieval. Files are the source of all information which is in possession of the system. Usually one will encounter customer files, employee files, vendor files, inventory files and many others. Files are made up of records such as customer's data or employee's data. Each record is composed of fields. For an example, the fields of an employee record would include name, address, employee number, salary, position and others as required by the system. These fields contain all the data known to the system about a record.

CHARACTERISTICS OF BUSINESS INFORMATION RETRIEVAL SYSTEMS

Obviously, data which can be extracted from a file at any cost is limited to the data which was put into the file. However, data which can be extracted quickly and efficiently is dependent on *how* the data was placed into the file. We are thus led to consider the factors involved in designing and operating a file for the retrieval of business information. There are three characteristics of an information retrieval system for business data: (1) prior planning of systems and file design, (2) data dictionary or file dictionary, (3) supporting software.

Planning for Information Retrieval

First, it should be understood that it is not possible to design a system which answers all the possible questions which a manager would have. Each transaction has many attributes, only a limited number of which are recorded and included in the file. To include all the attributes of data would be far too expensive. A more reasonable objective must be established.

There are two basic approaches to designing a business information retrieval system. One approach is to attempt to anticipate the nature of management's questions and to construct a file with records in approximately that order. Alternatively, and more realistically, indexes for anticipated questions can be developed. Obviously, this approach can only be used where questions can be reasonably anticipated. Also, it is best used in those situations where additions and deletions to the file are low (low file maintenance) compared with the number and complexity of questions (high retrieval ratio).

The second approach is to avoid anticipating the type of questions. In this situation, a record by record search is required for each question. This approach may be used where few special requests are anticipated and their nature cannot be known in advance. The main purpose of such a system is to account for additions and delineations, hence to update the file. Most systems in use today are of this type.

Sequential Versus Random Access Memory

The most important decision in designing a system responsive to management's needs for information rests on whether sequential (usually magnetic tape) or random access memory is to be used. A tape system is less expensive not only to design but to operate. A tape system can be used where 24-hour or limited response is suitable and ordinarily only one file is searched. Random access equipment should be used if immediate and complex searches are called for.

In a sequential system, the computer must look at (access) all the records in the file when a search is made. Then the computer must look at certain fields within each record. Efficient field arrangement is mandatory. Also, fixed length records are often required which many consider to be a handicap.

To illustrate this system, assume that management in a factory located in New Mexico needs an older foreman to train new workers. The foreman must be, among other things, Spanish speaking. The records in the employee file will look like this:

> Employee Number
> Name
> Address
> Sex
> Age
> Salary
> Position
> Date Started
> Foreign Language

The computer must look at each employee record. On each record the computer must look at the position field, the foreign language field, and the age field. Assume there are 30,000 employees and 8 foremen who speak Spanish. The machine must look at a great number of records and fields to find those persons in the proper category.

In random access systems, the computer does not need to access all records. Ordinarily, there is an index for every significant field which greatly reduces the amount of work which must be done by the computer. In the above example, assume that there are 138 foremen. The men in this position will be listed in an index of foremen. The computer merely has to go to the index and look at 138 records rather than 30,000. Note, however, that when a new foreman is added not only must his record be changed but all the indexes which concern him.

File Dictionary for the Manager

Data retrieval is the selection of records from a file according to a set of criteria applied to a field or fields. In a business retrieval system each manager must know what files are available, what records are in the files, and what fields are in the records. A dictionary of files, records, and fields is supplied to the manager. From the dictionary, the manager develops questions in the form of "and," "or," "greater than," "equal to" or "less than."

For example, a question might read: Print out the names of all female employees who have been with the company more than ten years *or* are 50 years old *and* make at least $900. The manager can specify the sequence of information. He may desire that all employees over 50 be listed before those under 50 but with 10 years' experience with the company. If desired, arithmetical functions may be performed. For example, it is possible to subtract the length of service from the age to determine the date the employee began with the company.

In contrast to the story at the beginning of this chapter, the manager making this request does not need the assistance of a programmer. In a well-planned business information retrieval system, his secretary can perform the necessary "programming." The manager's request is processed by the computer, usually at a specified time during the day. The next morning his special report will be on his desk, no more than 24 hours after he made the request.

Business information retrieval systems with less than 24-hour response time for "demand" reports are rare. Most managers accustomed to a three week response time are quite satisfied with one day "turn around." Theoretically, in real-time systems the manager has the potential of interacting directly with the computer and receiving immediate answers to requests for special reports. However, most experts agree that it will be some time in the future before the manager can sit down at a console and ask unstructured questions to which he will receive an immediate reply.

Software

The operation of a data processing system responsive to the information needs of management involves more than planning and a data dictionary. The third factor is computer software to maintain the file and process retrieval requests. There are three possible sources of such software. Many manufacturers supply information retrieval software with their computer. There is, however, a wide difference in effectiveness. Usually manufacturer's software is too general and needs to be tailored to the customer's own system. Independent software houses are available which will develop a system for the specific needs of the company. Such systems are often costly and require maintenance by the customer's own people. A company can develop its own information retrieval software if capable people are available. However, such a system requires better than average programming.

Examples of "Demand" Reports

One of the best generalized software support systems for business information retrieval has been developed by Scientific Data Systems. This system is oriented to the needs of management and is quite easy to use. The SDS system, called MANAGE, is described in the following illustrations.

Example 1: The personnel manager of the XYZ Corporation is making a study of the firm's wage and salary structure. As part of that study, he needs a report that includes data on certain employees who meet these specific criteria: (1) they are assigned to Department 543, 557, or 559; and (2) they have five or more years of employment with the company. He also needs the same information on employees assigned to Department 800 whose salary is $12,000 or more a year. The desired report is to consist of the following information as column headings for the selected employees: department number, salary, seniority, education, name, and title. The report is to be organized so that each entry is in sequence by department number, within department by salary amount in descending order, and for like salary amounts alphabetically by name of

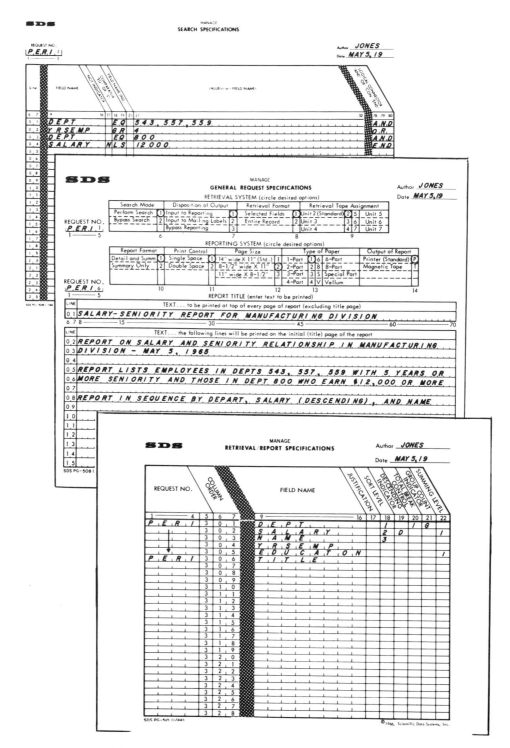

**Figure 9-1. MANAGE Specification Sheets.
Courtesy Scientific Data Systems.**

SALARY-SENIORITY REPORT FOR MANUFACTURING DIVISION

DEPART MENT	SALARY	NAME	EMPL OYME NT	EDU CAT ION	JOB TITLE
543	16,000	IBBAS, SAUL A	9	17	DEPT MGR
	15,000	DIXON, MERVAL G	8	16	SECT MGR
	15,000	WALLER, MORTIMER I	8	16	SECT MGR
	14,200	GALT, JOHN L	6	16	GRP LDR
	13,700	TILLOTSON, WID	6	16	SEN ENGR
TOTAL BY DEPT	73,900			81	
COUNT BY DEPT	5				
557	17,000	PRUDHOMME, RAOUL A	10	16	DEPT MGR
	15,500	GRETEL, HANSEL A	14	16	SEN ENGR
	11,400	RAY, BENTLEY C	8	14	GRP LDR
	10,200	BENTLEY, C RAY	6	12	INSP
	9,800	NEWMAN, ALFRED E	6	12	INSP
TOTAL BY DEPT	63,900			70	
COUNT BY DEPT	5				
559	14,000	NOTH, FISBIF H	7	16	DEPT MGR
	13,500	STANGLEY, CHARLES L	6	14	SEN ENGR
	11,000	BOMBERGER, PETER H	6	14	GRP LDR
	9,600	WINK, HORACE	6	12	FOREMAN
	5,800	POTTER, STIG H	8	4	JANITOR
TOTAL BY DEPT	53,900			60	
COUNT BY DEPT	5				
800	22,500	PASQUALI, PHILLIP A	13	14	DEPT MGR
	18,700	GUNDERSON, BEASLEY J	8	16	SEN ENGR
	15,500	BOGGIO, SILVIO L	10	16	GRP LDR
	15,500	STONE, EMORY M	9	16	GRP LDR
	13,000	SETTER, BART P	7	16	GRP LDR
	12,500	MC DALL, FINIAN G	6	16	GRP LDR
TOTAL BY DEPT	97,700			94	
COUNT BY DEPT	6				

Figure 9-2. "Demand" Report.
Courtesy Scientific Data Systems.

employee. Salaries and years of education are to be totaled by department, and the report is also to contain an item count for each department.

Available to the personnel manager is an Employee Master File on magnetic tape. The file contains employee information including data such as:

COLUMN HEADING	FIELD NAME
Employee Number	EMPNO
Name	NAME
Date of Birth	BIRTHDTE
Place of Birth	BIRTHPL
Education	EDUCATON
Department	DEPT
Salary	SALARY
Job Title	TITLE
Employment	YRSEMP

This file is in sequence only by employee number. The problem is first to find the employees meeting the specific criteria, then rearrange the data into the required sequence and format, accumulate the necessary totals, and print the results.

Method of Solution. To state the problem in terms that the computer can understand, the personnel manager need only fill out three specification sheets for MANAGE: (1) General Request Specifications, (2) Search Specifications, and (3) Retrieval/Report Specifications. (The procedure for filling out these forms can be learned in a few hours at most.) A key-punch operator converts this information to punched cards, which are then fed into the computer along with the MANAGE program tape. The computer automatically assembles the desired information, which is then printed out by a line printer under computer control. The MANAGE specification sheets as completed by the personnel manager are shown in Figure 9-1. The computer generated report is shown in Figure 9-2.

Example 2: During March the XYZ Corporation conducted market tests in Philadelphia and San Francisco on a particular product. The product in question, 14X27A, was sold at a lower price in the 1-, 5-, and 10-lb. sizes in those two markets during March only.

The sales manager wants to compare sales results of two offices (New York and Los Angeles) selling 14X27A at the regular price with sales results in the two test cities. For added control, sales information for all four offices during April is also desired.

The report is to be in summary form and should show the number of orders, the number of units, and the net revenue for each size, arranged first by month and then by sales office.

The only source containing the necessary data is the Invoice Master Tape File. This consists of the record of delivered sales, and the sequence of entries is by invoice number. For each invoice, it contains:

COLUMN HEADING	FIELD NAME
Invoice Number	INVNO
Date of Invoice	INVDATE
Customer Number	CUSTNO
Sales Office	SALEOFF
Salesman Number	SALENO
Gross Invoice	GRAMT
Net Invoice	NETAMT
Commodity Number	COMNO
Quantity	QTY
Size	SIZE
Description	DESC
Unit Price	UNITPR
Net Price	NETPR

As in the previous example, the sales manager prepares his request for the computer by writing it in the format provided on the three MANAGE specification sheets. Figure 9-3 shows how he stated his request on these sheets. A portion of the resulting report, as printed out by the line printer, appears in Figure 9-4.

Information retrieval systems for business involve much more than is presented here. The problems of file establishment, file maintenance, and sorting are immense. Insertion, deletion, and alteration of data are major programming problems. However, systems responsive to manager's needs are now in existence. Management will no longer tolerate the inflexibility of traditional data processing systems. Accountants should be familiar with what can be accomplished in this area and with the cost involved. Only the management will know if a responsive, flexible system is worth the cost. There are few quantitative guidelines.

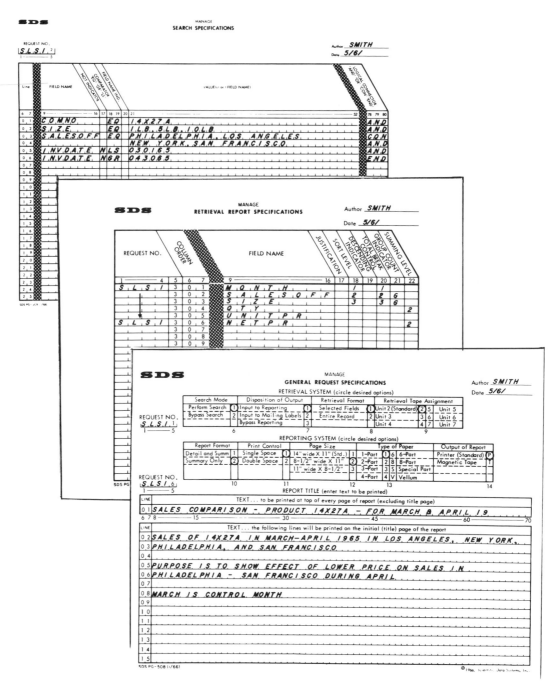

**Figure 9-3. MANAGE Specification Sheets.
Courtesy Scientific Data Systems.**

SALES COMPARISON-PRODUCT 14X27A-FOR MARCH + APRIL 1965

MONTH	SALES OFFICE	SIZE	QUANTITY	UNIT PRICE	NET PRICE
3	LOS ANGELES	1LB		.50	
TOTAL BY SIZE			1,500		750.00
COUNT BY SIZE		800			
		5LB		2.25	
TOTAL BY SIZE			1,125		2,531.25
COUNT BY SIZE		435			
		10LB		4.00	
TOTAL BY SIZE			610		2,440.00
COUNT BY SIZE		305			
TOTAL BY SALES OFFICE			3,235		5,721.25
COUNT BY SALES OFFICE	1,540				
	NEW YORK	1LB		.50	
TOTAL BY SIZE			1,100		550.00
COUNT BY SIZE		834			
		5LB		2.25	
TOTAL BY SIZE			1,222		2,749.50
COUNT BY SIZE		468			
		10LB		4.00	
TOTAL BY SIZE		605			2,420.00
COUNT BY SIZE		330			
TOTAL BY SALES OFFICE			2,927		5,719.50
COUNT BY SALES OFFICE	1,632				
	PHILADELPHIA	1LB		.45	
TOTAL BY SIZE			1,540		693.00
COUNT BY SIZE	1,251				
		5LB		2.00	
TOTAL BY			1,711		3,422.00

Figure 9-4. "Demand" Report.
Courtesy Scientific Data Systems.

10

Current
Trends in
Computer Reporting

As more and more business data is stored in electronic computers, accountants are seeking more efficient and more economical methods of getting information out of the computer and before the manager. This chapter covers three recent developments in computer reporting techniques which appear to have great potential for solving the information output bottleneck. These new techniques, cathode ray tube (CRT), computer linked microfilm, and computer connected graphic display, will cause accountants to re-think the content, format and standards for timeliness of management reports.

The cathode ray tube can display on a television screen any information stored in the computer. The information on display can be altered, added to, printed out, and returned to computer memory. Microfilm has been with us for many years as a method of storing inactive records. Now, technological advances have made microfilm a valuable reporting tool. Computer connected graphic display can print out information on bar charts and graphs just as quickly as in tabular form. This technique enables information to be placed before the manager in a form he can quickly grasp.

These three techniques for reporting computer stored information are in the development stage. They are not yet widely used as management reporting tools except in the largest companies. The greatest inhibitors to the expanded use of CRT, microfilm, and graphics are the costs of the equipment and computer programming. Where they are currently used in management reporting systems, the initial cost of acquisition has often been borne by some other operating system; thus their use in reporting is a by-product. However, the potential of CRT, microfilm, and graphic display for reporting to management is great, and a number of such systems are under study. Any accountant involved with computers today should acquaint himself with the advanced state of the art which will be the standard for tomorrow.

CATHODE RAY TUBES

The cathode ray tube, it is thought, will revolutionize man–computer interaction. For the first time, the manager can converse directly with the computer; he will operate in a truly dynamic environment. The instrument which will supposedly accomplish this is a small, television-like device with a keyboard attached. The keyboard has most of the characters found on a typewriter plus certain special keys through which instructions are issued to the computer. The CRT is connected directly to the computer or can be linked via communication lines.

The CRT unit can receive data from or transmit to the computer, and can display any data in computer memory. Alphabetic and numeric characters, punctuation marks, and specialized symbols can be displayed on some units while others are limited to numeric characters only. Usually, data is displayed in tabular form but more sophisticated units also display information in graphic form.

Up to 1,000 characters can be displayed at one time on a 9″ x 12″ or smaller screen. Each "page" may consist of as many as 30 horizontal lines depending upon the model used. Data called forth from the computer can be altered, added to, erased, and restored to its original place in memory. New data can be entered by using the typewriter to place it on the screen, sight verifying the result, and transmitting the displayed data to memory. Operators may be trained to use the CRT in a few hours.

Behind the extensive capabilities of the CRT is an enormous amount of systems and programming work. On-line and usually real-time computer systems are required to support CRT units. As a result, CRT installations are now quite costly and are used primarily for special purpose applications where there is considerable payoff.

However, as more CRT units are produced and experience gained in using them, the cost of such display systems will drop. Even now, most large companies are planning for CRT management reporting systems. The accountant must learn how this new technology can be used to prepare and communicate management information. This section outlines the ways in which CRT units are now being used and describes how such advanced reporting systems work.

File Scan Systems

There are two principal ways in which CRT units can be used for reporting information: (1) file scanning, and (2) management reporting systems. File scanning is where the current condition of an individual record is needed to make operating decisions. Usually such systems are found in organizations which interact with the public. Bank customer balances and airline reservations are examples. File scanning systems are also used in production and inventory control where minute-by-minute surveillance is necessary.

Most CRT file scanning systems are designed for special purposes and are not complete information systems. They are useful in those situations where line operators or first level supervisors need up-to-the-minute information on account balances or transactions.

Higher management typically needs summaries and analyses of file conditions and activities reported on a periodic basis.

CRT Management Reports

The objective of a CRT centered management reporting system is to make up-to-date information available at an instant's notice. Such systems are usually based on sets of reports which have been designed by the accounting department and stored in the computer. First, subreporting systems are established which deal with such categories as sales, financial, personnel, competition, etc. Within each subsystem the pyramid approach to reports is used. Starting from the basic file or files, successive reports summarize previous or lower level reports until the highest level is reached. Such a reporting system is described in detail in another chapter.

CRT reports either are updated manually, or automatically by the computer. Many systems under design today provide for the accounting department to manually control all updating of reports. Under this approach, each day the accountant obtains the necessary data from the underlying files or other sources. After verification, the data is inserted via the CRT unit into the proper report which is stored in the computer. Usually, instead of being destroyed, the reports for at least three prior periods are retained in memory.

Each manager has access to a CRT unit either in his office or at a central "control" room. Figure 10-1 shows a CRT unit in a conference room. Used in this way, answers to many questions can be obtained while the meeting is still in progress and adjournment for lack of information can be avoided.

Here is how a CRT based reporting system works. First, an executive activates the CRT unit by inserting an instruction code through the keyboard. An index of subreporting systems which are available to him is flashed on the screen.

FRAME I

	CODE
SALES	100
PRODUCTION	200
PERSONNEL	400
FINANCIAL	600
EQUIPMENT	800
PROFIT CONTROL AND ANALYSIS	900

Each subreporting system has numerous computer stored reports which provide information in increasing detail about the general topic. Assume that the executive wants to review financial reports. He inserts Code 600 into the CRT and Frame II appears. The data at the bottom of the frame indicates that the report is updated every seven days and that the last update was on August 21. Also, note that "Sales" is cross-indexed to Frame I.

**Figure 10-1. Cathode Ray Tube Used in Conference Room.
Courtesy of IBM Corporation.**

FRAME II

		THOUSANDS
610	CASH	4,820
620	RECEIVABLES	16,830
630	INVENTORIES	20,100
640	FIXED ASSETS	40,082
645	OTHER ASSETS	8,921
650	CURRENT LIABILITIES	20,921
655	LONG TERM LIABILITIES	30,112
660	EQUITY	39,720
100	SALES (NET OF C.G.S.)	90,821
680	BUDGET CONTROLLED EXPENSES	71,020
690	FIXED EXPENSES	10,200

U. D. 8-21-70   (7)

The executive is interested in the company's cash position. He inserts Code 610 into the CRT and Frame III appears showing a breakdown of "Cash" in Frame II. The total of "Cash" in Frame III does not equal "Cash" in Frame II because the former is updated daily and $400,000 has been added since August 21.

FRAME III

		THOUSANDS
611	CASH BUDGET 6 MONTH PROJECTION	
612	DEMAND DEPOSITS	3,320
613	U.S. SECURITIES	1,400
614	TIME DEPOSITS	500
615	SOURCE AND APPLICATION STMT.	

U. D. 8-24-70   (1)

The executive can review the projection of cash needs by inserting Code 611 or review the prior twelve months' source and applications of funds statement by inserting Code 615. If he wants a breakdown of maturities of U.S. Securities he inserts Code 613 and Frame IV appears. By inserting 613.2, a detail listing of securities maturing within 15 days would appear on the screen.

FRAME IV

	MATURITIES	THOUSANDS
613.1	7 DAYS	—
613.2	15 DAYS	100
613.3	30 DAYS	300
613.4	60 DAYS	400
613.5	90 DAYS	200
613.6	120 DAYS	400

U. D. 8-24-70   (1)

The hypothetical CRT reporting system described above is patterned after a similar system developed by The National Cash Register Company. Figure 10-2 shows four frames as they appear in the NCR system. Note that the fourth frame (lower right) indicates the steps followed to obtain the "Manufacturing Budget," i.e., (1) M.I.S. Index, (2) Financial Index, and (3) Budgets Index.

The CRT reporting system allows the manager to browse through each subsystem picking and choosing the information he needs for decision making. The information is always up-to-date and can be displayed as fast as the keyboard can be activated. If desired, a "hard copy" can be printed of any report appearing on the screen.

Next Step in CRT Reporting

Undoubtedly, the manual updating of reports will eventually be replaced by automatic updating by the computer. The computer will synthesize data obtained from underlying files and from figures fed into the system and insert the resulting information in the proper report. There is not sufficient experience with advanced systems of this type to attempt a description here.

Another concept often advanced in connection with CRT is to perfect it to the point

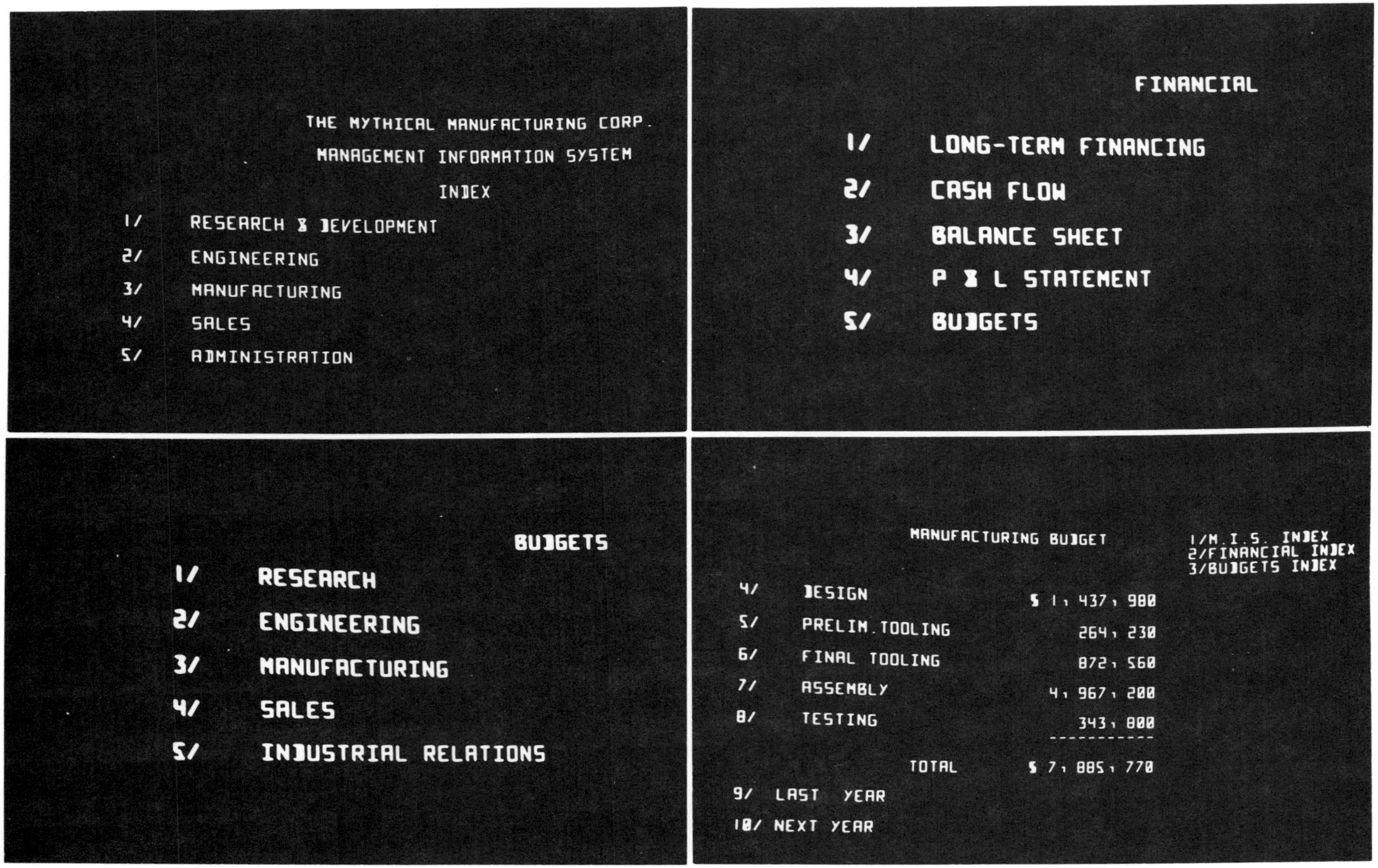

Figure 10-2. Frames from CRT Information System.
Courtesy of The National Cash Register Company.

where the manager can ask unstructured or unplanned questions and receive an immediate answer. This would require a system similar to the one described in Chapter 9. Most persons knowledgeable in the field believe that this phase is somewhat in the future.

Controls for CRT Reporting Systems

Despite the fact that CRT reporting systems are in their infancy, certain problems of control and operation are developing. In designing and operating such a system the accountant must be particularly alert in certain areas. The accounting department must maintain absolute control over changes in report content and format. Changes in the format of reports, including insertion of new reports, should be authorized by top accounting management. Changes in report content (updating) should be limited to designated accounting personnel. If these basic rules are not followed chaos will result and the system will be quickly discredited.

Reports on CRT should show the date to which information is current (update date) and, in many instances, the last transaction (cutoff). Any printout of information displayed must also be documented as to the effective date and last transaction covered. Access to information via CRT must be controlled. The computer can be programmed to accept input only from CRT units in the accounting department and to permit only authorized persons access to information. For example, executive salary information can be displayed only on CRT units in the offices of top management.

CRT Graphic Display

In addition to being able to display computer stored information in tabular form, some CRT units can project graphic information on the screen. Actually, complete pictures can be displayed but this feature has limited application for management reporting. Usually CRT graphic displays are fairly simple such as is shown in Figure 10-3. The operator in the exhibit is drawing a curve on the graph by using a light pen. The graph can then be stored in computer memory and retrieved by management when needed.

CRT display of graphic information requires quite complex programming. Some manufacturers of CRT units have built up libraries of programs for a variety of display formats. Programs for displaying bar graphs, contour plots, and scatter diagrams are available. Most graphic displays on CRT are used for engineering or scientific purposes. While business applications have been slow in developing, the use of CRT for this purpose has obvious potential in the graphic display of relationships existing in report data.

MICROFILM REPORTING SYSTEMS

The expanded use of microfilm for management reporting is inhibited by the fact that most people identify this process exclusively with the storage of large, inactive files. Microfilm has the image of a very slow, manually operated process which could not possibly compete with CRT display devices or even ordinary computer printing as a management reporting tool. This was true up until a few years ago. However, recent

**Figure 10-3. Cathode Ray Tube Graphic Display.
Courtesy of IBM Corporation.**

technological advances enable microfilm systems to be connected directly to the computer, thus providing speed and flexibility not possible before. This section discusses
some features of management reporting systems using microfilm.

How to begin a discussion of microfilm is a problem. There is a bewildering amount of
new equipment and techniques being marketed by over 100 manufacturers. Traditionally,
microfilm in reels of 100 feet were the standard. The filming process was slow and the
retrieval process not much better. Not only have techniques for handling reels of microfilm been dramatically improved but new storage media, such as microfiche and aperture
cards, have been developed.

Microfiche is a sheet of film carrying numerous micro images. There are many sizes
of microfiche but 4″ x 6″ is considered standard. Sheets of microfiche can be coded for
visual filing and retrieval. Aperture cards are tabulating cards with a frame of microfilm attached. The card is key punched for indexing. Searches for information are expedited by processing the cards through tabulating equipment. The microfilm viewer in

Figure 10-4 uses aperture cards. Because of the various storage media available, procedures utilizing these techniques are more properly termed "film" systems.

A Film System Illustrated

Because of the great number of film systems available, generalizations are inadequate to illustrate what can be done with this technique. Therefore, in this section one typical, although advanced, system is described in detail so that the reader can appreciate the potential of this new reporting media. This particular system, called MICROMATION, was developed by Stromberg-Carlson. Any organization interested in using film should thoroughly review all applicable systems and decide which one best meets its needs.

Normally, in order to be used in a microfilm system, computer generated data must be produced first in paper form and then photographed by various cameras. While fairly well automated, these cameras nevertheless cannot keep pace with the ever increasing speed of data processing machines. MICROMATION eliminates the need for first producing paper records.

To accomplish this, the system depends upon one of several electronic printers which accept computer codes, either on-line or from magnetic tapes. The codes are fed into the electronic printers which automatically translate the codes into ordinary language.

The data is then displayed briefly on a special cathode ray tube. The tube is built into the printer and in its operation is not visible to the user except for monitoring purposes. Instead, a microfilm camera is focused automatically on the tube face. As each page of data appears on the tube, the camera snaps a picture and automatically advances the film to the next frame. Then another page of data is presented on the tube and the picture-taking process is repeated.

Figure 10-4. Aperture Card Viewer.
Courtesy of IBM Corporation.

Types of Film Storage Available

Currently, three types of film can be produced with this system. The most popular form is 16mm microfilm which is stored in plastic cartridges or magazines after processing. Second is 35mm film. Normally, this film is cut into individual frames and attached to aperture cards.

The third form and one which is growing in application is microfiche. Instead of one frame or page of data being reproduced on each card, many pages can be recorded. For example, 72 pages could be recorded on the microfiche sheet by using 6 rows of 12 pages each. These microfiche sheets are sufficiently rigid to be filed just as aperture cards are now handled, except less space is required and more pages of data can be extracted from the files with a single card.

"Automatic" Custom Forms

In most business applications today, only letters, numerals and some special symbols are required. However, the user normally wants this data recorded on some special business form. For example, a firm might want its computer generated data printed over a report form bearing various headings, lines, boxes, and perhaps its company logotype. In the past, vast inventories of many different variations of such forms had to be pre-printed and stored.

The Stromberg-Carlson system eliminates this expense. Instead of preprinting the forms, a photographic slide is made of each desired form. The slide is then inserted into a special holder inside the printer. Simultaneously with the microfilming of the data on the tube face, light is passed through the slide containing the business form. In this way the camera records the lines and other static data on the form at the same time it records the computer produced data.

Graphics on Film

More sophisticated printers are capable of turning computer generated data directly into graphic form. In this case, management may desire charts showing sales or inventory curves, for example. The computer can be programmed to extract this information from its memory, and then the cathode ray tube can draw the chart on the face of its tube where it can be recorded by camera.

The speed possible with the cathode ray tube surpasses that of any other method. A complex chart, for example, can be drawn in a fraction of a second, making it feasible to put many composite reports in graph form which would have been impractical before.

Film Processing Speeds

One way of describing the speed of microfilm systems is in terms of 8½" x 11" pages of information translated from computer codes and recorded in a work day. The lower cost machines can record 20,000 pages or frames of data in one eight-hour shift while other equipment can increase this speed to 70,000 pages per shift.

With these speeds, even the most comprehensive system of management reports can be reproduced frequently. Because film is relatively inexpensive, reports which were formerly updated monthly can be reproduced weekly or even on a daily basis. Thus management and clerical help can have up-to-the-minute reports that were not available previously.

Duplicate and "Hard" Copies

Once the film is exposed, it must be processed. This is done automatically by special processors. If duplicate copies are needed they can be produced rapidly on automatic film copiers. Because of the low cost of film, an organization can afford to send duplicate reports to many different executives or offices, often to locations in other cities. Even the cost of postage involved in mailing film to locations in other cities is cheaper than sending paper records or using communications lines.

Even with filmed data, some organizations may require or desire paper copies of all data. Where a paper copy is required, the film may be run through another machine. This machine will handle microfilm at a rate of 60 feet per minute, producing report-quality paper records in page form of all the filmed data whether it is in alphanumeric or graphic form.

Paper Reports Not Needed

Most firms, however, will eventually dispense with bulky paper records entirely. Instead they will equip all possible users with inexpensive film viewing consoles. Each manager may have a viewing device in his office or located nearby. At these stations the user has all the up-to-date records in film form, either in 16mm cartridges, 35mm aperture cards or on microfiche. When he wishes to refer to a given record, the manager merely selects the cartridge or card containing that particular page and inserts it into the desk-top viewer.

The record is displayed on the screen and the data noted by the user. Should the user have need for a paper copy of that particular record, viewers can be installed which have a paper producing capability. By pushing a special control, a paper copy of the record is displayed on the screen. In this way, paper copies are made only when needed rather than producing hard copy records of all data. The storage savings alone can be sizeable.

Updating and Retrieval

In one company, information for management reports is maintained on magnetic tape files. Each week the computer stored reports are updated and the changed records are microfilmed. Inquiries can be processed by first locating the report number on an index which is also on microfilm. The index shows both the number of the film magazine, and the location of the frame that contains the microfilmed report.

Retrieval is made on high speed reader/printer systems which make paper copies for

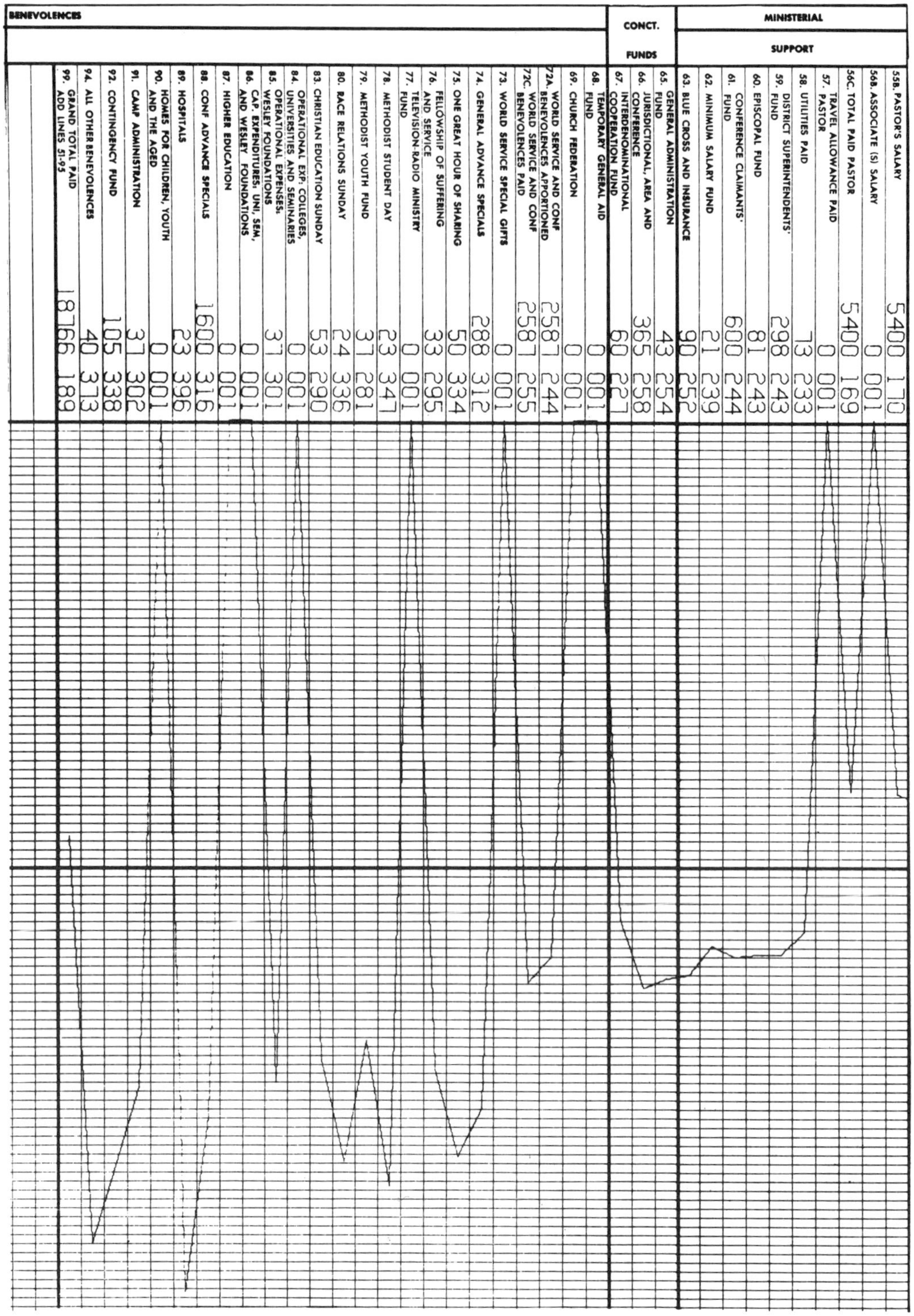

BENEVOLENCES		CONCT. FUNDS	MINISTERIAL SUPPORT

55B.	PASTOR'S SALARY	5400 170
56B.	ASSOCIATE (S) SALARY	0 001
56C.	TOTAL PAID PASTOR	5400 169
57.	TRAVEL ALLOWANCE PAID PASTOR	0 001
58.	UTILITIES PAID	73 233
59.	DISTRICT SUPERINTENDENTS' FUND	298 243
60.	EPISCOPAL FUND	81 243
61.	CONFERENCE CLAIMANTS' FUND	600 244
62.	MINIMUM SALARY FUND	21 239
63.	BLUE CROSS AND INSURANCE	90 252
65.	GENERAL ADMINISTRATION FUND	43 254
66.	JURISDICTIONAL, AREA AND CONFERENCE	365 258
67.	INTERDENOMINATIONAL COOPERATION FUND	60 227
68.	TEMPORARY GENERAL AID FUND	0 001
69.	CHURCH FEDERATION	0 001
72A.	WORLD SERVICE AND CONF BENEVOLENCES APPORTIONED	2587 244
72C.	WORLD SERVICE AND CONF BENEVOLENCES PAID	2587 255
73.	WORLD SERVICE SPECIAL GIFTS	0 001
74.	GENERAL ADVANCE SPECIALS	288 312
75.	ONE GREAT HOUR OF SHARING	50 334
76.	FELLOWSHIP OF SUFFERING AND SERVICE	33 295
77.	TELEVISION-RADIO MINISTRY FUND	0 001
78.	METHODIST STUDENT DAY	23 347
79.	METHODIST YOUTH FUND	37 281
80.	RACE RELATIONS SUNDAY	24 336
83.	CHRISTIAN EDUCATION SUNDAY	53 290
84.	OPERATIONAL EXP, COLLEGES, UNIVERSITIES AND SEMINARIES	0 001
85.	OPERATIONAL EXPENSES, WESLEY FOUNDATIONS	37 301
86.	CAP. EXPENDITURES: UNI, SEM, AND WESLEY FOUNDATIONS	0 001
87.	HIGHER EDUCATION	0 001
88.	CONF ADVANCE SPECIALS	1600 316
89.	HOSPITALS	23 396
90.	HOMES FOR CHILDREN, YOUTH AND THE AGED	23 001
91.	CAMP ADMINISTRATION	37 302
92.	CONTINGENCY FUND	105 338
94.	ALL OTHER BENEVOLENCES	40 313
99.	GRAND TOTAL PAID ADD LINES 51-95	18766 189

Figure 10-5. Graph Prepared by Digital Plotter.
Courtesy of Physical Sciences Laboratory, University of Wisconsin.

206

No.	Item	Published Amount	Rank
CHURCH MEMBERSHIP			
1.	TOTAL MEMBERS LAST YEAR	495	274
2.	RECEIVED THIS YEAR ON PROFESSION OF FAITH	3	174
3.	RECEIVED BY TRANSFER FROM OTHER METHODIST CHURCHES	4	231
4.	RECEIVED FROM OTHER DENOMINATIONS	2	231
5.	REMOVED BY TRANSFER TO OTHER METHODIST CHURCHES	4	193
6.	REMOVED BY QUART CONF ACTION OR WITHDRAWN	0	001
7.	REMOVED BY TRANSFER TO OTHER DENOMINATIONS	2	208
8.	REMOVED BY DEATH	6	346
9.	TOTAL FULL MEMBERS	492	275
10.	AVERAGE ATTENDANCE AT SUN MORNING WORSHIP SERVICE	188	296
11.	BAPTISMS; INFANTS PRESENTED BY PARENTS OR GUARDIANS	10	329
12.	BAPTISMS ALL OTHERS	0	001
13.	PREP MEMBERS NOW ON ROLL	275	356
CHURCH SCHOOL MEM.			
16.	TOTAL OFFICERS, TEACHERS, OTHER LEADERS	35	311
17.	CHILDREN (0-11 YEARS)	159	288
18.	NURSERY HOME MEMBERS	28	319
19.	YOUTH (12-21 YEARS)	70	287
20.	YOUTH HOME AND EXTENSION MEMBERS	8	352
21.	ADULTS (22 AND OLDER)	34	307
22.	ADULT HOME AND EXTENSION MEMBERS	8	329
23.	TOTAL CH SCHOOL MEMBERSHIP	342	291
ADD. INFO. ATTENDANCE			
24.	AVERAGE ATTENDANCE AT SUNDAY SCHOOL	207	326
25.	AVERAGE ATTEN METHODIST SUN EVENING FELLOWSHIP	0	001
26.	AVG ATTENDANCE ADDITIONAL SESSIONS OF CHILDREN	0	001
27.	SUNDAY EVENING MEETINGS AVERAGE ATTENDANCE MYF	14	180
28.	AVG ATTEN OF ADULTS IN CH SCH MEET OTHER THAN SUN SCH	0	001
32.	METHODIST PUPILS AND CONST IN VAC CHURCH SCHOOLS	107	348
33.	CH MEMBERS JOINING THE CHURCH ON PROF OF FAITH	0	001
34.	NUMBER OF CLASSES IN CHURCH SCHOOL	16	288
35.	NUMBER OF CLASSES USING METHODIST LESSON MATERIAL	16	294
36.	CHURCH SCHOOL OFFERING FOR WORLD SERVICE	117	284
WSCS			
37.	WSCS, MEMBERSHIP	114	302
38.	WSCS, AMT PAID FOR LOCAL CHURCH AND COM WORK	353	170
95.	WSCS CASH SENT TO DISTRICT TREASURER	803	268
40.	MEMBERSHIP IN METHODIST MEN'S CLUB	24	294
41.	NUMBER OF TOGETHER SUBSCRIPTIONS	21	226
LOCAL PROPERTY — EXPENDIT & ASSETS			
44.	ESTIMATED VALUE OF CHURCH BUILDINGS, EQUIP AND LAND	81000	141
45.	EST VALUE OF PARSONAGE, FURNITURE AND LAND	12000	122
46.	ESTIMATED VALUE OF OTHER ASSETS	3952	260
51.	PRINCP AND INTEREST ON OLD INDEBT; LOANS, MORTG, ETC.	0	001
52.	BUILDINGS IMPROVEMENTS	1323	235
53.	CHURCH SCHOOL; LESSON MATLS, SUPPLIES, ADMINIS	716	232
54.	OTHER CURRENT EXPENSES, ETC.	3896	174

return to the requester. If required, a report can be retrieved in less than one minute. A computer system without on-line retrieval capabilities can, in most instances, only provide overnight services.

Advantages of Film Systems

While not applicable to organizations producing only a few reports daily, microfilm systems are rapidly becoming accepted by firms inundated with voluminous reports. In many cases the users can obtain more up-to-date reports faster and at lower costs by using microfilm than by relying on paper printers. Cost savings come in the form of reduced paper inventories, storage costs and labor involved in handling records. In the near future most managers and supervisors, even factory foremen, may have viewers at their desks for reading reports.

Business use of CRT units (described in a previous section) is inevitable where instant access to a computer memory is required. However, in many organizations CRT costs are prohibitive in the foreseeable future for business applications. Film generally provides a cheaper storage medium than computer memory and film viewers are far less expensive than providing a CRT display for every user. The accountant should be alert to the possibility of using film reporting systems in his organization, and should understand what is involved in designing and operating such a system.

COMPUTER GRAPHIC DISPLAY

Most methods of retrieving computer stored business information provide for numerical tabulations in one form or another. This is not always the most useful format. Graphic display of information is often easier to understand, hence of more use to busy managers. In the past it was necessary to have a clerk transfer information from lengthy computer runs on to hand prepared charts and graphs. This process took considerable time, was subject to inaccuracies, and was not always attractively done.

A number of devices are available which will allow computer synthesized data to be printed out in graphic form. These devices can produce bar charts or graphs on stock paper, graph paper, or custom forms in the time it would take to print the same information in tabular form. Displays range in size from 5″ x 5″ to 20″ x 100″ and can be printed in a number of colors and different line types. Some graphic display devices can "draw" curves as well as straight, point-to-point lines. If desired, graphic display can be connected directly to a computer-microfilm system which is described in this chapter.

The most advantageous use of computer connected graphic displays is to quickly inform management of current developments. By a glance, the manager can identify trends and potential trouble spots. Usually, actual data is plotted against planned or budgeted figures, and any significant deviations spotlighted on the graph. A frequent use of graphic display is for projecting operations into the future. Variables can be introduced, and the computer quickly and accurately plots the effect of assumed changes in values. Graphic displays are often used to plot break-even points and other widely used business measurements.

Digital Plotters

Basically, two types of devices are available for graphic display of computer stored data. The digital plotter is the most widely used instrument for this purpose. Digital plotters can be operated on-line or off-line and can be used in a card only system. The capabilities of plotters vary widely as do the prices. Most plotters are used primarily for engineering and scientific purposes; few are installed for purely business information display. However, where the accountant has access to digital plotters or where the accountant's exclusive use would warrant it, definite thought should be given to utilizing their capabilities for management reporting.

A graphic report prepared by a digital plotter is shown in Figure 10-5. This report is used by a church organization to evaluate the progress of local churches under its jurisdiction. The status of each local church is plotted for 99 different categories. Measurement units involve services to persons or money collected or disbursed, and are printed adjacent to each category. The rank of each church in relation to other churches is also shown. The graph is plotted in terms of percent of quota or budget attained.

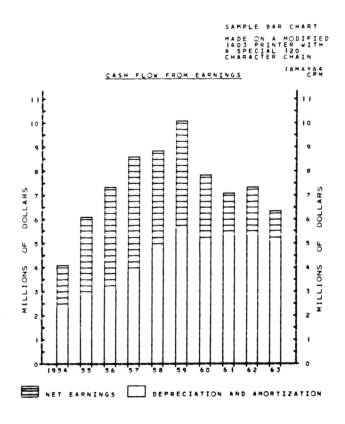

**Figure 10-6. Bar Chart Prepared by Computer Printer.
Courtesy of IBM Corporation.**

Graphs by Computer Printer

Charts and graphs can also be prepared by specially equipped computer printers. IBM has developed a printer which can do almost anything a digital plotter can do except print in more than one color. A special print chain is provided with graphic display symbols. The printer can be used for ordinary alphanumeric printing by simply changing print chains. Figure 10-6 shows a bar chart depicting cash flow information which was prepared on a computer printer. Computer printers are not as widely used as digital plotters for graphic display although the use of both is increasing.

One factor which inhibits the use of computer connected graphic display is the cost of programming such a system. The cost of computer programming may exceed the cost of the additional equipment needed for graphic display. Manufacturers of digital plotters are developing packaged programs for certain types of graphs and charts. If these "canned" display formats can be utilized for management reporting, substantial costs can be avoided.

One recent development is the emergence of time shared computer graphic displays. A computer manufacturer and a maker of digital plotters have joined forces to set up a network of computer connected digital plotters throughout the nation. Organizations may purchase only the time they need for graphic display work thus avoiding the purchase price and upkeep expense on equipment. As the use of time sharing increases, more companies may avail themselves of this means of producing graphic information for management decisions.

11

Typical
Accountants'
Reports

Every reporting situation is unique, and the report prepared on the covered events should be unique. The report should be tailored specifically to the purpose it serves, to the use it will be put, and to the person who will receive it. Even though every report is unique in these three characteristics, we may generalize somewhat. The examples of accountants' reports presented in this chapter are "typical." Like the "average," they may never be found exactly in this form in real life. Nonetheless, the examples represent starting points from which you may be able to devise a similar report which will be useful in your unique reporting situation.

The reports illustrated here are presented without extended comment on the procedures used to make the specific analyses embodied therein. These procedures are to be found in current industry practice, in cost accounting and managerial accounting textbooks, and in accounting encyclopedias and handbooks. Presentation of form is the primary purpose of the illustrations.

After presenting various forms of general-purpose statements and reports to aid in decision making, reports for several functional areas of the business are given. These include sales, credit, purchases, personnel, inventory, and production. Also illustrated are examples of forecasts.

You should keep in mind several questions while reviewing these illustrations:

- In your own reporting situation, could your using exception reporting be more effective?
- Could you use any of the techniques described earlier to make your effort be more eye-appealing, creative, and useful?
- Every report you prepare should be the basis for some action; do your reports meet this test?

THE MODERN MANUFACTURING COMPANY, INC.

CONSOLIDATED POSITION STATEMENT

December 31, 1969

<u>Assets</u>	(000)	<u>Equities</u>	(000)
Current Assets:		Current Liabilities:	
Cash...........................$ 2,000		Accounts Payable...............$ 300	
U. S. Government Securities... 1,000		Taxes Payable.................. 800	
Accounts Receivable		Wages, Interest and other	
(less allowance).............. 2,000		accrued expenses payable..... 370	
Inventories (lower of cost		Total Current Liabilities...$ 1,470	
or market)..................... 2,000			
Total Current Assets.......$ 7,000		First Mortgage Sinking Fund Bonds,	
		4½%, due 1979.................... 2,000	
Property and Plant:		Capital:	
At Cost.........$ 8,000		5% preferred stock ($100 par,	
Less Depreciation		10,000 shares authorized	
Allowance..... 5,000		and issued).................. 1,000	
Net Property...............$ 3,000		Common Stock (no par,	
		authorized and issued	
Investments:		50,000 shares).............. 1,000	
Investments in Unconsolidated		Paid-in Capital in Excess of	
Affiliates (current equity,		Stated Value of Capital Stock 1,900	
$ 350), cost................. 200		Retained Earnings	
Plant Improvement Fund........ 550		Reserved for contingencies... 200	
Other Investments (current		Available for dividends...... 3,530	
value, $130) at cost........ 100			
Other Assets:			
Prepayments................... 50			
Deferred charges.............. 100			
Patents, Goodwill............. 100			
Total Assets....................$11,100		Total Equities....................$11,100	

Figure 11-1.

212

THE MODERN MANUFACTURING COMPANY, INC.

CONSOLIDATED POSITION STATEMENT

December 31, 1969

Assets

	(000)	(000)
Current Assets:		
Cash..	$ 2,000	
U. S. Government Securities..................................	1,000	
Accounts Receivable (less allowance)......................	2,000	
Inventories (lower of cost or market).....................	2,000	
Total Current Assets....................................		$ 7,000
Plant and Property:		
At Cost...	$ 8,000	
Less Depreciation Allowance...............................	5,000	
Net Property..		3,000
Investments:		
Investments in Unconsolidated Affiliates (current equity,		
$350), at cost..	$ 200	
Plant Improvement Fund....................................	550	
Other Investments (current value, $130), cost...........	100	
Total Investments....................................		850
Other Assets:		
Prepayments..	$ 50	
Deferred charges...	100	
Patents, Goodwill..	100	
Total Other Assets..................................		250
Total Assets..		$11,100

Equities

Current Liabilities:		
Accounts Payable..	$ 300	
Taxes Payable..	800	
Wages, Interest, and other accrued expenses..............	370	
Total Current Liabilities............................		$ 1,470
First Mortgage Sinking Fund Bonds, 4½%, due 1979...........		2,000
Capital:		
5% preferred stock ($100 par, 10,000 shares).............		1,000
Common Stock (no par, 500,000 shares).....................		1,000
Paid-in Capital in excess of stated value................		1,900
Retained Earnings:		
Reserved for contingencies........................	$ 200	
Available for dividends...........................	3,530	3,730
Total Liabilities and Capital...............................		$11,100

Figure 11-2.

GENERAL-PURPOSE FINANCIAL STATEMENTS

General-purpose financial statements usually include the position statement (balance sheet), income statement (profit and loss statement), and several supporting statements analyzing the equities' or funds' flow.

Position Statement

The position statement, or balance sheet, traditionally shows the assets, liabilities and owners' equity of the firm. Figure 11-1 shows the "account form" with assets on the left and equities on the right side. The equality of the two groups is emphasized in this form. Where appropriate, parenthetical notes have been added to disclose additional information. Often, statement footnotes are needed to disclose certain details more completely in narrative form. Forecasted and prior-year comparisons may also be included for more usefulness.

The position statement may be simplified by using lay language in place of the technical terms. For example, instead of "Current Assets," you could use "Cash and Other Items Owned Convertible into Cash Within a Year."

Figure 11-2 recasts the same information into the "report form." Assets are listed first; equities follow below. Because of their positioning the assets are stressed in this form. On the other hand, working capital is stressed in the position statement in Figure 11-3. Current liabilities are subtracted from current assets in the first section, thus highlighting working capital. Other assets are then added to form a total "capital," which is matched in dollar amount in the "sources of capital" section that follows.

The right-hand money column in Figure 11-3 shows the adjusted amounts for each item. The adjustments are based on net realizable market value, price-level changes, or discounted present value, as appropriate. The last item on the statement, "unrealized changes in assets and liabilities," accounts for the difference between the adjusted figures and recorded equity. If possible, additional information such as this should be included; it makes the report into a "true position" statement. Most probably it would be more meaningful and useful to the reader.[1]

Other forms of the position statement could be devised to highlight certain items. Public utilities, for example, have traditionally placed their plant and equipment ahead of current assets, since the former comprise the bulk of the assets. Likewise, long-term debt is usually listed ahead of current liabilities for the same reason. Tradition should not

---

[1] The authors realize the difficulty generally encountered in obtaining such figures as realizable market values or discounted present values. Historical cost amounts, adjusted for price-level changes, are more easily obtained; lacking the former values, you are encouraged to show adjusted price-level amounts. Procedures for so translating and reporting adjusted historical cost amounts are detailed in the *Accounting Research Study No. 6,* "Reporting the Financial Effects of Price-Level Changes," by the American Institute of Certified Public Accountants, 1963, 278pp. The Accounting Principles Board of the AICPA, at this writing, is considering the release of a statement recommending certain procedures to be used in adjusting and reporting price-level-adjusted historical cost figures.

THE MODERN MANUFACTURING COMPANY, INC.

CONSOLIDATED POSITION STATEMENT

December 31, 1969

Corporate Capital	Cost (A)	Adjusted (B)
Current Assets:		
Cash...$	2,000	$ 2,000
U. S. Government Securities...........................	1,000	1,200
Accounts Receivable (less allowance).....................	2,000	1,800
Inventories..	2,000	2,900
Total Current Assets.............................$	7,000	$ 7,900
Current Liabilities:		
Accounts Payable.......................................$	300	$ 300
Taxes Payable...	800	800
Wages, Interest, and other accrued expenses.............	370	370
Total Current Liabilities.........................$	1,470	$ 1,470
Working Capital...$	5,530	$ 6,430
Plant and Property:		
Original Cost...$	8,000	$ 12,000
Less Depreciation Allowance............................	(5,000)	(7,500)
Net Plant and Property...........................$	3,000	$ 4,500
Investments and Other Assets:		
Investments in unconsolidated affiliates................$	200	$ 350
Plant Improvement Fund.................................	550	800
Other Investments......................................	100	• 50
Prepayments..	50	50
Deferred Charges.......................................	100	100
Patents, Goodwill......................................	100	600
Total Investments and Other.......................$	1,100	$ 1,950
Total Corporate Capital.....................................$	9,630	$ 12,880

Sources of Capital		
First Mortgage Sinking Fund Bonds, 4½%, 1979.................$	2,000	$ 1,800
5% Preferred Stock ($100 par, 10,000 shares).................	1,000	1,000
Common Stock (no par, 500,000 shares).......................	1,000	1,000
Retained Earnings:		
Reserved for contingencies.............................	200	200
Available for dividends................................	3,530	3,530
Paid-in Capital in excess of stated value..................	1,900	1,900
Unrealized changes in assets and liabilities...............		3,450
$	9,630	$ 12,880

(A) Assets at cost or lower of cost or market.
(B) Current assets at net realizable value; fixed assets at price level (1940=100) adjusted cost; liabilities at discounted present value.

Figure 11-3.

215

THE MODERN MANUFACTURING COMPANY, INC.

CONSOLIDATED INCOME STATEMENT

For the Year Ended December 31, 1969

```
Sales Revenues:                                                      (000)
    Gross Sales.............................................$  11,000
    Less:  Sales Returns and Allowances......................$   750
           Sales Discounts..................................    250        1,000
    Net Sales..............................................$  10,000

Cost of Sales:
    Beginning Inventory.....................................$ 2,000
    Purchases...........................$ 8,500
        Transportation in.............     500
        Purchase Returns..............    (250)
        Purchase Discounts............    (750)       8,000
    Goods Available for Sale..............................$ 10,000
    Less Ending Inventory...................................   3,000
        Cost of Sales.....................................$  7,000      $  7,000

Gross Margin on Sales.....................................................$   3,000

Operating Expenses:
    Selling, Administrative and General.....................$    500
    Depreciation............................................     200
    Maintenance and Repairs.................................     400
    Taxes -- Other than Income..............................     300      $  1,400

Income from Operations....................................................$   1,600

Other Income and Expense
    Other Income:
        Royalties and Dividends...........................$     250
        Interest Earned....................................      25
                                                         $     275

    Other Expense:
        Interest on Funded Debt.......$     70
        Other Interest...............      20         $    (90)      $     185

Income Before Federal and State Income Taxes............................$   1,785

Less:   Income Taxes Expense.............................................      678

Net Income Before Extraordinary Items...................................$   1,107

Extraordinary Items:
    Gain on sale of fixed assets (net of tax)................$    200
    Loss from fire in plant (net of tax effect)..............   (200)        -0-

Net Income..............................................................$   1,107
```

Figure 11-4.

216

THE MODERN MANUFACTURING COMPANY, INC.

CONSOLIDATED INCOME STATEMENT

For the Year Ended December 31, 1969

(A)

Revenues:		(000)
Net Sales..		$ 10,000
Royalties and Dividends..		250
Interest Earned...		25
Total Revenues..		$ 10,275

Expenses of Operation:		
Cost of Sales...	$ 7,000	
Selling, Administrative, and General......................	500	
Depreciation...	200	
Maintenance and Repairs..................................	400	
Taxes -- Other than Income..............................	300	
Federal and State Income Taxes..........................	678	
Funded Debt and Other Interest.........................	90	
Total Expenses of Operation..............................		$ 9,168

Income Before Extraordinary Items.. $ 1,107

Extraordinary Items:		
Gain on Sale of Fixed Assets (net of tax)................ $	200	
Loss from Plant Fire (net of tax effect).................	(200)	-0-

Net Income.. $ 1,107

(B) (Continued from above)

Net Income.. $ 1,107

Retained Earnings -- Beginning of Year........................ $	3,083	
Less: Additional Taxes Assessed on prior year's income........	(10)	
Adjusted Beginning Balance of Retained Earnings............................		$ 3,073
Total..		$ 4,180

Less Dividends:		
Preferred Stock ($5 a share)............................. $	50	
Common Stock ($1 a share)................................	400	
	$ 450	
Less Addition to Reserve for Contingencies...................	200	650

Retained Earnings -- End of Year... $ 3,530

Figure 11-5.

217

necessarily govern practice, however. You should emphasize by position and other devices the important things in your report.

Income Statement

The income statement may be prepared either in multiple-step or single-step form, and may or may not be combined with a summary of changes in retained earnings. Personal preferences should dictate the form to use. The multiple-step form is illustrated in Figure 11-4. There are several groups of amounts above net income before extraordinary items. More detail is shown for the groups, and more intermediate totals are presented. All revenues and all expenses are separately grouped in the single-step form shown in Figure 11-5.

In both statements, the extraordinary items are set out separately, according to the form prescribed in the AICPA Accounting Principles Board *Opinion No. 9,* "Reporting the Results of Operations." The (B) part of Figure 11-5 shows the addition of information on retained earnings. If this were made an integral part of the presentation, it would be retitled "Consolidated Statement of Income and Retained Earnings." If it were presented separately, it would be a "Statement of Changes in Retained Earnings." As in the case of the position statement, adding comparative information and certain statistics may make the statements more meaningful and useful.

Supporting Statements

In addition to the Statement of Changes in Retained Earnings presented in the previous section, there are several other statements included in the general-purpose category that might be mentioned.

A "Statement of Changes in Capital Stock" might be prepared. This would show the beginning balances of each type of stock, the changes therein, and the ending balances. An extension of this statement would include other equity accounts, such as paid-in capital and retained earnings (separately, that appropriated and available for dividends). This latter statement would be called a "Statement of Changes in Stockholder Equity." It is especially helpful when there have been numerous changes in the equity accounts, such as in a merger or reorganization.

The "Change in Working Capital Funds Statement" has become a familiar presentation in published annual reports. It is seen in various forms and known by several names: Funds Statement, Source and Application of Funds Statement, Statement of Resources Provided and Applied. This statement provides the link between the position and income statements. The net change in working capital (current assets minus current liabilities) must equal the net change in the non-working capital accounts. Therefore, the statement will detail the changes in the non-working capital items and show that the net change equals the increase or decrease in working capital. This may be presented in a number of ways:

- Source of Funds = Application of Funds (including the working capital increase as a balancing item)

- Source of Funds — Application of Funds = Increase in Working Capital
- Working Capital at beginning of year + Increases from Sources — Decreases from Applications = Working Capital at end of year.

An example of the second presentation is given in Figure 11-6; this form seems to be the easier of the three to interpret. A reconciliation between beginning and ending balance of working capital is also provided in Figure 11-6.

The income statement and funds statement are especially adaptable to graphic presentation. Bar charts and pie charts are most easily used. An accompanying table usually gives the specific percentages and/or dollars for the current year only or on a comparative five- to ten-year basis.

REPORTS TO AID IN DECISION MAKING

Actually, all reports in some way should aid in decision making and action taking. A report that does not, should not be prepared. But decision making may require both general information (for broad policy making) and specific information (for implementation directing). The reports that cover general information usually may be standardized to a large extent. Reports covering information to be used in specific decisions are less adaptable to standardization. The content and format of these reports depend upon the specific problems requiring the action taking. The reports should highlight the information upon which action is required. The examples presented herein, therefore, must be modified to suit your specific situation—your problem, your reports structure, your users.

Specific decisions must be made in and for all functional areas of the business. Specific decisions involve capital investments, production, sales, personnel, and finance. For all these specific decisions, there is an underlying common characteristic. This is that alternatives are weighed and the best one chosen. The alternatives usually involve either a comparison of future revenues and costs, and/or cash flows. The costs are normally divided into variable and fixed. A further division into variable, programmed, and standby costs facilitates establishing the alternatives.

Variable costs are those that will change in direct proportion to an activity base: sales, production, hours, input units, etc. Programmed costs are discretionary with management, but once decided upon, commit the organization for a fixed amount over a relatively long period. Standby costs are those that will continue even if all activity stops, since they are required to maintain the operation unimpaired until normal activity resumes.

The revenues and costs to use in this type of analysis, we must emphasize, are expected future revenues and costs. These may be determined either on a total basis or differential (or marginal) basis. Projecting only the past is usually not a satisfactory basis for estimating the future; an estimate of future conditions must be made. Moreover, cash or cash equivalent costs are usually more relevant and preferable to costs which include some noncash items.

THE MODERN MANUFACTURING COMPANY, INC.

STATEMENT OF CHANGES IN WORKING CAPITAL

For the Year Ended December 31, 1969

Sources of Working Capital: (000)
    Income Before Extraordinary Items.........................$ 1,107
        Add Back Expense for Depreciation not
        requiring use of funds.............................   200
        Total Funds Provided by Operations................................$ 1,307
    Net Proceeds from Sale of Common Stock.................................   150
    Increase in Long-term Debt, Less Construction Funds on Deposit......... 1,450
    Sale of Certain Investments...   50
    Net Book Value of Plant and Property Sold.............................   500
        Total Sources of Working Capital..................................$ 3,457

Uses of Working Capital:
    Expenditure for Plant and Property....................................$ 850
    Reduction in Long-term Debt, due in 1969.............................. 2,000
    Increase in Patent Expenditures.......................................   75
    Investment in Unconsolidated Affiliate................................   50
    Cash Dividend Paid..   450
        Total Uses of Working Capital.....................................$ 3,425
Net Increase in Working Capital...$ 32

Beginning Balance of Working Capital......................................$ 5,498
Add Net Increase for Year...   32
Ending Balance of Working Capital...$ 5,530

Figure 11-6.

ALTERNATIVE 1

(A)

Year	Investment Actual	Discounted 15%	20%	Additional Revenue	Costs ✦	Net Cash Flow *	Discounted Cash Flow 15%	20%
0	200,000	200,000	200,000			-0-		
1	50,000	43,500	41,650	60,000	50,000	10,000	8,700	8,330
2				85,000	65,000	20,000	15,120	13,880
3				120,000	80,000	40,000	26,320	23,160
4				200,000	120,000	80,000	45,760	38,560
5	6,000	2,982	2,412	320,000	220,000	100,000	49,700	40,200
6				530,000	410,000	120,000	51,840	40,200
7				660,000	530,000	130,000 **	48,880	36,270
	256,000	246,482	244,062			500,000	246,320	200,600

✦ Includes tax, excludes depreciation (non-cash charge).

* Revenue less costs and tax, plus depreciation.

** No salvage value assumed.

(B)

Year	Investment Actual	Discounted *	Net Cash Flow Actual	Discounted *
0	200,000	200,000	-0-	-0-
1	50,000	45,450	10,000	9,090
2			20,000	16,520
3			40,000	16,040
4			80,000	54,640
5	6,000	3,726	100,000	62,100
6			120,000	67,680
7			130,000	66,690
		249,176		292,760

* At 10% average earnings rate

Return 292,760 / Invested 249,176 = $1.18 per $1.

(C)

	Discounted Cash Flow - estimated rate of return (A)	Present Value at 10% return - est. return per invested dollar (B)	Payback Period **
Alternative 1	15%	$ 1.18	3.6 yrs.
Alternative 2 *	9	.93	2.3
Alternative 3 *	12	1.10	4.8

* Not illustrated

** Net investment divided by average cash flow

Figure 11-7.

221

Capital Investment Decisions

There are many ways to evaluate capital investment projects: discounted cash flow method, present value method, average return on investment, average return on average investment, and payback period. Each of these has its advantages and disadvantages; you must judge which is most relevant to your situation.

Figure 11-7 illustrates three of these methods. Part A of the figure shows the discounted cash flow method. Since the rate of 15% equates (almost) the present values of the total investment with the total net inflow, this is the rate to be earned by this alternative. In Part C, two other alternatives are compared with the illustrated alternative. Either a larger discount percentage (e.g., 20%) or a smaller percentage (e.g., 10%, illustrated in Part B), causes a greater degree of difference between the present values of the investment and net inflows, so these are inaccurate in measuring rate of return.

Part B of Figure 11-7 illustrates the present value method. Here 10% is selected as the rate by which to discount the investment and net cash inflows. This percentage is the actual average earnings rate on existing investments, so is considered a "bench mark" for prospective investments. Since the present value of the inflows exceeds the investment, this tells us that the project would earn over 10% (actually 15%, as shown in Part A). It would earn a $1.18 return for every $1 invested. This is contrasted in Part C with competing investment opportunities.

Part C of Figure 11-7 also shows the payback period for the three competing alternatives. As indicated, a low payback period does not necessarily indicate the more desirable investment.

Production Decisions

Make or Buy Components. This is a decision frequently faced by management. The decision to make is required when the expected cost savings provide a higher return on investment than can be obtained from using these funds in an alternative investment bearing the same risk. The approach is similar to that illustrated above; in this case the least cash outflow is the focus rather than net cash inflow.

Figure 11-8 illustrates a make or buy computation. If the duration of the project were to be four years, the net cash inflow (on a discounted basis at 20%, the acceptable minimum rate of return) would be $13,493. If the investment required to make the components exceeded this figure, the venture would be unprofitable and the decision would be to buy the components. If the investment required were less than the $13,493, making the components would be a profitable investment. Given the amount of the investment, one may find the actual rate of return by using the procedures illustrated in Figure 11-7.

The decision involved in making or buying or leasing production facilities is similar to the one required for components, illustrated above. Costs for each alternative must be estimated; the alternative with the greatest cost savings on a discounted basis would be the one chosen.

Retain or Drop or Add Products. This decision hinges on many external and internal

Make or Buy Information

	1969	1970	1971	1972
Estimated parts required	10,000	15,000	20,000	10,000
Estimated cost to buy	50,000	75,000	100,000	50,000
Estimated cost to make: *				
Material A	10,000	15,000	20,000	10,000
Material B	15,000	22,500	30,000	15,000
Direct labor	5,000	7,500	10,000	5,000
Indirect labor	10,000	12,000	15,000	13,000
Electricity	2,000	4,000	6,000	4,000
Repairs	1,000	4,000	6,000	4,000
Supplies	500	800	1,000	500
Insurance	500	600	700	500
Space	1,000	1,200	1,400	1,400
Total	45,000	67,600	90,100	53,400
Estimated net cash flow	5,000	7,400	9,900	(3,400)
Total present value of net cash flows @ 20% = 13,493 =	4,165	5,136	5,831	(1,639)

Figure 11-8.

Add or Drop Products

	Actual		Projected	
	Prior Year	Current Year	Next Year	2d Year
Units produced	30,000	40,000	50,000	20,000
Ending inventory in units	2,000	3,000	4,000	2,000
Sales in units	28,000	37,000	46,000	18,000
Average sales price per unit	10	9	8	12
Sales revenue	280,000	333,000	368,000	216,000
Variable production costs	110,000	135,000	165,000	153,000
Variable selling costs	30,000	43,000	68,000	63,000
Contribution margin	140,000	155,000	135,000	-0-
Direct fixed costs	35,000	65,000	85,000	24,000
Direct product profit	105,000	90,000	50,000	(24,000)
Market share attained	22%	25%	28%	10%
Contribution margin to sales	50%	47%	37%	0%
Direct profit to sales	38%	27%	14%	-11%
Direct break-even point ($)	70,000	138,297	229,729	216,000
Direct capital investment	50,000	60,000	70,000	60,000
Return on direct capital investment	210%	150%	70%	-40%
Turnover of direct investment (times)	5.6	5.5	5.3	3.6

Figure 11-9.

223

factors that must be estimated. Figure 11-9, for example, shows an analysis of a product in terms of its actual and projected sales, profitability, and return on direct capital investment. Likewise, acceptable levels of performance must be established for such measures as sales revenue, contribution margin, direct profit, and return on direct capital investment. It is fairly clear that the projection next year is marginal and the second following year is unacceptable. Unless the items in the projection are controllable to a large extent, the product should probably be dropped. But other factors must also be considered, such as the effect upon other sales and costs. As a matter of fact, the evaluation of these other factors is in itself the most critical element of this type of decision. Arriving at a determination of the projected effects of certain decisions is difficult and risky, but it must be done. This is one place where agreement must be reached, even though it is based on opinions and projections. Statistical techniques using probabilities are constantly being refined; this area of decision making may well be a fertile ground for applying these techniques. In any event, the "whole picture" must be considered, however fuzzy the edges or imprecisely distinguishable the figures.

The report of an analysis of the alternatives to add or not to add a product would be similar to the projection in Figure 11-9. If the measures exceed the acceptable minimum levels, and other considerations do not negate these, then the product would be added.

Other analyses may be made relating to production decisions. These include determining plant location, optimizing product mix, selling or processing further, and minimizing inventory investment. These will not be illustrated since the approach to them is similar to the examples above.

Product Distribution Decisions

Decisions in this area affect both the size of the revenue produced and the efficiency with which it is produced. Cost alternatives must be evaluated when deciding what, where, and when to sell. Reports for management in this area weigh the alternatives involved in decisions on customer type, size and category, salesmen, channels of distribution, product pricing, and in many other specific problem areas.

Profit Contribution by Customers. Analyses may be made to determine the profit contribution by customers, in terms of customer type, customer order size, or customer category. As in several of the examples above, the focus is upon the revenue produced and the direct identifiable costs.

Figure 11-10 illustrates a report on profit contribution by customer types. Although not included in this figure, budget figures and percentage calculations for each type would increase the usefulness of the report. Bench marks of acceptability should also be included; return on investment, for example, would help to tell whether the company store is more profitable than it appears from the dollar amount of contribution.

Customer order size profitability may be computed to determine where the selling emphasis should lie. For the retailers and/or wholesalers, for example, the past invoices could be analyzed by order sizes of less than $100, $101–300, $301–500, $501–700, $701–900, and over $900. Identifying revenues and costs with these groups would derive a direct contribution margin per order size. This would tell you, for instance, that 40%

Profit Contribution by Customer Types

For Year Ended Dec. 31, 1969

	Retailers	Whole-salers	Company Store	Mail Order	Total	% of Sales
Sales - Product A	25,300	53,200	20,200	16,700	115,400	33
Sales - Product B	98,200	120,400	8,100	10,500	237,200	67
	123,500	173,600	28,300	27,200	352,600	100%
Direct costs:						
Cost of sales	37,400	69,400	7,300	10,800	124,900	35
Entertainment expense	8,200	10,300			18,500	5
Catalogues and literature	1,300	3,700		2,600	7,600	2
Salesmen's salaries	26,800	34,900	15,200		76,900	23
Salesmen's commissions	9,400	14,800	2,300		26,500	8
Travel expense	10,200	8,200			18,400	5
Direct mail advertising				4,500	4,500	1
Bad debts	2,100	1,500			3,600	1
Total	95,400	142,800	24,800	17,900	280,900	80
Direct contribution margin	28,100	30,800	3,500	9,300	71,700	20
Indirect costs:						
Sales office salaries					6,200	2
Selling supplies					500	0
Storage					4,200	1
Order filling and shipping					2,300	1
Credit, billing, collection					5,100	2
Advertising space & salaries					10,300	3
General & administrative					14,000	4
All taxes					10,000	3
Total					52,600	15
Net Income					19,100 ·	5
Direct contribution margin as % of total	39%	43%	5%	13%		

Figure 11-10.

Profit Contribution by Salesmen

For Month Ended Dec. 31, 1969

Salesman	Over (Under) Quota		Net Sales Billed	Cost of Sales	Salary & Expenses	Profit Contribution Amount	Over (Under) Budget		% of Sales
Able	(10,000)	(25%)	30,000	21,300	3,500	5,200	(600)	(4%)	17.3
Baker	6,000	15%	46,000	32,600	5,100	8,300	700	9%	18.0
Cook	16,000	20%	96,000	71,700	10,100	14,200	1,500	12%	14.8
Dodd	(5,000)	(10%)	45,000	33,200	5,000	6,800	(800)	(5%)	15.1
Evans	13,000	22%	73,000	54,800	7,800	10,400	400	4%	14.2
Fox	1,000	2%	68,000	50,900	7,300	9,800	200	21%	14.4
Gunn	(7,000)	(7%)	93,000	70,600	9,800	12,600	500	4%	13.5
Hitt	2,000	4%	52,000	41,100	5,700	5,200	(800)	(13%)	10.0
Zack	(5,000)	(20%)	25,000	19,900	3,000	2,100	(400)	(16%)	8.4
Totals	11,000	2%	528,000	396,100	57,500	74,600	700	1%	14.1
District Overhead						6,800	(800)	(13%)	1.3
District Profit Contribution						67,800	(100)	0%	12.8

Figure 11-11.

Profit Contribution of Alternative Sales Channels

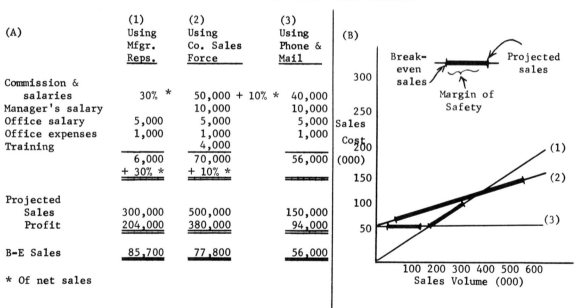

(A)	(1) Using Mfgr. Reps.	(2) Using Co. Sales Force	(3) Using Phone & Mail
Commission & salaries	30% *	50,000 + 10% *	40,000
Manager's salary		10,000	10,000
Office salary	5,000	5,000	5,000
Office expenses	1,000	1,000	1,000
Training		4,000	
	6,000 + 30% *	70,000 + 10% *	56,000
Projected Sales	300,000	500,000	150,000
Profit	204,000	380,000	94,000
B-E Sales	85,700	77,800	56,000

* Of net sales

Figure 11-12.

of the retail trade consists of orders between $101–300, but that this group's contribution margin is only 25%.

Profit Contribution by Salesmen. Figure 11-11 demonstrates a typical report on the profitability of salesmen. The actual sales are contrasted against quota for one measure of efficiency. Profit contribution over or under budget provides another measure. Profit contribution provided as a percent of sales is still another. Teams of salesmen, or the district's sales force performance can be matched against other teams or districts in the same fashion. But merely providing the figures is not enough. They must be interpreted: Is 7% under sales quota necessarily undesirable? What conditions caused this variance?

Profit Contribution by Distribution Channel. Many possibilities for analyses exist in this problem area. Usually a measure of least cost will be a determining factor in the various alternatives. But other factors must be considered, such as projected sales in Figure 11-12. Because of the personal effort exerted, alternative (2) would produce the greatest sales and profit, but it also has the highest break-even point. Below $56,000 sales, alternative (1) would produce the greatest profit; after that, for each $1 of sales added, alternative (3) is best. If other alternatives can push sales over (3)'s potential, another evaluation of alternatives is in order.

Personnel and Financing Decisions

In deciding upon employee compensation plans, management must weigh the many alternatives open to them. Different plans will ordinarily produce different results, especially if they are based in whole or part upon built-in incentives. Figure 11-13 illustrates the projected unit manufacturing cost under alternative compensation plans. If the projected output figures prove valid, plan B would be preferable; at other output levels, another plan would be the best alternative. Perhaps in this case it would be well to report to management the costs under each plan at various levels of production.

Cost analysis in the area of financing operations is necessary for intelligent management decisions as well. If additional capital is needed for expansion, for example, an analysis of the costs of various alternatives would be relevant. The alternatives could include long-term debt, preference or common equity, short-term borrowing, internal generation through retained earnings, or a combination of any or all of these. The analysis would identify (on a discounted cash flow basis) the cash inflows and outflows of the provision, use, and repayment of the funds.

SALES AND DISTRIBUTION REPORTS

There are many possible ways of analyzing sales and distribution revenues and costs. In its 1951 *Research Report No. 19,* the National Association of Accountants listed the following:

- by products or product lines
- by geographical area of distribution
- by administrative divisions of the sales organization
- by distribution channels

Projected Unit Manufacturing Cost Under

Alternative Compensation Plans

| | Cost Per Unit | | |
	Plan A	Plan B	Plan C
Direct Material	1.500	1.500	1.500
Direct labor (1)	.200	.250	.229
Applied Overhead (2)	.600	.494	.520
Total Manufacturing Cost Per Unit	2.300	2.244	2.249

(1) Plan A: Hour rate compensation. Output has been 600 units per week, at $3 per hour for 40 hours. This equals $120 or $ .20 per unit.

Plan B: Piece-rate compensation. Output estimated to be 750 units per week. Operator is paid $ .25 per unit; no maximum, no minimum output.

Plan C: Combination hour and piece-rate. Output estimated to be 700 units per week. Operator is paid base salary of $1.50 per hour for 40 hours, plus $ .50 per unit over 500 units.

(2) Overhead is applied by interpreting annual flexible budget for one week at the stated production levels, divided by the weekly output.

Figure 11-13.

Product Sales Performance

| | Product A | | | | Product B | | | |
	Forecast	Actual	Budget	Actual YTD	Forecast	Actual	Budget	Actual YTD
January	400	184	350	184	2,000	2,040	2,050	2,040
February	500	468	450	652	1,900	1,835	1,800	3,875
March	600	710	550	1,362	1,800	1,580	1,700	5,455
•	•	•	•	•	•	•	•	•
•	•	•	•	•	•	•	•	•
•	•	•	•	•	•	•	•	•
November	3,200	3,010	3,100	17,068	500	538	500	32,394
December	3,600	3,232	3,500	20,300	400	406	400	32,800
	24,500	20,300	22,000	20,300	33,000	32,800	32,000	32,800

Figure 11-14.

228

- by methods of solicitation
- by methods of delivery
- by individual salesmen or salesmen's groups
- by individual customers or customers' groups
- by warehouses
- by order size.

Oftentimes a single analysis is inconclusive. Many views of the problem (for example, high sales but low profits) must be taken by preparing many analyses similar to those named above. The whole picture, then, coupled with available relevant external information, must be considered before constructing alternative solutions to the problem and deciding on one of those alternatives.

For all these analyses, you must decide just how each would fit into your reporting structure. Should they all be on a pyramid basis up to the president? May some be prepared on an exception basis? Are they appropriately compared to budget or projected figures, with last year, or with year-to-date figures? Are they presented with additional ratio, percentage and turnover interpretations? Are they eye-appealing and "digestible"? Are the analyses more understandable in graph or chart form?

Several analyses of sales revenue and costs were presented earlier in this chapter. You should make the analyses most meaningful in your situation. Costs may be analyzed alone, or revenues may be presented separately, as in Figure 11-14. Although the illustration shows only two products, this may be expanded as needed or grouped into product lines. Forecasted and budgeted figures are shown; perhaps these supplemented with percentages of total may be more meaningful. A calculation of the difference between actual and budget, and statistical measures of standard deviation may aid in understanding. A similar report showing an analysis of expenses could be prepared. A detailed listing of direct expenses related to products A and B, for example, could be summarized by months similar to the form in Figure 11-14. Combining this and the Figure 11-14 information would derive a profit contribution statement by month on an actual, year-to-date, forecast and budgeted basis. This could further be analyzed by territory, salesmen, or any other of the bases listed at the beginning of this section.

It would be desirable in your firm to have a definite understanding among report receivers about certain definitions. This subject was explored in the earlier chapter on Narrative Reports, but a further note is necessary here. For example, the meanings of *forecast, budget,* and *actual* are frequently misunderstood or misinterpreted. Different firms use these terms in different ways for different purposes, so no universal definition may be stated. The authors recommend, however, that they be used just as their names imply: forecast—what is expected to happen; budget—what ought to happen; actual—what finally did happen. The difference between forecast and budget is subtle, and pivots upon the controllability of the factors involved. A budget attempts to predict the results of decisions made and actions taken toward a specific goal, under relatively tightly controlled conditions. A forecast attempts to predict the results of decisions made and actions taken, but under the assumption that the environment is relatively uncontrolled. *Actual,* as a term, is not always as definite as it implies. The figures purported to be "actual" may have been the result of several allocation operations, so in effect it is a form of estimate as well. Moreover, there are some costs (such as opportunity and imputed costs) that the accounting system does not normally attempt to measure, yet these may be important considerations in comparing actual budget or forecast. In terms of emphasis in comparison, therefore, we feel that the actual figures should always be compared with budget first, then with the forecast, and finally budget against forecast. This procedure highlights the difference between the effort (budget) and the accomplishment (actual) as the most important, and between the effort (budget) and the expected (forecast) as the least important.

A daily report and analysis of scheduled, shipped, and backlog of sales orders is presented in Figure 11-15. This analysis is in terms of numbers of orders; the report could be prepared also on the basis of total dollars in each category. Such a report could help establish sales quotas, adjust product mix, point out bottlenecks in material flow, and establish production levels.

CREDIT AND COLLECTION REPORTS

The credit and collection cycle provides a number of items upon which reports to management would be proper. These may include:

- number of requests for credit, number granted, number rejected and reason for rejection
- turnover of accounts; accounts opened and closed; accounts inactive
- list of charges and credits to accounts receivable, and reasons for credits if exceptional
- list of delinquent accounts or other aging; write-offs listing
- cash flow forecast
- budgeted and actual departmental costs.

The *aging of accounts receivable* is a fairly well-known report on the current status of each account. From this you might prepare a report on the major delinquent accounts; this becomes an exception report, in effect. Figure 11-16 illustrates this report on delinquent accounts, showing the amounts, the percentages they represent of total receivables and of total past due, and the action taken on them to date.

A *report on forecasted collections of receivables* is frequently helpful in cash planning and financing decisions. Figure 11-17 illustrates a summary of receivables due and their projected collection date. A further study of those accounts being collected beyond the normal 30-day period may reveal habitual credit term offenders, or a too-lax collection policy being followed, or a too-lax credit granting policy in force.

A daily credit department report may cover some or all of the other items listed at the beginning of this section. Such a report is shown in Figure 11-18. This report is easily adapted to each firm's particular situation.

PURCHASE DEPARTMENT REPORTS

The purchasing department keeps abreast of external market conditions and develop-

Daily Report on Scheduled, Shipped, and Backlog of Sales Orders

	Scheduled			Shipped			Backlog		
Product	Today	MTD	LMTD	Today	MTD	LMTD	Today	MTD	LMTD
A	35	860	790	30	850	765	5	10	25
B	10	420	380	13	390	375	20	30	5
C	90	1,320	1,280	90	1,285	1,275	0	35	5
D	63	650	750	70	620	735	10	30	45
E	81	780	1,200	102	790	1,150	8	25	30
Total	279	4,030	4,400	305	3,935	4,300	43	130	110

* MTD = month to date; LMTD = last month to date

Figure 11-15.

Major Delinquent Accounts Receivable *

Customer Name	Past Due Total	Days Past Due			Action Taken
		30	60	Over 60	
Adams	1,350	1,350			3d letter, phoned him 3/10/69
Blue	4,320	320	1,500	2,500	On cash basis, note in transit
Cook	2,580			2,580	Creditor claim entered in court
Dodd	690	300	390		On cash basis
Evans	3,750		2,500	1,250	In hands of collecting agency
Fuller	6,500			6,500	In hands of attorney
	19,190	1,970	4,390	12,830	

% of total
receivables   1.5%   0.1%   0.4%   1.0%   * Over $500

% of total
past due   85.5%   45.2% 56.0% 97.0%

Figure 11-16.

Accounts Receivable Collection Forecast

For the Month of December, 1969

Sales in:	Receivable Total 12/1/69	Collection Forecast			
		December	January	February	March
Prior to					
September (over 120 days)	4,500	4,000	500		
September (over 90 days)	8,300	8,000	300		
October (over 60 days)	33,000	31,500	1,500		
November (over 30 days)	184,500	163,000	19,500	2,000	
December (current)	135,000 *	28,000	105,000	1,000	1,000
Total	365,300	234,800	126,800	3,000	1,000

* Projected
  30 day terms normal

Figure 11-17.

231

ments through published sources and personal contacts. These external conditions must then be related to internal operations. Sales estimates and production forecasts and schedules form the basis for purchasing department plans. Management of the department and others in the hierarchical structure can be kept informed for decision and control purposes through a number of reports. A sample of these reports would include the following:

- market conditions, including current and anticipated future price and supply developments
- inventory position, including stocks on hand, turnover, and anticipated demand
- purchase commitments, by inventory category, showing orders placed, and delivery schedules
- open-to-buy, the amount of additional inventory that can be ordered without exceeding anticipated sales and inventory positions
- open requisitions, awaiting processing into purchase orders
- survey of vendor performance, showing inspection information, lapsed time between order and receipt, percentage of items backordered
- summary of purchases by vendor and by expense, to identify the major suppliers of particular items
- expense and activity analyses, detailing the activities of the department in dollar and other quantitative measures.

This last analysis is illustrated in Figure 11-19. The budgeted and actual expenses are indicated on a responsibility basis for the three identifiable activities. This is supplemented by activity indicators of various types. For these latter items, in addition to actual experience, year-to-date or last month or same month of last year could be shown in contrast. For the dollar amounts of expense items, these could be presented on a unit cost basis compared with standards or past averages to obtain more control over the department's operations.

PERSONNEL AND PAYROLL DEPARTMENT REPORTS

Since payroll and personnel activities are frequently recurring, and because these are service operations, they are often overlooked as cost control centers for their own expenses and as valuable information suppliers about employees in other departments. Being routine, payroll and employee variations and exceptions should be highlighted in all reports to management. This may be accomplished through reports such as the following:

- departmental payroll costs, showing direct and indirect labor by department and relating this to departmental operations and standards or budgets
- employee turnover and number of employees, by department
- employee absenteeism or idle time, by department, and reasons including illness and accidents
- employee status changes, such as promotions, transfers and salary grade increases
- employment department expenses and activity, detailing the departmental activities in dollar and quantitative measures.

Credit Department Report

December 18, 1969

		Month to Date		Year to Date	
	Today	This Year	Last Year	This Year	Last Year
Credit orders received					
Number	20	350	320	4,300	3,950
Amount *	12	180	165	2,155	1,975
Orders approved for credit					
Number	18	330	290	4,280	3,940
Amount *	10	168	140	2,150	1,980
Credit orders awaiting approval					
Number	5	24	35	26	30
Amount *	3	14	15	12	17

Accounts receivable outstanding *

	Today	Comments
New York Office	120	
Los Angeles	60	This is decrease of $30,000 compared
New Orleans	30	with this date last year, which is
Atlanta	40	favorable in light of increased
Seattle	20	sales of about $80,000.
Total	270	

Number accounts receivable

Active	860	This is an increase of 60 over the
Inactive	220	same time last year, an increase
Total	1,080	of 6%. Accounts opened and closed
Accounts Opened	2	is normal.
Accounts Closed	(0)	
Total approved open accounts	1,080	

Accounts Receivable -- amount *

In hands of collection agents	2	This is normal this time of year
Charged off	1	
% of O/S A/R	0.4%	Below budget by 0.1%
Collections	46	Collections running 25% over normal

* In thousands of dollars

Figure 11-18.

Purchases Department

Expense and Activity Analysis *   Month of December, 1969

	Production Raw Material		Production Parts		Non-production Materials		Total	
	Budget	Actual	Budget	Actual	Budget	Actual	Budget	Actual
Purchasing Agents' salaries	12.0	12.1	10.2	10.2	13.2	13.1	35.4	35.4
Buyers' salaries	25.3	24.8	16.0	15.2	12.3	14.1	53.6	54.1
Direct office salaries	10.6	12.2	8.4	9.1	7.2	7.1	26.2	28.4
Direct office supplies	.4	.4	.2	.3	.4	.4	1.0	1.1
Total	48.3	49.5	34.8	34.8	33.1	34.7	116.2	119.0
Indirect salaries							5.8	6.4
Office space							12.2	12.2
Office supplies							.9	.8
Storage							14.2	14.3
Total							33.1	33.7
Total expenses							149.3	152.7
Number:								
Orders placed		42		28		53		123
Orders received		38		34		62		134
Salesmen interviewed		14		23		19		56
Time lapse: days								
Reg. - order		5		4		3		12
Order - receipt		30		25		10		65
Receipt - release		2		3		2		7
Percentage:								
Orders received before prom. date		12		4		2		18
Returns to total purchase order		3		12		1		16
Back ordered items		8		14		3		25
Freight charge per Dollar net purchases		0.04		0.12		0.005		0.165

* Dollar amounts in thousands

Figure 11-19.

234

Inventory Summary

December 31, 1969

Divisions, Departments, Responsibility Centers	Inventory on hand at FIFO cost		Change in Inventory on hand				Next Quarter Forecast	%(2) Change	Replacement Cost of Inventory on hand
	Amount	%(1)	Quarter		Year				
			Amount	%	Amount	%			

Notes:
(1) % to sales for next calendar quarter.
(2) % change over last year, same quarter.

Figure 11-20.

235

INVENTORY REPORTS

Inventory reports are an important part of the indispensable tool kit for management use. They are required to provide information by which to evaluate the effectiveness of day-to-day inventory operations and controls.

Inventory reports help control the investments in inventories, their proper use, their condition, and their value. Proper control over inventories results from the proper control over purchasing, manufacturing, and sales activities. Inventory levels, use, condition, and value are the result of management decisions and actions. Reports on these phases of inventory control should emphasize the relationship between previous management decisions and the current status of the inventory. By showing this relationship the reports become useful as a guide to future decisions. Moreover, inventory valuation is significant in income and financial position determination, and its analysis in various ratios is useful in evaluating operating and financial results. In Figure 11-3 earlier in this chapter it was noted that supplementary current-value information was frequently valuable in decision making. That point is re-emphasized here; a current value for inventory is usually an important factor in evaluating current asset position and for planning purposes.

Many different types of inventory reports are possible. The following would be typical:

- inventory analyses by item class, age, value, or department
- purchase commitments and open-to-buy amounts
- analyses of obsolete, damaged, stolen, slow-moving, or frequently re-stocked items
- material price and quantity variance analyses, to reveal market price trends, purchasing efficiency, and efficiency in use of inventory items
- analyses of scrapped and reworked items
- analyses of turnover and investment in particular classes or items
- analyses of differences between physical count and book amounts of inventory to reveal accuracy in accounting for and handling of items.

The first report mentioned above may be prepared fairly easily by divisions, departments, or other responsibility segments of the firm. If the items in inventory are relatively few in number, the report may show both units and dollar value; usually, however, only dollar amounts are given. The report would be constructed similar to the column titles in Figure 11-20. In addition, a comparison report may be presented showing the inventory position last month and/or last quarter and their percentage of next quarter (or some period) sales. You should use your imagination in seeking out information that will be useful to management in making decisions on controlling and investing in inventories.

Another example of an inventory status and projection report is given in the following section.

PRODUCTION DEPARTMENT REPORTS

Production department reports relate both to quantities and dollars of production per time period. On this basis, production reports cover actual output of finished goods, subassemblies, parts, rework, and other statistics. These may be compared with cost and production standards, budgets and schedules. Production control and cost control are all-important to efficient operations; effective management reports will help in making accurate and timely decisions.

As many reports are possible as exist variations in production methods. In general terms, the following are typical accounting reports:

- costs of production summarized by division, factory, departments, responsibility centers
- costs of production, performance and efficiency variances, analyzed by cost elements of material, labor, direct and indirect overhead
- summary of production and other operational details by responsibility centers, compared with planned quantities
- summary by responsibility centers of quantities and costs of scrap, waste, defective units, and reworked units
- tool and die status summary and projection
- capacity requirements of facilities, personnel and materials for forecasted shipping and production schedule.

Figure 11-21 presents a detail of the inventory planning information flow and several management reports produced from the inventory data bank. These five selected reports cover sales performance and projection (Report 1 of Figure 11-21), style performance (Report 2), stock expedite (Report 3), factory production (Report 4), and raw material inventory projection (Report 5). The note on each report explains its function.

COMPANY STATUS REPORTS

Management should have for their use a periodic Company Status Report. This is for information purposes to top and middle management. It provides an operations-oriented analysis geared to current planning, which in turn provides a basis for timely data-based management decisions. The Status Report emphasizes early identification of deviations from plans and their effects on other planning elements. It also emphasizes corrections in order to minimize the impact of undesirable events. Key data is identified concerning the long-term forecasts and goals and is used as a framework for short-term decisions.

The Company Status Report should be made at different times during the year:

- *Annual Report,* reviewing established goals and strategy
- *Semiannual Report,* relating actual progress to the plans
- *Quarterly Report,* comparing the short-run plans with actual performance on a total company basis
- *Monthly Report,* by division managers, of their actual performance compared with short-term plans.

The specific content of each of these reports was presented in Figure 7-1, to which the reader is referred.

ABLE MANUFACTURING COMPANY

DETAIL OF INVENTORY PLANNING INFORMATION FLOW

SHOWING SELECTED HIGH LEVEL REPORTS

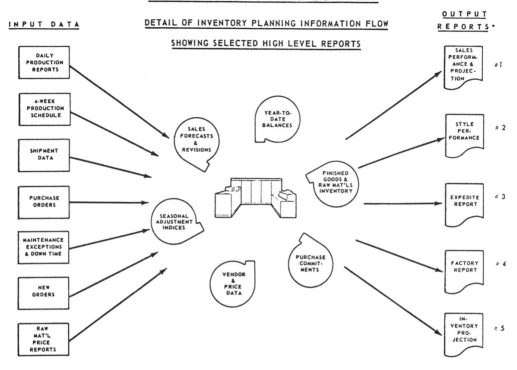

REPORT I

Able Manufacturing Company, Sales Performance vs. Plan
September 30, 196X, (000 omitted)

	YEAR TO DATE SALES			THIS MONTH SALES		
		DEVIATION FROM			DEVIATION FROM	
	AMOUNT	ORIGINAL FORECAST	LATEST REVISION	AMOUNT	ORIGINAL FORECAST	LATEST REVISION
PRODUCT LINE A	$ 778	$ 58	$ 4•	$ 86	$ 7•	$ 2•
B	907	21	5	98	6	1•
C	829	19	2	90	3	3
D	786	9•	2•	85	4•	2
E	800	15	6	86	6•	3•
F	691	11	1	75	9	6
G	850	12•	3•	92	3	1
H	1,123	17	4	122	11	4
I	878	9	1	95	2	6•
J	987	25•	7	107	5	4
OTHERS	$43,868	$329	$54	$4,899	$178	$ 8
TOTAL	$52,497	$433	$71·	$5,835	$200	$16

•Below plan
†Based on year to date sales after seasonal adjustment

Figure 11-21. Reprinted with permission from J.W. Konvalinka and H.G. Trentin, "Management Information Systems," *Management Services* (New York: American Institute of Certified Public Accountants), September–October, 1965, pp. 34–39.

Able Manufacturing Company
Weekly Expedite Report
September 30, 196X (week 39)

STYLE	SAFETY STOCK (units)	PROJECTED STOCK-OUT NEXT SIX WEEKS¹		ITEM NOW RUNNING AT PLANTS NO.	CAPACITY TO COVER STOCK-OUT AVAILABLE AT		HOURS NEEDED TO RESTORE TO SAFETY
		WEEK	QUANTITY SHORT		PLANT NO.²	LINE	
XDZG	25	41	31	1-6-3	4-6	1,7,15	192
YHQN	40	42	60	1-6-3	4-6	2,3,5	568
GBEN	100	42	153	2-7	–	–	791
JLMD	60	41	68	4-7	–	–	213

¹ Based on year to date sales (after seasonal adjustment) and existing production plan

² Based on existing production plan, subject to any prior special orders

Note: This report expands on expected stock-outs disclosed in Report 2, showing available plant capacity and amount of inventory and production hours needed to restore safety stock and cover planned requirements.

Note: As well as reporting monthly sales by product line, this report shows the expected and actual results against the original forecast and all revisions. By the application of standard gross profit rates, the profit effect of all deviations can be measured, and revisions in the profit and production plans can be recognized and made on a timely basis.

PROJECTED DEVIATION OF FUTURE SALES†						EXPECTED AT YEAR END		
OCTOBER		NOVEMBER		DECEMBER			DEVIATION FROM	
ORIGINAL FORECAST	LATEST REVISION	ORIGINAL FORECAST	LATEST REVISION	ORIGINAL FORECAST	LATEST REVISION	TOTAL SALES	ORIGINAL FORECAST	LATEST REVISION
$ 8•	$ 3	$ 5•	$ 2•	$ 15•	$ 2	$ 1,011	$ 30	$ 1•
3	1	7	2	10	6	1,180	41	14
5	2•	3•	1	12	4	1,078	33	5
9	3	15	3	8	4	1,022	23	8
7	4	6	1•	11	5	1,040	39	14
6	3	9	4	2•	3	898	24	11
2•	2	7	2	4	2•	1,105	3•	1•
5	4	12	2	9	5	1,460	43	15
1•	1	2•	2•	12	4	1,141	18	4
2	2	4	1	3	2•	1,283	16•	8
$115	$10	$230	$30	$247	$21	$58,782	$ 921	$115
$141	$31	$280	$40	$299	$50	$70,000	$1,153	$192

Figure 11-21 (Continued).

239

Able Manufacturing Company
Style Performance Report
September 30, 196X (week 39)

PRODUCT LINE B

STYLE	YEAR TO DATE DEVIATIONS FROM PLAN[1]			THIS MONTH DEVIATIONS FROM PLAN[1]		
	SALES	PRODUCTION	ENDING INVENTORY	SALES	PRODUCTION	ENDING INVENTORY
XAGO	$ 300•	$ 3,600	$ 3,900	$ 200•	$ 500	$700
XDZG	600	—	600•	350	—	350•
YHQN	2,200	1,600	600•	400	200	200•
ZMVO	400	1,200	800	450	800	350
APET	1,900	4,000	2,100	200	400	200
DUFH	800•	3,000	3,800	175•	200	375
GBEN	1,100	—	1,100•	250	—	250•
JLMD	900	—	900•	325	—	325•
WBPN	100	2,400	2,300	190	680	490
PTSY	500•	1,400	1,900	300•	290	590
RVWB	1,000	2,700	1,700	510	470	40•
OTHER STYLES	14,400	18,500	4,100	4,000	3,350	650•
TOTAL	$21,000	$38,400	$17,400	$6,000	$6,890	$890

• Below plan
[1] Based on year to date sales after seasonal adjustments
[2] And existing production plan

REPORT 2

Able Manufacturing Company
Factory Report — September 30, 196X
(000 omitted)

	YEAR TO DATE				THIS MONTH	
	EARNED HOURS		PLANT UTILIZATION		EARNED HOURS	
	NUMBER	DEVIATION FROM PLAN	%	DEVIATION FROM PLAN	NUMBER	DEVIATION FROM PLAN
PLANT 1	98	3•	78	2•	11	.4•
PLANT 2	139	6•	84	1•	15	.7•
PLANT 3	117	5	86	6	13	.5
PLANT 4	81	2	61	14•	9	.2•
PLANT 5	108	9•	84	3•	12	1.1•
PLANT 6	144	4	82	2	16	.5
PLANT 7	126	1	90	1•	14	.2

• Below plan

REPORT 4

Able Manufacturing Company
Weekly Raw Material Inventory Projection
September 30, 196X (week 39)

RAW MATERIAL CODE	END OF WEEK		LEAD TIME	SAFETY STOCK	ON ORDER DUE IN WEEK						
	MATERIAL ON HAND	DEVIATION FROM PLAN			40	41	42	43	44	45	46
281	2,758	204	2	1		600		450			
282	204	816•	3	2			1,400		1,400		1,800
284	421	286•	2	1		100		400		400	
290	575	55	1	1	75		75		75		75
301	1,008	122•	2	1		350		450		550	
350	900	500•	3	2			1,500		1,500		1,500
423	847	47	2	1		500		400		300	
424	3,100	100	2	1							1,500
500	290	90	1	1	40	40	40	40	40	40	40
501	1,949	49	1	1	900			600		600	

• Below plan
[1] Based on existing production plan
[2] For quantity sufficient to restore safety stock

REPORT 5

Figure 11-21 (Continued).

Note: This report expands on Report 1. It relates sales performance of a style to its production and inventory levels, to maintain maximum flexibility in production scheduling. Where a style is falling below its sales forecast, the basis is provided for curtailing production on that item and shifting the resulting available capacity to where it may be needed. (Total sales for the entire product line, Product Line B, are shown on Report 1.)

PROJECTED INVENTORY LEVEL USING LATEST FORECAST[1,2]							
END OF WEEK 40		41		42		43	
UNITS	DAYS' SALES	UNITS	DAYS' SALES	UNITS	DAYS' SALES	UNITS	DAYS' SALES
38	8	43	10	50	12	56	13
17	4	(6)	(1)	(2)	(1)	(6)	(2)
19	4	16	4	(20)	(4)	(24)	(5)
20	4	20	4	26	5	30	7
21	5	25	5	27	5	32	7
39	8	65	16	74	18	78	19
61	15	46	11	(53)	(13)	(60)	(15)
31	7	(8)	(1)	(2)	(1)	(5)	(1)
12	3	20	4	21	4	28	5
25	5	4	1	20	4	23	5
45	10	18	4	9	2	3	1
320	80	270	68	250	63	298	75
648	153	513	125	400	94	453	109

Note: This report focuses on plant utilization and pinpoints variations from plan as well as the major reasons for those variations. The information here comes from the same source as the information on Report 3 relative to plant capacity for certain lines.

THIS MONTH		LOST HOURS DUE TO			AVAILABLE HOURS NEXT MONTH
PLANT UTILIZATION					
%	DEVIATION FROM PLAN	UNPLANNED DOWN TIME	SCHEDULE GAPS	PRODUCTION BALANCE	
78	2•	.4	—	—	11.9
82	3•	.2	.4	.1	16.4
82	2	—	—	—	14.2
65	10•	.1	.1	—	9.6
88	1	.5	.6	—	13.7
87	2•	—	—	—	17.3
90	5•	—	—	—	14.3

Note: This report helps ensure that the production plan and finished goods inventory levels can be met. Changes in either of these plans are reflected in this report, and attention is drawn to any exceptions in the planned level of raw materials inventory.

PROJECTED USAGE IN WEEK[1]							PROJECTED STOCK-OUT[1]		INDICATED PURCHASE PRICE[2] VARIANCE
40	41	42	43	44	45	46	WEEK	QUANTITY	
45	45	40	42	46			—		—
400	400	400	400	400	400	400	40	996	5.5¢
150	150	150	150	150	150	150	43	79	14.7¢
80		80		80		80	—	—	—
	600		600		600		—	—	—
500	500	500	500	500	500	500	41	600	11.2¢
	90		210		660		—	—	—
375	375		375	375		375	—	—	—
90		90		90		90	—	—	—
300	300	300	300	300	300	300	—	—	—

Figure 11-21 (Continued).

Distribution Procedure. These reports are distributed as indicated in their titles above. After distribution to the key top and middle management personnel involved, at least two meetings are held to discuss and review the report. Then a final meeting of top and middle management takes place for a complete review using view graph and slide or other visual aids to show further statistical support and to present recommendations in light of current events.

Report Format. These periodic Company Status Reports are all with a standard cover and format; the cover would identify the period involved. The report is divided into several sections related to organizational responsibilities. The information is in tabular, graphic and narrative form. Graphs and charts come first, giving the overall picture. This is followed by narrative giving explanations and then by tabular data giving more detail about the operations. Understandability is stressed in each presentation.

It is not possible to present here a complete Company Status Report. In Chapter 6, "Graphic Reporting Techniques," a number of graphs and charts used in the Status Report described above are illustrated and discussed.

Index